SAMUEL BOUGH R.S.A.

THOMAS BUSHBY

BARBARA CRYSTAL COLLINGWOOD

JOHN DOBSON

JOSEPH FAULDER

DANIEL GARDNER

JOHN HARDEN

ROBERT HARRINGTON

JOHN JAMES HODGSON

Tom Mayson.

The Artists of
Cumbria

an Illustrated Dictionary

William Havell: Lodore on the Banks of Keswick Lake, 1826.
Oil $14\frac{1}{2} \times 21\frac{1}{2}$. Anthony Dallas Ltd.

George Romney 1734-1802.
Self Portrait. Oil $49\frac{1}{2} \times 39$. National Portrait Gallery, London.

The Artists of
Cumbria

an illustrated dictionary
of Cumberland, Westmorland,
North Lancashire and North West Yorkshire
painters, sculptors, draughtsmen and engravers
born between 1615 and 1900

by Marshall Hall

Artists of the Regions Series: Volume Two

MARSHALL HALL ASSOCIATES

26 Jesmond Road, Newcastle upon Tyne NE2 4QP

for Jennifer and Nicholas

©

Marshall Hall
published 1979

ISBN 0 903858 01 0

Printed in Great Britain by Titus Wilson and Son Ltd.,
28 Highgate, Kendal.

Contents

*Notes: * at the beginning of an artist's entry indicates that his, or her, work is illustrated; + following a reference in an entry to a particular work, or type of work, produced by an artist, signifies that this work is illustrated; all dimensions shown in captions are given in inches, height preceding width. All Cumbrian place names mentioned in the Introduction, and in artists' entries, have been set in capitals for ease of identification, thus: AMBLESIDE.*

Acknowledgements

The assistance of the following art galleries, organisations and individuals in the compilation and illustration of this dictionary is hereby gratefully acknowledged.

The Abbot Hall Art Gallery, Kendal; James Alder Ltd., Newcastle upon Tyne; The Armitt Trust, The Armitt Library, Ambleside; Art Gallery and Temple Newsam House, Leeds; Carlisle Library; Carlisle Museum & Art Gallery; Christie's, London; B. Cohen & Sons, London; Cumbria Magazine; Anthony Dallas Ltd., Reading; Darlington College of Technology; The Dean & Chapter of Carlisle Cathedral; The Dean & Chapter of Durham Cathedral; Dean Gallery, Newcastle upon Tyne; Eastbourne Fine Art, Eastbourne; Fitz Park Museum & Art Gallery, Keswick; Fitzwilliam Museum, Cambridge; Gomshall Gallery, Gomshall, near Guildford; Richard Green Galleries, London; Hatton Gallery, University of Newcastle upon Tyne; The Iveagh Bequest, Kenwood, London; Laing Art Gallery, Newcastle upon Tyne; Mr. & Mrs. Paul Mellon, U.S.A.; Roy Miles Gallery, London; Morgan & Brown Ltd., Newcastle upon Tyne; B. & R. Moss, Brampton; National Gallery of Ireland, Dublin; National Portrait Gallery, London; Newcastle upon Tyne City Library; Norham House Gallery, Cockermouth; Northgate Gallery, Newcastle upon Tyne; N. R. Omell Gallery, London; Phillips, London; The Ruskin Galleries, Bembridge School, Isle of Wight; The Ruskin Museum, Coniston; Rydal Mount, Ambleside; F. T. Sabin Gallery, London; Shipley Art Gallery, Gateshead; Simon Carter Gallery, Woodbridge; Sotheby's, London; Spink & Sons, London; Tate Gallery, London; Ulster Museum, Belfast; Victoria & Albert Museum, London; Walker Art Gallery, Liverpool; Whitehaven Museum; Christopher Wood Ltd., London.

In particular I should like to thank the Abbot Hall Art Gallery, and Carlisle Museum & Art Gallery, for placing their excellent files on Cumbrian artists completely at my disposal for the purpose of documenting and illustrating this book, and various members of their respective staffs for their helpful assistance. Among the latter I should especially like to thank Mary Burkett, Director of the Abbot Hall Art Gallery, and her Deputy, Vicky Slowe, for their unfailing help and encouragement, and Denis Perriam, Museum Assistant, Carlisle Museum & Art Gallery, for his generous assistance at every stage of the planning, compilation and illustration of *The Artists of Cumbria*, and for kindly reading and correcting my typescript of the artists' entries.

Others whom I should like to single out for my special thanks, are Daniel Hay, former Borough Librarian at Whitehaven, and Keeper of Whitehaven Museum, Harry Fancy, present Curator of Whitehaven Museum, and Annie Robinson of Maryport Maritime Museum, for their great help in researching the work of Cumbrian marine and other artists, and Iain Bain, Publications Manager of the Tate Gallery, and Oliver Turnbull, Director of Titus Wilson & Son Ltd., Kendal, for their expert technical advice in connection with the production of this dictionary.

Finally, I must thank Allan Graham, Director of the Dean Gallery, and Graham Graphics Ltd., Newcastle upon Tyne, for personally photographing for me the many fine works from his gallery which are illustrated in these pages, and for giving me much invaluable guidance on the presentation of my material. To all those mentioned above, and to the many more whom space does not permit me to mention by name, I tender my sincere thanks.

Introduction

Marshall Hall

Probably no other region of Britain has produced as many talented painters, sculptors, draughtsmen and engravers in ratio to its number of inhabitants, as the region embraced by modern Cumbria (see map page 101). Some of the best known names in British Art are associated with the scattered towns and villages of this giant new County which stretches from the Solway to Morecambe Bay, the Irish Sea to the Pennines, and there is hardly an aspect of this art in which a Cumbrian has not distinguished himself as master, pioneer, teacher or writer.

Let us look a little more closely at Cumbria's contribution to British Art, and the fortunes and misfortunes of some of its artists, over the centuries covered by this dictionary . . . .

Portrait painters

Portrait painting, notoriously dependent for its promotion on human vanity and wealth, was slow to emerge in Cumbria during the centuries when it was gaining popularity elsewhere in Britain. The seventeenth century saw Richard Gibson (see "Miniature painting") leave for Mortlake, and occasional visits from itinerant portrait painters such as John Bracken, but there seems to have been neither the vanity nor the wealth in Cumbria to sustain a native school of portrait painters before the eighteenth century. But then what an explosion of talent in portrait painting this seemingly unlikely area of Britain was to witness in the space of only a few decades. From the FURNESS area in the first decade of the century sprang the remarkable James Cranke, Senior, who, after some years in London, established himself as a successful portrait painter in Cumbria just as two young men who were later to set the whole area agog with their artistic and other activities were making their first acquaintance (Christopher Steele and George Romney); while by the end of the century there were at least half a dozen Cumbrians who had either established themselves as portrait painters in London, or were in the process of doing so. The cause of this explosion was a happy coincidence of available talent, and burgeoning opportunity.

The focal point of the explosion was KENDAL, in the mid-eighteenth century fast becoming "one of the most flourishing towns in Northern England", with a wealth based not only on wool, but a diversity of industries "ranging from manufacturing snuff to the making of horn and leather". CARLISLE to the north of the region had to wait until the early nineteenth century to experience a similar explosion, and though it was eventually to eclipse KENDAL in terms of its number of fine portrait painters, the greater practitioners of the art were certainly associated with Cumbria's southern capital. Romney, of course, was undoubtedly the region's most outstanding portrait painter, but his one-time master Steele can not be dismissed lightly, and Daniel Gardner achieved an artistry in the use of crayons for his portraits which has led to his description by one authority, as one of "the three chief masters of the crayon . . .", and of these ". . . the most distinguished and at the same time the most original . . .". The past century has, of course, seen the practice of portrait painting superbly represented by John Scott, and Joseph W. Simpson of CARLISLE, and James Bateman of KENDAL, to mention only three of the many fine Cumbrian portraitists of more recent years.

Miniature painting

Miniature painting in Britain was little more than a century old when Richard Gibson left his native Cumberland for Mortlake in Cheshire, and there laid the foundation for the skill which was shortly afterwards to make him one of the country's earliest painters of portrait miniatures. And a more successful and intriguing debut for a provincial artist on the stage of fashionable British Art could scarcely be conceived. Quickly befriended by one of the country's most successful portrait painters (Lely), and patronised by royalty, his was the almost classic story of the local boy who made good. Gibson left a brood of artistically talented children to practise the art of miniature painting, but it was not until well after the death of the last of these that another native Cumbrian, in the person of Thomas Carlyle, Senior, once more brought lustre to the region's association with the art. And again it was not in Cumbria, but in a thriving metropolis (in Carlyle's case, Edinburgh) that the artist was to bring his art to fruition. Carlyle's emergence as a painter of portrait miniatures was, however, soon to be eclipsed in terms of success and achievement by that of another son of Cumbria – Thomas Heathfield Carrick, whose career was to encapsulate the whole rise of Victorian miniature painting, and its virtual extinction by photography towards the end of the century. But even long after the decline of direct portrait miniature painting, Cumbrians remained attracted to the art, and with its revival in popularity after the turn of the century, several of the region's women artists, notably Edith Mary "Dorothy" Collingwood, and Mary Slee, distinguished themselves as worthy practitioners of this, Britain's earliest form of popular portrait painting.

Painters of history

Cumbria has produced few painters of history, and then mainly artists whose heads were turned only briefly by this grand idea of painting subject matter inherited from the French Academy, and warmly championed in England by Sir Joshua Reynolds. George Romney, already referred to under "Portrait painters", settled in London just as enthusiasm for history painting in Britain was approaching its peak, and such was the spell which it cast over him that within a few years he had tackled some of the most popular history subjects of the day. Among these was his *The Death of Rizzio* (David Rizzio, murdered at Holyrood, 1566), and possibly the first true history painting by an artist born in Cumbria. His success as a history painter was not ever to fulfil his ambitions, however, and it was left to fellow Cumbrian, Robert Smirke, R.A., to make something of a success of the art – though, like Romney, he could not survive by it alone. Others of Cumbrian birth who flirted with history painting, albeit contemporary history rather than ancient, were Romney's one-time pupil Thomas Robinson, whose *Battle of Ballinahinch* (1798), was a reconstruction of a battle fought not far from his home at Lisburn, in Northern Ireland, and Guy Head, whose *Nelson receiving the French Admiral's sword after the Battle of the Nile,* 1798, must be regarded as one of his rare excursions into the field of history painting, apart from his work as copyist. Others of later years who were drawn to history painting or illustration of the contemporary type, were William Henry Nutter and Herbert Lees, who recorded local events, and Joseph W. Simpson, and James Bateman, both of whom became distinguished war artists in the present century.

Landscape painters

As an area possessing some of the finest scenery in Britain, Cumbria has inevitably inspired thousands of fine landscapes, but there was little demand for these landscapes before the end of the eighteenth century, and local artists were obliged to seek their views, and their patronage elsewhere in Britain. What little demand there was for landscape work consisted of views of Cumbria's leading towns, and most impressive buildings, commissioned by those responsible for the development of these towns, or the construction of the buildings. Thus we have Matthias Read, Cumbria's earliest landscape painter of note, painting views of WHITEHAVEN for Sir John Lowther, whose family had much to do with establishing the town as a leading West of England seaport. And the situation did not alter much until the interest on the part of Englishmen in the antiquities and topography of their native countryside discussed under "Draughtsmen and engravers" began to create another and more numerous sort of patron. Among those Cumbrian landscape painters who early benefited from this fascination on the part of their countrymen, was Robert Carlyle, Senior, of CARLISLE, many of whose views were engraved. Several other CARLISLE artists also

enjoyed success in this field, notably Carlyle's pupil, Matthew Ellis Nutter. Meanwhile several other Cumbrian artists had chosen to follow their interest in landscape painting outside the area, some as a relaxation from their principal career, as with Captain John Bernard Gilpin, and his son the Rev. William Gilpin; others as full-time professionals like John "Warwick" Smith and James Baynes.

By the early decades of the nineteenth century, thanks to the examples of Turner, Constable and others, landscape painting had become popular in its own right, though still with at least a hint of the human presence to enable the spectator to identify with the subject. A shift in the character of this presence had been achieved, however, from the antique to the contemporary; from glimpses of ruined castles and quaint old buildings being inspected by worthy gentlemen and ladies, to ordinary folk pictured at their daily work, or weekend play. No Cumbrian artists were to take greater advantage of this shift than Jacob Thompson and Samuel Bough, whose landscape work – the former's in particular – was to draw heavily on spectator interest in human activity. Bough tried vainly to make a living in Cumbria with his views of the area, finally quitting it in 1845 with the observation: "There is little chance of every growing fat by landscape painting in Carlisle". Thompson, returning to Cumbria at much the same time as Bough left it, and after spending much of his life out of the area, found himself able to settle there successfully on the basis of a reputation made mainly in London. Both made their moves little suspecting that their native heath was shortly to become one of the most popular landscape painting areas in Britain, with a national market for its produce. This came about as a result of the discovery of the Lake District by tourists and holidaymakers, and their consequent interest in possessing reminders of its beauty in the form of paintings. But native artists were not the only ones to benefit from this bonanza. Many artists such as Edward Tucker, Senior, and Alfred Heaton Cooper, moved into the area with their families to take advantage of the demand for views, and what might have become a boon to native artists alone, merely attracted greater competition. The end of Victoria's reign saw the popularity of the Lake District unabated, but the art of photography, and new techniques of producing prints of artists' views, were beginning to diminish the demand for relatively expensive original works. Landscape painting in Cumbria became more and more the forte of amateurs who did not need to sell their work to earn a living, or professionals not solely dependent on landscapes for their income. But the change must not be counted a loss, for some of Cumbria's finest landscape painters of the past three quarters of a century have fallen into one or other of these two categories.

Marine painting

The development of marine painting in Cumbria, as with its development elsewhere in Britain, closely followed the growth of local seaport and shipbuilding facilities. And, as with its development in other regions, its most expansive period was in the nineteenth century, when Britain's might as a maritime nation was approaching its zenith. The major focal point of this expansion in Cumbria was WHITEHAVEN, which ". . . already in the third quarter of the eighteenth century had temporarily outstripped Liverpool and Bristol, and was rivalling London for business...". The earliest known marine painting associated with the town (excepting the views of Matthias Read, some of which contained both sea and shipping, and were painted in the early eighteenth century), is a watercolour of *c.* 1780, thought to have been painted by one of the several visiting marine painters known to have been attracted to WHITEHAVEN by its increasingly busy shipping scene. The next painting of note was: *Two Armed Merchantmen leaving Whitehaven Harbour* (1800), painted by a man born just a few years before the *c.* 1780 watercolour was executed. This was Robert Salmon, a silversmith's son who was later to become Cumbria's outstanding marine painter, and to exert a strong influence on both British and American Marine Schools.

Salmon was the area's first marine painter to try and make his living in London, and exhibited at the Royal Academy the earliest recorded example of a Cumbrian subject marine work; his *Whitehaven Harbour, Cumberland,* shown in 1802. Salmon left behind him a number of young artists who also were to specialise in marine painting, but while some, like Salmon, and later Joseph Heard, went to London or Liverpool to launch their careers, by far the greater number preferred to serve the shipowners and shipbuilders of their native Cumbria in the production of shipping scenes and ship portraits. None was to produce anything like the number of marine works which can be safely attributed to Salmon, except William Mitchell of MARYPORT, whose very lengthy working life, and evident industry, enabled him to produce well in excess of the 1000 works thought to have been painted by Salmon. Mitchell painted almost until sailing ships ceased to visit Cumbrian ports, his work over the last three decades of the nineteenth century portraying some of the most glamorous days of sail. WHITEHAVEN and MARYPORT were not, of course, the only Cumbrian ports to flourish in the eighteenth and nineteenth centuries, but it was with these two that the majority of the area's marine painters remained associated until the last artist of note, George Nelson, Junior, practised virtually alone at WHITEHAVEN in the early twentieth century.

Animal and sporting painters

Probably the earliest representations of animals in the work of a Cumbrian artist are those contained in the views of WHITEHAVEN by Matthias Read, and it is interesting that quite the most outstanding painter of animals which the area has produced to date received his tuition indirectly from this artist: Sawrey Gilpin. Read's interest in the horses which he placed so statuesquely in his views may have been inherited from his supposed master, Jan Wyck, and appears to have lasted only a few years. Gilpin, on the other hand, began painting views under Samuel Scott the marine painter, and follower of Canaletto, and succumbed to animal and sporting painting for the rest of his life. Scope for specialisation in animal and sporting painting in Cumbria remained poor until well into the eighteenth century, and its popularisation elsewhere in Britain by Gilpin, Stubbs, and others; wealthy patrons were few in the North West corner of England until this time, and horse racing and livestock breeding had not yet created an interest in the animals concerned. By the end of

the century, however, the race and hunt meetings which were becoming features of Cumbrian life, the extension of coaching facilities, and the national obsession of landowners with unusually large, or otherwise distinctive bulls, cows, sheep and other livestock, were beginning to offer artists opportunities for their skills as animal painters. No other Cumbrian artist, with the exception of James Bateman in the present century, was to make anything like the same impact in animal and sporting painting outside of the area, as Sawrey Gilpin, but artists like Matthew Ellis Nutter, and his one-time pupil Robert Harrington, were able to make reasonable livings from this type of work — the latter even finding employment painting animals into the pictures of fellow artists such as Samuel Bough, and Jacob Thompson. The heyday of the animal painter in Cumbria, and, indeed, Britain generally, was over by the turn of the century, though artists like William Brown of CARLISLE, William Taylor Longmire of AMBLESIDE, and visiting artist George Vernon Stokes, still found a ready enough market for their animal and sporting works until well into the twentieth century.

Sculptors, stonemasons and woodcarvers

The demand for portrait busts and statuary in Cumbria until the late eighteenth century gave little encouragement to its sculptors to remain at home. Like portrait painting, the production of such works depended mainly on human vanity and wealth, and the two did not occur in a satisfactory combination as far as sculpture was concerned, until the early nineteenth century. What did offer employment to their skills in the years before this came about, however, was a demand for tombstones and commemorative tablets in some of which can be perceived a talent, which, in more affluent times, would undoubtedly have found expression in much grander and significant works. Many of Cumbria's early sculptors did not, indeed, even bother to adopt the title to which the quality of their work entitled them, using instead the title "stonemason" without embarrassment. Also the art of sculpture was practised alongside a miscellany of other arts like architecture, reminiscent of the way in which Renaissance artists like Da Vinci and Michelangelo moved easily and unselfconsciously from one artistic discipline to another, though of course with much more spectacular results. Those sculptor-stonemasons, and wood carvers whose skill became particularly noticeable in these early days were quickly snapped up by the local aristocracy to help restore, or improve the ornament of their castles and homes. Some, indeed, were encouraged by their patrons to work on buildings far removed from their native Cumbria, and the hand of several sculptors and woodcarvers from the area is evident in the stone and wood carving of some of Britain's finest architecture. Among these early sculptors and woodcarvers were John Teasdale, Senior, and Thomas Carlyle, both of whom came under the patronage of the Duke of Norfolk through his ownership of Greystoke Castle, near PENRITH, and subsequently worked in various parts of Britain.

With the arrival of the nineteenth-century portrait sculpture in Cumbria became almost as popular as portrait painting, and nowhere in the area did it become more popular than in CARLISLE, where the Artists' Academy established in 1823 gave local sculptors their first opportunity to show their work publicly. The most outstanding of these local sculptors (though he was not, in fact, born in Cumbria, but in a neighbouring county), was David Dunbar, Senior, who later became one of the most prolific and successful British sculptors of the nineteenth century. His skill inspired several young Cumbrian sculptors, but none with more telling effect than Musgrave Lewthwaite Watson, who, after briefly studying under Dunbar, embarked on a professional career which was to eclipse that of his teacher. Watson's example was followed by George Nelson, another pupil of Dunbar, and the century was to witness Cumbrian sculptors producing some of their finest and most widely acclaimed work. By the end of the century, however, sculpture had lost much of its appeal as a means of portraiture, and statuary had become largely relegated to use in war memorials, or other public works, leaving little demand for other commissions. Fortunately, a new type of patronage began to emerge at this time in the form of the public art gallery, and Cumbrian Francis Derwent Wood, for instance, became only one of many British sculptors to benefit from the purchases of the Tate Gallery.

Draughtsmen and engravers

The discovery of Britain embarked upon by cultivated Englishmen from the mid-eighteenth century onwards, and the resulting interest in antiquarian and topographical studies, was to have a profound influence on the type and number of books handled by the country's publishers. The printed word alone, or crudely illustrated by means of wood cuts, quickly lost popularity in favour of large books, lavishly illustrated by means of engravings, first on steel or copper, later through the artistry of men like Thomas Bewick, on wood. Cumbrian artists responded magnificently to the demand for accurate drawings, and competently executed engravings of such drawings, eventually numbering among their ranks some of the best known names in the production of both. Sometimes the draughtsman was his own engraver, as in the case of William Green and William James Linton, both of whom produced illustrations of Lake District scenery for use in books, and broke new ground in engraving terms. Green is said to have been the first British artist to etch scenery on the spot, and Linton the first draughtsman involved in guide-book illustration to interpret his own work in the form of wood engravings. But these are only two of the more obvious names in Cumbrian draughtsmanship and engraving. The areas's connections with the former practice extends from the antiquarian drawings of the Rev. Thomas Machell in the late seventeenth century, through to the book and newspaper illustrations of John James Hodgson, Alfred Heaton Cooper and William Irving, of the twentieth century, while in the field of engraving Cumbria can claim to have produced down the centuries some of the country's finest practitioners of the art; William Pether and Wilson Lowry in steel engraving,

Isaac Nicholson and George Francis Reiss in wood engraving, and Thomas Sibson and Joseph W. Simpson in etching, to name only a few.

Exhibiting societies, institutions, and galleries

No brief introduction to the achievements of Cumbria's artists would be complete without reference to the important role played in presenting these achievements, by the various exhibiting societies, institutions and galleries to which they sent their work.‡ Most of these organisations did not come into existence until after the middle of the eighteenth century, but from this point forward their influence on the careers of Cumbria's artists, and, indeed, British artists generally, became of paramount importance. Through their exhibitions the work of previously little known artists was brought to the attention of wealthy and influential patrons; critics and commentators of the day were able to single them out for praise or condemnation, and at the very least – and no matter what the leading pundits might say of their exhibits – artists were almost sure of glowing press comment back at home!

At first there were problems in transporting exhibits to the venues of the exhibiting organisations, and this, together with the lure of the schooling which many of them were able to offer, accounted for the steady migration of artists to the cities which possessed such organisations. Indeed, several Cumbrian artists played important parts in the foundation of the leading exhibiting organisations, and later held teaching or administrative posts. Few could afford to ignore their influence on the making or breaking of careers, and as transport facilities for exhibits improved, so the exhibiting organisations multiplied, and attracted larger, and yet larger volumes of provincial artists' work. Before this came about, however, several provincial cities – Carlisle among them – decided to create exhibition venues of their own, and although they had left it somewhat late in the day, bearing in mind the improvements in transport facilities which were shortly to be offered by the railways, the Academy opened at Carlisle in 1823, for instance, not only became a magnet for Cumbrian artists, but for dozens of nationally famous artists.

The Carlisle Academy survived only a few years, but exercised a lasting effect on the careers of many of Cumbria's artists. Some other provincial academies survived longer, and successfully competed with the London and Edinburgh based exhibiting organisations in attracting artists to send their work. But it was undoubtedly the major metropolitan exhibiting organisations, whose exhibitions determined the career prospects of artists generally, and as will be seen from the following entries, not only did most Cumbrian artists show their work through these organisations, but many rose to acquire the coveted titles of member, or associate, which some were able to offer by election.

‡ *See notes page 102.*

The Artists

ABBATT, Robert (fl.1821)
Painter of architectural subjects and townscapes in watercolour. His only known work is his *Town Hall and other buildings on the east side of Stricklandgate, in 1821*, in the collection of the Museum of Lakeland Life & Industry, KENDAL. The watercolour shows Kendal's Moot Hall and various old buildings replaced in 1826, and was included in "The Artists' Kendal" exhibition at the Abbot Hall Art Gallery, KENDAL, Summer, 1975.

ABBOT, John (1884-1956)
Landscape painter in oil and watercolour. Abbot was educated at Corpus Christi College, Oxford, and later studied art under Francis Hodge. He did not, however, become a full-time painter until his retirement from the Indian Civil Service in 1932. He exhibited at the Royal Academy, the Royal Institute of Oil Painters, and the New English Art Club, all six of his contributions to the Royal Academy being sent from his home at GRASMERE, between 1937 and 1945. His first contribution was entitled: *Blindtarn, Grasmere*; his final: *Butter Crags, Grasmere.*

AIREY, William (fl.1795-1815)
Stonemason and sculptor. A "William Airey", mason of KENDAL, is referred to in the *Cumberland Pacquet*, 10th February, 1795, and a marble tablet to Anne Steward-son‡ (d. 1815), signed "Airey of Kendal", is in Holy Trinity Church, KENDAL.
‡ *Mother of Thomas Stewardson (q.v.).*

ALLEN, Mrs. O. (fl.1873)
Painter of figure studies in watercolour. Allen contributed one work to the Suffolk Street Gallery in 1873 from her home at GRASMERE. Her contribution was entitled: *The Gentle Friend.*

ALSOP, John (1789-1849)
Painter of portraits, miniatures and altar-pieces. Alsop practised in WHITEHAVEN in the second quarter of the 19th century following tuition from George Sheffield Senior (q.v.), while the latter was resident in the town. In 1826 he painted the altar-piece for the New Catholic Chapel at Warrington, Lancashire, copying the *Ascension* of West. "In short, we have seldom seen a picture of its magnitude in which the colours are better laid on, and in which there is harmony in every part: it will be an ornament to the chapel in which it is placed, and a lasting monument of the Artist's taste and abilities", commented the *Cumberland Pacquet,* on its completion. In 1829 his workshop was at Scotch Street in WHITEHAVEN, while in 1847 he was painting at Queen Street. He was the brother or father of William Leigh Alsop (q.v.).

ALSOP, William Leigh (fl.1839-1883).
Painter of inn-signs and religious subjects in oil. The brother or son of John Alsop (q.v.), Alsop began practising as a painter in April 1839, when he attracted considerable local interest with his sign for the *Whittington and his Cat*, in Lowther Street, WHITEHAVEN. In 1841 he painted a copy of an Old Master Crucifixion as an altar-piece for the Catholic Chapel in the town's Duke Street. He was working in WHITEHAVEN in 1883, according to Bulmer's *West Cumberland Directory* of that year.

ANDERSON, Joshua (1791-1846)
Sculptor and surgeon. Anderson was probably born at WIGTON, and after qualifying at The Royal College of Surgeons at the age of twenty-two he decided to follow his profession in CARLISLE. Here he practised for some thirty-three years, becoming surgeon to the New Gaol, and evidently taking a keen interest in the setting up of the Carlisle Academy in 1823, for he purchased several

1

pictures from its first exhibition and is said to have been much influenced by the works in sculpture which he saw there. Following the 1823 exhibition of the Academy he apparently resumed his spare-time hobby of modelling in clay with renewed enthusiasm, producing busts of Joseph Saul, the Reverend Fawcett, and Robert Cowan, and himself exhibiting at the Academy in 1825. Anderson later sculptured his bust of Saul in marble, possibly with the help of his friend, and probably teacher, David Dunbar Senior (q.v.). The bust is in Holm Cultram Abbey, the remains of which are now used as the Church of St. Mary, ABBEY-TOWN. He died at CARLISLE, his obituary stating that he had left "indubitable proofs of superior talents as a modelist, besides being a first class doctor . . .".

ANSTEY, Harriet (1816-1903)
Copyist of portraits in oil. The daughter of Jarrard Edward Strickland (1782-1844), of SIZERGH, Anstey was not a professional artist, but produced in 1869 a large version in oil on canvas, of a miniature portraying her father. This work was included in the exhibition: "Cumbrian Characters", at the Abbot Hall Art Gallery, KENDAL, in 1968.

*ARDEN, Edward – see TUCKER, Edward, Junior

ARMSTRONG, Miss E. J. (fl.1901)
She was listed in a directory of 1901 as an artist living at Ellenborough Place, MARYPORT.

ASKEW, T. or J. (fl.1789)
Marine painter in watercolour. Two of his watercolours of the harbour, WHITEHAVEN, in a primitive style, are in Carlisle Library.

ASPLAND, Theophilus Lindsey (1807-1890)
Landscape painter in watercolour. He was born in London, and became a pupil of George Cooke the engraver and aquatinter. He worked in Manchester and Liverpool until 1848, when he retired to a house on Esthwaite Water to concentrate on painting Lake District Views. While living at Liverpool both Aspland and his wife contributed works to the 1846 exhibition of Carlisle Athenaeum. Following their move to the Lake District they both showed works at the 1850 exhibition of the Athenaeum. Represented: British Museum.

ATHERTON, James (1869-1938)
Landscape painter in watercolour; art teacher. He was born at Bradford, and later became a pupil and teacher at the city's art school. He subsequently spent four years at the Royal College of Art, where he was a contemporary of Septimus E. Scott and Philip Connard, and received many prizes and medals for his work. At the age of twenty-nine he moved to CARLISLE to take up the position of Headmaster at the Carlisle School of Art, retiring in 1926 due to failing health. He exhibited at the Royal Academy, and the Royal Institute of Painters in Water Colours, and regularly showed his work at local exhibitions until his death. Carlisle Art Gallery has thirty-five of his Royal College of Art student sketches, and one of his water colours. He died at CARLISLE, his obituary in the Cumberland News, 23rd July, 1938, remarking: ". . . Fortunate possessors of examples of his work will value them as reminders of an artist who lent distinction to the city and of a man whose courage was proof against ill-fortune".

ATKINSON, Thomas K. (fl.1823-1826)
Topographical draughtsman. Atkinson's view of the opening of the Canal Basin, CARLISLE, in 1823, was engraved for the Carlisle Canal Company's Share certificate. He was one of the patrons of the Carlisle Academy 1823, Treasurer in 1824, and member of the committee in 1825. He is believed to have been a solicitor by profession, and to have died before the opening of the 1826 Carlisle Academy exhibition, as a toast at the opening referred to him as "the late T. K. Atkinson". His portrait by James Ward of Kendal (q.v.), was exhibited at the Carlisle Academy 1825 exhibition.

Edward Arden (Tucker):
The Swan Inn, Windermere.
Watercolour 10½ × 16.
Dean Gallery.

BAILY, Robert M. (fl.1846-1874)

Landscape painter. This artist practised at PENRITH, and in London during the third quarter of the 19th century. He exhibited at Carlisle Athenaeum in 1846 and 1850, and in London in 1874.

BAKER, James (1750-1826)

Painter of portrait miniatures. This little known artist came to WHITEHAVEN from London in 1825, and began to undertake portrait commissions in miniature on ivory. His health soon deteriorated, however, and he died about six months later. The *Cumberland Pacquet*, 6th February, 1826, published an obituary describing him as a "gentleman of considerable literary attainments, and ... high as an artist; he was also the inventor of that ingenious instrument the Tintegraph".

*BANNER, Delmar Harmood (b.1896)

Landscape, portrait and figure painter in oil and watercolour. Born at Freiburg-im-Breisgau, Banner studied at the Regent Street Polytechnic School of Art, and later became a professional artist. He has exhibited at the Royal Academy, the Royal Institute of Painters in Water Colours, the Royal Society of Portrait Painters, and in the provinces. One of his Royal Academy exhibits was his portrait of Sir Charles Wheeler, President of the Royal Academy. Banner lived initially in the south of England, but has now lived for many years in Little Langdale, near AMBLESIDE, with his sculptor wife

JOSEPHINE DE VASCONCELLOS (b. 1904). He has produced many landscapes and portraits while living in the area. One of his best known portraits is that of Beatrix Potter (q.v.). The National Trust has one version of his portrait; the National Portrait Gallery another, given by the artist in 1948. Represented: Victoria and Albert Museum; National Portrait Gallery; Fitzwilliam Museum, Cambridge, and various provincial and overseas art galleries.

BANNER, Hugh Harmood (b.1865)

Portrait and landscape painter in oil and watercolour; etcher and mezzotinter. Banner was born at Glasgow, the son of art teacher Alex Banner, and studied at Glasgow School of Art, and the City of London School. He exhibited at the Glasgow Institute of Fine Arts, the Royal Society of Portrait Painters, Walker's Gallery, London, and in the provinces. He lived at Glasgow, Maxwelltown, Dumfries, and CARLISLE.

BARNES, Joseph, A.R.Cam.A. (1835-1915)

Landscape painter in oil. Barnes was born at Epworth, Lincolnshire, the son of a printer and bookseller. He ran away from home to study in Paris (where he eventually exhibited at the Salon), and later toured widely throughout the continent as part of his art education. On returning to England he began exhibiting his work at various art establishments, including the Royal Cambrian Academy, the Walker Art Gallery, Liverpool, and Carlisle Art Gallery. During this period he lived mainly at KESWICK and CARLISLE, and became an associate of the Royal Cambrian Academy. While living for a period at Epworth he painted and exhibited to the public a diorama measuring some 120 yards in length, and consisting of

Delmar Harmood Banner:
Scafells from Dore Head.
Oil 20×30.
Darlington College of Technology.

3

Views of the finest English Lake and Mountain Scenery, with the effects of Daylight, Moonlight, Sunrise, Summer, Winter &c . . ., as a poster described it. He is said to have met John Ruskin (q.v.) while painting at CONISTON, and to have so impressed the latter with his work that Ruskin not only purchased several examples, but showed him the Turners at Brantwood, and presented him with a number of etchings to help him in future study. H.R.H. Princess Louise, Duchess of Argyll, is also said to have patronised his work. He died at CARLISLE. Represented: Abbot Hall A.G., Kendal.

*BATEMAN, James, R.A., R.B.A., A.R.W.S., A.R.E. (1893-1959)

Landscape, cattle and portrait painter in oil and watercolour; wood engraver, etcher and sculptor. One of Cumbria's most outstanding landscape and cattle painters of this century, Bateman was born at KENDAL, the son of a well known local farming family. He studied art first at Leeds, then went to the Royal College of Art, where he studied sculpture. On returning from the First World War badly wounded, however, he gave up sculpture for the less strenuous art of painting. He next studied art at the Slade School, and shortly after reaching the final of the Prix de Rome in 1920, he took up a position as painting master at Cheltenham School of Art, and later visiting master at Hammersmith School of Art. His first contribution to the Royal Academy in 1924, was a self portrait, but by 1929, with his *Pastoral* (purchased for the Tate Gallery by the Chantrey Bequest), he had started to exhibit the type of work for which he eventually became best known; pastoral scenes and paintings of auctions and farmyards incorporating cattle and horses.# One of these works: *Commotion in the Cattle Ring*, shown at the Royal Academy in 1936, was also purchased for the Tate. He exhibited at the Academy until 1960 (in the last year posthumously), showing some 122 works in oil, or in the form of wood engravings, and also showed at the Royal

Scottish Academy, the Royal Hibernian Academy, the Royal Society of British Artists, the Royal Society of Painter-Etchers, the New English Art Club, and the Fine Art Society.

In 1940 the War Artists Advisory Committee commissioned him to paint several pictures of the war effort on the land, notable among which was his work: *Silage.* He also produced in this period several portraits of serving officers of the armed forces. Many of his landscapes featured Cumbrian subjects, and he was a frequent visitor to his birthplace, taking a keen interest in Kendal Art Society, and serving as President for several years. During his distinguished career as a professional artist Bateman was elected a member of the Royal Society of British Artists (1930), a member of the Royal Academy (1942), and an associate of the Royal Water Colour Society (1948), in addition to becoming an associate or member of several other art societies and institutions. A major exhibition of his work was held at Kendal Town Hall, in March 1960, to commemorate his death, and at which were shown more than fifty examples of his work ranging from a bronze head to wood engravings. Represented: Tate Gallery; Abbot Hall A.G., Kendal; Laing A.G., Newcastle, and various provincial and overseas art galleries.

*BAYNES, James (1766-1837)

Landscape painter in watercolour. Born at KIRKBY LONSDALE, Baynes displayed a talent for art at an early age, and was taken by a patron to study in London under George Romney (q.v.). He later studied at the Royal Academy Schools, and became a successful professional artist, showing his work at the Royal Academy, the Suffolk Street Gallery, and the Old Water Colour Society continuously from 1796 until his death. Most of his work consisted of landscape, sometimes with cattle or figures, and featured views of Norfolk, North Wales, Cumberland and Kent. Some of his views in Wales were made in the

James Bateman:
Field Byre.
Oil 24×36.
*Tyne & Wear County Museums,
Laing Art Gallery.*

4

James Baynes:
The Bridge.
Watercolour 12½ × 17.
*Tyne & Wear County
Museums,
Laing Art Gallery.*

company of John Varley, one of the two artists who are said to have unmasked Baynes in his practice as a highly successful drawing master of submitting his own work as that of his pupils. Represented: British Museum; Victoria and Albert Museum; Laing A.G., Newcastle, and various provincial art galleries.

BELL, John (fl.1847-1850)

Landscape painter He was listed in a directory of 1847 as an artist living at 10 Church Street, CARLISLE. He exhibited one work at Carlisle Athenaeum in 1850.

BELL, Joseph (fl.1856)

Amateur artist. Bell was sub-Postmaster at ARMA-THWAITE for many years, drawing in his spare time. Little is known of him beyond what is stated in a report of his work in the *Carlisle Patriot,* 13th September, 1856. The report stated that his "skill with the pencil though known and appreciated by the nobility and many of the gentry of the county" was not yet known to the general public. "His many pieces are numerous and various. What is wanting in originality is amply compensated by the general finish of the picture . . .". The report then remarked on "his copies from Rembrandt and Vandyke", and went on to claim as his patrons "the Earl of Carlisle, Sir George Musgrave, Sir James Graham, the Hon. Charles Howard, Mr Howard of Corby, and many principal men of the county".

*BLACKLOCK, William James (1816-1858)

Landscape painter in oil and watercolour; lithographer. Blacklock was born in London, the son of a bookseller from CUMWHITTON who had established a business in the capital. His father's health soon deteriorated, however, and when Blacklock was only four he was taken back to CUMWHITTON, where his father died in 1823. Blacklock Senior had been a close friend of CARLISLE bookseller and printer Charles Thurnam, and William James was

apprenticed to the latter at an early age. During his employment with Thurnam he first began to exhibit his work by sending a landscape to the 1833 exhibition of the Carlisle Academy, and learnt the use of lithography, having several examples of his work in this medium published as part of a series of local views before he left for London.

Back in London by 1836 he began to exhibit at the Royal Academy, the British Institution, the Suffolk Street Gallery, and Carlisle Athenaeum, some of the many landscapes in oil and watercolour which he was to produce in his short lifetime. His work was highly praised by Turner, David Roberts, Thomas Creswick and by William Bell Scott – who introduced him to the Pre-Raphaelite collector James Leathart. Leathart, who recognised the strong Pre-Raphaelite influence of Blacklock's work, bought several examples, and visited the artist when increasing ill-health drove him to return to CUMWHITTON in 1850. Home in Cumbria Blacklock's health progressively deteriorated to the point where he was obliged to give up painting, and he shortly afterwards married, and settled at Dumfries, where he died at the early age of 42.

Geoffrey Grigson, author of one of the most comprehensive studies of the artist's work to date, published in *Country Life,* 4th July, 1974, has said of Blacklock in *Britain Observed,* Phaidon, 1975, that he was "one of the few English artists who have made acceptable pictures out of the Lake District", and that ". . . but for his early death Blacklock might have matured into a landscape painter of great power". Thirteen of the artist's works in oil and watercolour were shown at Carlisle Art Gallery's "Cumberland Artists 1700-1900" exhibition, in 1971, including the work illustrated in this volume. Represented: National Gallery of Ireland; Carlisle A.G., and York A.G.

William James Blacklock: Catbells and Causey Pike.
Oil $12\frac{3}{4} \times 21\frac{3}{4}$.
Carlisle Museum & Art Gallery.

BLAIN, Joseph (died c.1837)
Stonemason and sculptor. Blain practised as a monumental stonemason and sculptor at CARLISLE during the early 19th century. In 1827 he took over the free stone quarries of the Earl of Egremont at CHALK, near DALSTON, formerly in the possession of Paul Nixson (q.v.). A tablet of 1828 by "Blain of Carlisle" is in St. Cuthbert's Church, Beltingham, Northumberland.

BLAND, Benjamin (fl.1900-14)
Architectural and landscape painter in watercolour. Bland practised as a painter of architectural subjects and landscapes in watercolour in KENDAL in the first quarter of the 20th century, showing his work at the Royal Cambrian Academy, and the Walker Art Gallery, Liverpool.

BLAND, John Selkeld (1840-1867)
Landscape and plant draughtsman; amateur poet. Bland was born in Westmorland, the son of William Bland, and nephew of Thomas Bland (q.v.). Only a small proportion of the work which he produced in his short lifetime has been identified. This includes an album of pencil drawings sold at Sotheby's in 1963, and an album of plant drawings in Carlisle Library (this library also has a manuscript containing his poems).

BLAND, Thomas (d.1853)
Amateur animal painter. Thomas Bland of PENRITH published *A Portrait of the Short-Horned Ox* belonging to Sir George Musgrave of nearby EDENHALL. "Judges of the animal", commented the *Carlisle Journal,* 27th May, 1843, "have invariably pronounced the Print an exact Portrait". His obituary in the same publication, dated 29th April, 1853, recorded that "... Mr. Bland coach builder,

had resided in Penrith for several years where he has carried on the business of coach maker and livery stable keeper. He was a man eminent in his profession as a coach builder and his genius as an amateur painter was not to be surpassed".

BLAND, Thomas (1799-1865)
Sculptor, painter, and composer of music. Bland was born at REAGILL, near SHAP, the son of a yeoman farmer, and became a self-taught artist. Little is known of his work prior to 1837, when he decorated his garden with examples of his sculpture and paintings in oil, and opened it to the public in celebration of Queen Victoria's accession to the throne. Annually, on the anniversary of the accession, he is said to have repeated this activity, also lecturing on art and providing a band for entertainment. David Cox Junior was evidently so impressed by Bland's work in painting that he offered to introduce him to the art world. Bland declined his offer. His principal surviving work consists of his sculptural additions to the Queen Victoria Monument at SHAP (see "A Westmorland Sculptor", *Manchester Guardian,* 2nd May, 1955; also Pevsner's *Cumberland and Westmorland*), and several albums of sketches featuring local scenery, etc. Represented: Carlisle A.G.; Carlisle Library.

BLAND, T. (fl.1890)
Landscape painter in oil. The Museum of Lakeland Life and Industry, KENDAL, has his *The Fish Market & Pump Inn,* dated 1890. The Pump Inn stood at the top of the town's Finkle Street until its removal in 1878.

6

BOUGH, James Walker (1828-1859)

Landscape painter in oil and watercolour. Born at CARLISLE, the younger brother of Samuel Bough (q.v.), he first worked as a solicitor's clerk, making pen and ink sketches in his spare time. When his brother left the city for Manchester to become a scene painter, James Walker accompanied him, and also obtained work at the Manchester Theatre Royal. He made a success of his work in this field, and followed his brother to Glasgow and Edinburgh, also painting and exhibiting landscapes executed very much in the style of his brother. He exhibited at the West of Scotland Academy in 1849, and the Royal Scottish Academy in 1857. On a visit to Manchester he was brutally attacked and robbed, ending his days in a mental hospital at Preston, Lancashire, as a result of brain damage sustained in the attack. His *Penton Linns, c.* 1843, in grey wash (private collection), was included in Carlisle Art Gallery's "Cumberland Artists 1700-1900" exhibition, in 1971.

*BOUGH, Samuel, R.S.A. (1822-1878)

Landscape painter in oil and watercolour. Probably Cumbria's most successful and prolific landscape painter of the 19th century, "Sam" Bough was born at CARLISLE the son of a shoemaker, and received his early artistic training from Matthew Ellis Nutter (q.v.), and John Dobson (q.v.). After first trying to make his living as an artist, and working in a lawyer's office in CARLISLE, he was introduced to engraving, and was encouraged by his father to go to London to study under Thomas Allom (1804-1872). He stayed with Allom only a short time,

however, and finding that he could not afford the fare back home he is said to have walked all the way.

Back at CARLISLE at the age of eighteen he contributed nine drawings to the *History of Leath Ward in the County of Cumberland,* by Samuel Jackson, a local bookseller, and was befriended by a Major Aglionby, who introduced the young artist to influential friends in the south, and let Bough stay in his London chambers while copying works by Gainsborough and Rubens in the National Gallery. During this period, and based in CARLISLE, he went on many sketching tours, meeting William Wordsworth (1770-1850) in the Lake District, and forming friendships with many members of the Northern School of Painters which were to last a life-time. By 1843 he had become recognised as a talented young artist, but discouraged by the lack of opportunities for his skill in his native CARLISLE he left for Manchester to take up a position as assistant scene painter at the Theatre Royal. His work in this field was greatly admired and was to leave an indelible effect on his style of landscape painting, much as scene painting work is said to have affected the work of other artists such as David Roberts, Clarkson Stanfield, etc., etc. While at Manchester he did not confine himself solely to scene painting, sending works to the Royal Manchester Institution in 1847, Liverpool and Worcester, and winning at Manchester a silver medal for the best watercolour.

He was not satisfied with the progress he was making in Manchester, however, and towards the end of 1848 he took up a position as scene painter at the Princess Theatre, Glasgow, meeting there his future wife, and marrying in 1849. His experience of scene painting in Glasgow, and subsequently Edinburgh, did not convince him that he would do well to remain in the profession, and when his *Baggage Waggons — Carlisle in the distance*[+] was popularly acclaimed at the 1849 exhibition at the West of Scotland Academy, he decided to become a full-time

Samuel Bough: Baggage Waggons – Carlisle in the distance.
Oil 35×60½.
Carlisle Museum & Art Gallery.

landscape painter. Most of the remainder of his life was spent in Scotland, during which period he exhibited at the Royal Academy, the Royal Scottish Academy, and at Carlisle Athenaeum. All except one of his Royal Academy exhibits featured Scottish scenery, but throughout the many years he exhibited at the Royal Scottish Academy (including three years' posthumously), he regularly showed work featuring Cumbrian scenery. Other work shown in Scotland featured Norway, (which he visited with Alexander Fraser), Scotland and various parts of the South of England. He made many artist friends in Scotland, several of whom later became famous, and through their friendships and his growing popularity as a landscape painter he was elected an associate of the Royal Scottish Academy in 1856, and a member in 1874.

His work throughout his some thirty years as a professional artist was widely acclaimed and fetched good prices. Much of it was in oil, but he was a prolific and able painter in watercolour, becoming President Elect of the Royal Scottish Society of Painters in Water Colours in the year of his death at Edinburgh, and earning a detailed study of his work in this medium in Martin Hardie's *Water-Colour Painting in Britain*, Vol. III. A major exhibition of Bough's work was held at his birthplace in 1896, and several examples have been included in the recent exhibitions of Carlisle Art Gallery, notably its "Cumberland Artists 1700-1900" exhibition, in 1971. Sydney Gilpin's *Sam Bough*, 1905, contains an account of his life and work. Represented: British Museum; Victoria and Albert Museum; National Gallery of Scotland; Abbot Hall A.G., Kendal; Carlisle A.G., and various provincial art galleries.

*BOUSFIELD, John (1793-1856)

Portrait, animal and rustic painter in oil. Bousfield has been described as the most celebrated artist in WHITEHAVEN in the first half of the 19th century, painting portraits of local gentry and worthies, their favourite horses, cats and dogs. One of his best known works was his painting of Mr Daniel Bird's "Solway" and "Bess", in a landscape (1842). He is also known to have painted decorations for the chancels of Trinity and St. James's Church, WHITEHAVEN. Represented: Whitehaven Museum.

*BOWNESS, William (1809-1867)

Portrait, figure and genre painter in oil and watercolour. Born at KENDAL, Bowness probably learnt to paint in the company of the town's several early 19th century portrait painters, and shortly after his twentieth birthday went to London to practise as a portrait and figure painter. He spent the remainder of his life in the capital, exhibiting at the Royal Academy, the British Institution, the Suffolk Street Gallery, and Carlisle Athenaeum, showing portraits, groups, narrative and genre works. Among his portrait subjects were Hartley Coleridge, son of poet Samuel Taylor Coleridge, and Thomas Allom (1804-1872). Typical of his figure work was *The Keepsake*, shown at the Royal Academy in 1836. He visited his birthplace throughout his life, sometimes painting figure and genre subjects which he later exhibited in London, as with his *Pride of Patterdale, Cumberland Beggar,* and *A Westmorland Lassie,* shown at the Suffolk Street Gallery in the 1840's, and producing a number of poems in

John Bousfield:
Man with animals outside Whitehaven Castle.
Oil 18×26. *Whitehaven Museum.*

William Bowness: John Grayson.
Oil $22\frac{1}{4} \times 19\frac{1}{2}$. *Abbot Hall Art Gallery.*

Westmorland dialect which were later collected and published under the title: *Rustic Studies in Westmorland Dialect, with other scraps from the sketchbook of the artist* (London and Kendal 1868). While visiting his birthplace he also painted a portrait of its Mayor for the period 1852-3, John Hudson. This portrait (together with two paintings believed to be self portraits), is at Kendal Town Hall. He died in London. Represented: Abbot Hall A.G., Kendal.

*BRACKEN, John (fl.1665-1668)

Portrait painter in oil. Bracken was an itinerant artist who painted portraits of Sir Daniel le Fleming and his family, at Rydal Hall, near AMBLESIDE, in the second half of the 17th century. These portraits were painted as part of the refurbishment of Rydal Hall, following its partial

Samuel Bough: The Hayfield, 1859. Oil 16×26. *Richard Green Galleries.*

Samuel Bough: Cricket Match at Edenside, Carlisle *c.*1848. Oil 24½×34¾. *Carlisle Museum & Art Gallery.*

William Brown: Canal Basin, Carlisle, 1823. Oil 38½×62½. *Carlisle Museum & Art Gallery.*
William Brown: Launch of the Collingwood from Kelsick Wood's Yard, Maryport, 1819. Oil 27×39⅞. *Walker Art Gallery.*

destruction by Cromwell's troops during the Civil War. Sir Daniel's account books (County Record Office, County Hall, KENDAL) for the period contain some interesting details of the transactions between the artist and the family in respect of the portraits. One of the portraits mentioned, "Cousin Ambrose, sometime Rector of Grasmere", is in the collection of the Abbot Hall Art Gallery, KENDAL; this gallery also has his *Lady Anne Clifford.*# Represented: Abbot Hall A.G., Kendal.

John Bracken: Lady Anne Clifford, Countess of Dorset, Pembroke and Montgomery, 1670.
Oil 29½×24¼. *Abbot Hall Art Gallery.*

BRADE, Daniel Frank (fl.1883-1894)
Architectural draughtsman. Brade practised as an architect in KENDAL, during the last quarter of the 19th century, sending four drawings to the Royal Academy between 1883 and 1894. His last contribution was a drawing for *St. John's Church, Bassenthwaite Lake.*

BRAGG, Miss Jane (fl.1816-1834)
Genre painter; drawing mistress. She practised at WHITEHAVEN from at least 1816, when she opened a day school in the town with a relative, Mary Bragg. She exhibited eight genre works at the Carlisle Academy between 1824 and 1830, evidently studying in London in the early part of this period, for in 1825 she was advertising classes in drawing, stating: "... from having studied in London during the last summer, under some of the first masters" she was enabled "to afford varieties in the art which have not generally claimed the attention of students here ...". She was still giving drawing lessons at WHITEHAVEN in 1834, according to Pigot's *Directory of Cumberland* for that year.

BRAITHWAITE, Samuel Hartley (b.1883)
Landscape painter and etcher. Born at EGREMONT, Braithwaite studied at Bournemouth Municipal School of Art, and subsequently practised as a professional artist at the resort. He exhibited at the Royal Academy and the Fine Art Society, chiefly showing south country landscapes.

BROMLEY, John (1772-1840)
Stone cutter and engraver. The father of William Bromley (q.v.), he practised at WHITEHAVEN in the town's Irish Street, advertising "Head stones cut, seals and cyphers". His son's obituary refers to him as "that eminent stone cutter".

BROMLEY, William (1811-1861)
Sculptor. He was the son of John Bromley (q.v.), and practised at KESWICK. The *Carlisle Journal*, 30th December, 1843, describing his tombstone to the memory of poet Robert Southey in the old churchyard at St. Kentigern's, CROSTHWAITE, near KESWICK, said: "This handsome memorial, which is of elegant workmanship, was executed by William Bromley, son of that eminent stone cutter the late Mr. John Bromley, and is finished with a degree of taste which it would be impossible to surpass".‡ Two large headstones at St. Kentigern's are also attributed to William Bromley: Joseph Dover (d. 1810), with *Hope* at the top (illustrated plate 58, Pevsner's *Cumberland & Westmorland*), and Joseph Cherry (d. 1818), with *Father Time.*

‡ *Southey's grave was extensively restored in 1961, with financial assistance from the Brazilian Government (the poet wrote the first official history of Brazil).*

BROOK, Alfred Newton (fl.1858)
Art master. He was a master at Carlisle School of Art in 1858, later becoming headmaster of the drawing department at the training college at Cheltenham, Gloucestershire.

BROOKER, James (fl.1846-1876)
Wood carver. He was possibly born at Sunderland, Co. Durham, and moved to MARYPORT as a young man to follow the profession of carver of ships' figureheads, and other decorative features. He had a workshop in the town's Eaglesfield Street from the early 1840's and in the next thirty years was responsible for carvings for many of the ships built at MARYPORT, and nearby HARRINGTON and WORKINGTON. In a letter dated "Maryport, July 21st., 1846", from K. Wood & Sons, Shipbuilders, who had for many years employed Brooker, he is described as "inferior to none – but superior to most" in his carving of "Figure Heads and Sterns and all other carved work belonging to Vessels". His work is now finding its way into maritime museums throughout the world.

*BROWN, William (fl.1811-1837)
Marine, landscape and genre painter in oil and watercolour. Brown is first recorded as an artist in watercolour practising at MARYPORT in 1811. By 1819 he was painting in oil on large canvases, and developing considerable ability as a marine painter. In 1823 he was in CARLISLE, where his oil of the city's canal basin of that

year earned the description in the *Carlisle Citizen*: "Our clever townsman, Mr Brown, has just finished his painting of the Carlisle Canal Basin. It adds much to his former well-earned fame, and does, we think, credit to our city ...".# Although Brown's work is, perhaps, best known through his marine paintings, he contributed seven genre works to the Carlisle Academy between 1823 and 1828, and also painted the oil of *Kendal from Thorny Hills, 1819*, at Kendal Town Hall. He has sometimes been described as a Liverpool artist, but is more likely to have been born at MARYPORT. Represented: Carlisle A.G.; Walker A.G., Liverpool.

BROWN, William (1854- c.1940)
Sporting painter. Brown studied art under Robert Harrington (q.v.), and subsequently became a successful sporting artist, practising at CARLISLE. One of his sporting paintings was *Stainforth – Winner of the Cumberland Plate, c. 1936*. He also painted a portrait of Harrington wearing the Beaver hat in which the latter is said to have returned from London. Brown enjoyed a considerable reputation as a sporting painter in CARLISLE, though apart from showing three of his works at Carlisle Art Gallery in 1896, he appears to have confined himself to exhibiting at his studio at West Tower Street. Here he also had on permanent display works by many other fine sporting artists, including several by his former master. He lost his sight in 1933, but it was restored by an operation in 1936. Represented: Carlisle A.G.

BROWN, William Morrison (fl.1851)
He is listed in the *Directory of Westmorland*, 1851, as an artist of Church Walk, ULVERSTON.

BUCKLER, Edward H. (fl.1864-1879)
Architectural draughtsman; lithographer. Buckler produced a lithograph of WHITEHAVEN in 1865, following the publication of a series of his views of churches and buildings in Lancaster. He also made several drawings of Carlisle Cathedral. One of his church studies was exhibited in London in 1879. Represented: Carlisle A.G.; Carlisle Library; Lancaster Museum and A.G.

BULMAN, Henry Herbert, R.B.A. (1871-1928)
Landscape, genre and portrait painter in oil and watercolour. Born at CARLISLE, Bulman had moved to London by 1907, where he became a successful professional artist. He showed seventeen works at the Royal Academy between 1907 and 1929 (in the last year posthumously), and in 1916 he was elected a member of the Royal Society of British Artists. He also exhibited at the New English Art Club, and was a member of the Langham Sketching Club. He died in London. Represented: Carlisle A.G.

BUNBURY, Henry William (1750-1811)
Amateur caricaturist and landscape draughtsman; rustic and landscape painter in watercolour. The *Cumberland Pacquet*, 14th May, 1811, records Bunbury's death at KESWICK as: "Wednesday last at Keswick (where for some years he had chiefly resided), Henry Bunbury, Esq., the celebrated caricaturist (doubtless the greatest genius in that line of his day) and brother to Sir Charles Bunbury, Bart." Bunbury's home for most of his life was at Mildenhall, Suffolk, but about 1800 he moved to

KESWICK, where he is believed to have continued producing his well known caricatures. He exhibited at the Royal Academy while still resident at Mildenhall, showing not only caricatures but landscapes. His work was praised by Sir Joshua Reynolds, President of the Royal Academy, and was engraved for publication by leading professional engravers, sometimes anonymously. Many examples of his work are reproduced in M. Dorothy George's *Hogarth to Cruickshank – social change in graphic satire*, Allen Lane, The Penguin Press, 1967. Represented: British Museum; Victoria and Albert Museum; National Gallery, Scotland.

*BUSHBY, Thomas (1861-1918)
Landscape painter in watercolour. Born at Eccleshill, near Bradford, Bushby's first employment was in a woollen mill before the age of ten. At eleven he began taking art lessons at the local Mechanics' Institute, and at sixteen he was apprenticed to a lithographer in Bradford. He next moved to London, but in 1884 he went to CARLISLE to take up a position as a designer with Hudson Scott and Sons, now the Metal Box Company. His employers encouraged him in his painting, and his work attracted the attention of George Howard, 9th Earl of Carlisle (q.v.), who is said to have admired its Pre-Raphaelite detail. He exhibited at the Royal Academy, the Royal Scottish Academy, the Royal Cambrian Academy, the Royal Institute of Painters in Water Colours, Walker Art Gallery, Liverpool, and Carlisle Art Gallery. One of his works was purchased by

Thomas Bushby: Wood Gatherers.
Watercolour 12×10. *Carlisle Museum & Art Gallery.*

the Art Union in 1908. He travelled abroad whenever possible, sketching in Norway, France, Switzerland, Italy and Holland. He also produced many watercolours and pencil drawings of local landscapes and buildings, including among the latter his *Carlisle Academy of Art,* painted in 1895. This work, together with several other of his local subjects, was shown in the "Thomas Bushby" exhibition, of that year, in CARLISLE, and in Carlisle Art Gallery's "Cumberland Artists 1700-1900", exhibition, in 1971. He died in CARLISLE. Represented: Carlisle A.G.

CAIRD, Dr. Andrew J. (fl.1926-1935)
Etcher of street scenes. He exhibited at the annual exhibitions of local art at Carlisle Art Gallery between 1927 and 1935, and at the Royal Scottish Academy between 1926 and 1932. Represented: Carlisle A.G.

CALVERT, Charles (1785-1852)
Landscape painter in oil and watercolour. Calvert was born at Glossop Hall, Derby, the son of the Duke of Norfolk's agent, and became a cotton merchant before developing into a talented landscape painter. He contributed four works to the 1833 exhibition of the Carlisle Academy from Manchester, and became a founder member of the Royal Manchester Institution. Later in his life he lived at BOWNESS-ON-WINDERMERE, dying there in 1852. Represented: Victoria and Albert Museum; Manchester City A.G.

CALVERT, Raisley (1773-1795)
Sculptor. A friend of William Wordsworth (1770-1850), to whom he bequeathed on his death £900, Calvert was the son of a steward of the Duke of Norfolk, at GREY-STOKE, near PENRITH. He is known to have been admitted to Magdalene College, Cambridge in 1793, but left after a short time to educate himself by travelling on the continent. In 1791 he inherited several farms, including one at ORMATHWAITE, a mile north of KESWICK. Most of his income came from these farms while he evidently dabbled in sculpture. Wordsworth rewarded Calvert for his generosity with a sonnet, part of which reads: "O Worthy shortlived youth . . .".

CALVIN, Ann (1747- *c.*1785)
Plant, flower and bird painter. The daughter of William Calvin, a house painter, she was born at PENRITH, and possibly received some tuition in art from her father. She was noticed by Pennant in his *Tour of Scotland,* 1769, the latter stating: "in this town lives Miss Calvin, of exquisite skill and accuracy in the painting of plants and flowers: a heaven-born genius obscure and unknown". She was later patronised by Lady Lonsdale, and exhibited one work entitled: *Two Birds,* at the Royal Academy in 1773, while still living at PENRITH. Following this, Lady Lonsdale encouraged her to go to London, where she is believed to have died shortly afterwards. She was the sister of William Calvin (q.v.).

CALVIN, William (1752-1830)
Landscape painter in watercolour; decorative artist. Calvin was born at PENRITH, the son of William Calvin, a house painter, from whom he possibly received some tuition in art. He was first noticed by Pennant in his *Tour of Scotland,* 1769, and some of his work appeared in that publication. He was also described by Walker, in his *History of Penrith,* as an "artist of some merit". In the field of decorative painting he often received commissions from the Earl of Lonsdale, and is known to have painted parts of the interiors of Ullesmere House, and Lowther Castle, in Cumbria. He was the brother of Ann Calvin (q.v.).

*CARLISLE, 9th Earl of – see HOWARD, George.

CARLISLE, Isabella, Countess of (d.1795)
Amateur etcher. She was the daughter of William, fourth Lord Byron, and in 1743 married the 4th Earl of Carlisle.

George Howard: 9th Earl of Carlisle. Pompeii. Oil 7×15. *Roy Miles Gallery.*

CARLYLE, George (1797- after 1830)

Landscape, figure and flower painter; art teacher. He was born at CARLISLE, the son of Thomas Carlyle Senior (q.v.), the miniature painter, and brother of Thomas Carlyle Junior (q.v.), and Robert Carlyle Junior (q.v.). He is presumed to have received tuition from his father, and to have later worked in both Edinburgh, and CARLISLE, giving art lessons at the latter between 1828-30. He exhibited at the Royal Scottish Academy in 1828 and 1829, the Carlisle Academy in 1824, 1825 and 1828, and at the Institute for the Encouragement of Fine Arts, Edinburgh, almost every year from 1821 to 1829. One of his painted vases was bought for Greystoke Castle near PENRITH, in 1828. George, his father, and his brother Thomas Junior, evidently toured Cumbria on joint painting ventures, one of their newspaper advertisements (*Carlisle Patriot,* 18th October, 1828) reading in reference to a visit to WHITEHAVEN: "Miniatures as usual by T. Carlyle – Landscape, Figure and Flower Drawing taught by G.C. in Chalk, Pencil, and Colours . . .". Another and later advertisement (*Carlisle Patriot,* 25th October, 1830) finds him identified in an announcement about artistic services available from his father, and Thomas Junior, as being ready to teach "the new style of enamelling . . . also the fashionable Art of Oriental tinting . . .".

*CARLYLE, Robert, Senior (1773-1825)

Landscape and architectural painter in pen and watercolour. Born at CARLISLE, the son of Thomas Carlyle (q.v.), sculptor and wood carver, and brother of Thomas Carlyle Senior (q.v.), the miniature painter, Carlyle became a largely self-taught artist. At the age of nineteen he won a silver medal for his drawings of Carlisle Cathedral, and in 1794, he was commissioned by Hutchinson to illustrate the latter's *History of Cumberland.* Several other examples of his work were also engraved for publication, including his views of CARLISLE in 1797, and 1821, and various illustrations for *The Beauties of England and Wales,* 1803, and Storer's book on Cathedrals, in 1816. He took a close interest in the foundation of the Carlisle Academy, and is said to have exercised a considerable influence on the work of younger landscape painters, notably that of his nephew Robert Carlyle Junior (q.v.), and Matthew Ellis Nutter (q.v.), both of whom were his pupils. He exhibited at the Carlisle Academy in 1823 and 1824, the Institute for the Encouragement of Fine Arts, Edinburgh, in 1824, and posthumously at the Dumfries Exhibition of 1828. He was a close friend of the poet Robert Anderson and wrote a book of verse entitled *De Vaux* or *The Heir of Gilsland,* which he published in 1817. His work in painting was patronised by the Duke of Norfolk, and Henry Howard of Corby Castle. He died at CARLISLE and is buried beside his father in the grounds of Carlisle Cathedral. Represented: Carlisle A.G.; Carlisle Public Library.

CARLYLE, Robert, Junior (1800- after 1858)

Landscape painter in watercolour. He was born at CARLISLE, the son of Thomas Carlyle Senior (q.v.), the miniature painter, and brother of Thomas Carlyle Junior (q.v.) and George Carlyle (q.v.). He was tutored in art by his father, and by his uncle, Robert Carlyle Senior (q.v.), and subsequently exhibited at the Carlisle Academy in 1824, 1825, 1826 and 1828, the Dumfries Exhibition of 1828, the Institute for the Encouragement of Fine Arts, Edinburgh, in 1822, 1824-1829, and at the Royal Scottish Academy in 1829. He appears to have left CARLISLE at an early age to live with his father in Edinburgh, but he later moved to Preston, Lancashire. By 1836 he appears to have moved from Preston, and in 1850 he was at GRASMERE, where he took a daguerrotype of William Wordsworth (1770-1850). In 1858 he was living at Prestwich, Lancashire. His *Six Views of Furness Abbey* were engraved and published by Ackermann in 1835.

Robert Carlyle, Senior:
A View of Carlisle from the North East, *c.*1792.
Watercolour $10\frac{5}{8} \times 14\frac{1}{2}$.
Carlisle Museum & Art Gallery.

CARLYLE, Thomas (1734-1816)

Sculptor and wood carver. He was born at CARLISLE and began to display a talent for wood carving at an early age. To develop this talent he went to London and took up a position with a firm of organ builders, carrying out carving on the casings of their instruments. In 1765 he returned to CARLISLE to handle a commission to restore the woodcarvings in Carlisle Cathedral to the designs of Thomas Pitt (Lord Camelford). In 1789 he was commissioned by the Duke of Norfolk to sculpt a life-size horse for the grounds of Greystoke Castle, near PENRITH. He also sculptured two greyhounds for the gate piers of Crofton Hall, at THURSBY (now demolished). His most notable work is said to have been his statue of Sir Hugh de Morville, for Brayton House. No identifiable examples of his work have survived. He was the father of Thomas Carlyle Senior (q.v.), and Robert Carlyle Senior (q.v.).

CARLYLE, Thomas, Junior (1795- after 1870)

Miniature painter in watercolour. He was born at CARLISLE, the son of Thomas Carlyle Senior (q.v.), the miniature painter, and brother of George Carlyle (q.v.), and Robert Carlyle Junior (q.v.). He is presumed to have received tuition from his father, and to have subsequently joined the latter in Edinburgh, where he exhibited at the 1826 exhibition of the Institute for the Encouragement of Fine Arts. In 1827 he is believed to have been working in MARYPORT and in 1830 he was practising in CARLISLE. Thomas Junior, his father, and his brother George evidently toured Cumbria on joint painting ventures, one of the brothers' newspaper advertisements (*Carlisle Patriot*, 18th October, 1828) reading in reference to a visit to WHITEHAVEN: ". . . Miniatures as usual, by T. Carlyle – Landscape, Figure and Flower Drawing taught by G.C. . . .". He appears to have joined his other brother, Robert, at Preston, Lancashire, at some point in his career for he is listed as a Lancashire artist associated with that town in *Four Centuries of Lancashire Art*. He is believed to have died at GRASMERE some time after 1870.

*CARLYLE, Thomas, Senior (1762- after 1837)

Miniature painter in watercolour; painting and drawing master. He was born at CARLISLE, the son of Thomas Carlyle (q.v.), sculptor and wood carver, and brother of Robert Carlyle Senior (q.v.). He began his career in art as a pattern drawer in CARLISLE, later moving to Edinburgh, where by 1817 he was teaching painting and drawing in schools and to the gentry. He exhibited at the Carlisle Academy from 1825 to 1828, the Dumfries Exhibitions of 1828 and 1830, the Royal Scottish Academy in 1829, the Institute for the Encouragement of Fine Arts, Edinburgh, in 1821 and 1822, and from 1827-1829; and at Liverpool Academy 1829, 1831, 1832 and 1834. He appears to have made periodic visits to his native city while living at Edinburgh, for newspaper advertisements attest to his presence in CARLISLE on a number of occasions during this period, and his 1828 exhibit at the Carlisle Academy was, for instance, contributed from a CARLISLE address. In 1830 he was in CARLISLE, advertising in the *Carlisle Patriot* on 25th October, that he intended to reside in the city, and that "Mr Carlyle Senr., has commenced his CLASSES in all the various Branches of DRAWING . . .". It is presumed that he was with his wife when she

Thomas Carlyle, Senior: John Lowry, 1816.
Miniature 3 × 2½. *Carlisle Museum & Art Gallery.*

John Mulcaster Carrick: The Lily Pond, 1877.
Oil 5¾ × 7¾. *Spink & Son.*

died in Liverpool in 1833, however, and he is recorded as living there in 1837. He was also at Dungarven, Ireland, in 1837, but his movements after that date are unrecorded. His only work in a public collection is a miniature on ivory of John Lowry, dated 1816*, but there are many examples in private collections. His work was invariably well received at the exhibitions at which it was shown. He was the father of Thomas Carlyle Junior (q.v.), George Carlyle (q.v.), and Robert Carlyle Junior (q.v.). Represented: Carlisle A.G.

*CARRICK, John Mulcaster (1833- after 1884)

Landscape, figure and marine painter in oil; etcher. Carrick was born at CARLISLE, the son of Thomas Heathfield Carrick (q.v.), and possibly received his early tuition from his father. He is known to have accompanied the latter to Newcastle upon Tyne (1834), and by 1841 to

London, from which in 1854, he first began exhibiting at the Royal Academy, showing his *From Barrow Common, looking towards Borrowdale, Cumberland*. In this year he also showed one work, a figure study, at the British Institution, following this in 1856 with his only contributions to the Suffolk Street Gallery: *Black Game*, and *Derwentwater, Borrowdale in the distance*. He exhibited at the Royal Academy until 1871, showing Cumbrian, French, Swiss and Spanish landscapes, and a number of figure studies. Two of these exhibits, *The Village Postman* (1856), and *Rydal* (1857), earned the praise of John Ruskin (q.v.). He appears to have spent the remainder of his life based in the London area, travelling widely throughout Britain, and abroad, in search of subjects for his landscapes, and later seascapes and coastal views, such as his *The East Cliff, Dover*, 1884, sold at Sotheby's in 1964. Also while living in London he became a member of the Hogarth Club, which sympathised with Pre-Raphaelite ideas, and joined the Junior Etching Club, for which he illustrated Hood's poems, in 1858, amongst others.

CARRICK, R. (fl.1707-1714)

Carrick is recorded as a painter of WIGTON, who painted the King's Arms in St. Mary's Church, WHITBECK, near MILLOM.

*CARRICK, Thomas Heathfield (1802-1874)

Painter of portrait miniatures in watercolour. Cumbria's outstanding painter of portrait miniatures in the 19th century, Carrick was born at UPPERBY, CARLISLE, the son of a china merchant. After education at Carlisle Grammar School he became a chemist, but found himself increasingly attracted to painting and drawing, showing his first exhibited work at the Carlisle Academy in 1827. In 1830 he first began painting miniatures on marble, an innovation which was to earn for him the Silver Isis Medal of the Society of Arts in 1838, and a medal from Prince Albert in 1854. On leaving CARLISLE in 1833/4 to become a full-time professional artist, Carrick moved to Newcastle upon Tyne, where he appears to have remained until moving to London at the end of the decade. During this period in Newcastle he showed work at the Newcastle exhibitions of 1834 and 1835, and produced portraits of several leading local and North Country celebrities, including Richard Grainger, the builder, and Thomas Miles Richardson Senior, the landscape painter. He also painted portraits of the Rev. W. Turner, Robert Jameson,* and Mr. Buddle, the celebrated geologist, all of which were subsequently engraved. In London he became an immediate success, painting miniatures of Lord John Russell, Daniel O'Connell, Thomas Carlyle, Wordsworth, Longfellow, and Sir Robert Peel. During the twenty-five years 1841-1866 he exhibited no fewer than 140 works at the Royal Academy, but with the introduction of photography he found it increasingly difficult to find sitters.

In 1858 he decided to leave London, and give in to the popularity of photography by becoming a colourist for Scarborough photographer and art patron Sarony. This proved so successful that he decided to set up a photographic establishment in London, returning there by 1862, where he opened a business in Regent Street. Here

Thomas Heathfield Carrick: Robert Jameson.
Watercolour $7\frac{3}{8} \times 5\frac{7}{8}$.
Tyne & Wear County Museums, Laing Art Gallery.

he advertised himself as a "photographer and miniature painter, on ivory, marble and the photographic base", and enjoyed success for some years. By 1866, however, the business had collapsed and he was forced to retire to Newcastle, on the Turner annuity granted to him, dying there eight years later. He was the father of John Mulcaster Carrick (q.v.), and among the several portraits of fellow artists which he produced was that of William James Blacklock (q.v.); Carlisle Art Gallery has both the latter, and a self portrait. Represented: Victoria and Albert Museum; Carlisle A.G.; Laing A.G., Newcastle.

CARRUTHERS, Richard (1792-1876)

Portrait painter in oil; copyist. Born at CROSBY ON EDEN, near CARLISLE, Carruthers went to London at an early age, and attended the Royal Academy Schools, where in 1816 and 1817 he won prizes for his copies of works by the Old Masters. He subsequently exhibited at the Royal Academy, showing his first work: *A child sleeping*, in 1816, and a variety of portraits until 1819. One of his portrait exhibits was William Wordsworth (1770-1850), shown 1818. His portrait of Wordsworth is worth noting as it was the first to be executed under the eyes of the poet's wife and sister, and the first to be engraved; until Wordsworth was 61 any likeness which appeared in public was a version of this (see also F. Blanshard, *Portraits of Wordsworth*, 1959). He showed only one work at the British Institution, in 1817, this being the same work as that shown at the Royal Academy in 1816. About 1819 he was advised to leave CARLISLE for health reasons, and settled in South America, where he amassed a considerable fortune. He showed two portraits at the 1825 exhibition of the Carlisle Academy in this period, presumably while visiting the city from South America, or another of his business bases, Lisbon, but did not return permanently until 1837, subsequently taking a leading role in arranging exhibitions of work by British artists at Carlisle Athenaeum, in 1850. He built his own home Eden Grove, at CROSBY, and spent the remainder of his life fishing and painting.

CARRUTHERS, *of Ulverston* (fl.1819)

Landscape painter. He painted two views of *Gooseholme – from the north and south,* in the collection of Kendal Town Hall. The views were painted in 1819, and portray a riverside area at KENDAL.

CLARKE, William (1805-1823)

Clarke is recorded in the *Carlisle Patriot,* 31st May, 1823, as a "young artist of promise", who died of consumption in KENDAL at the age of eighteen. Nothing more is known of this artist.

CLEMENTSON, John (*c.*1780-1841)

Marine and figure painter in oil. He was born at WHITEHAVEN, the son of Thomas Clementson, and is thought to have become apprenticed to the same master as Robert Salmon (q.v.). He became a successful painter of marine subjects, and achieved something of a reputation as a teacher, one of his pupils being Oliver Ussinon Hodgson (q.v.). Salmon, Clementson and Hodgson are among the best known members of the Whitehaven School of Marine Painters. The work of all three is said to have marked stylistic similarities. He died at WORKINGTON.

COLLIER, Thomas (1734-1825)

House and decorative painter. He painted the Royal Arms for St. James Church, HUTTON-IN-THE-FOREST, while working as a painter at PENRITH.

COLLINGWOOD (Altounyan), Dora (b.1885)

Portrait painter in oil. The eldest daughter of William Gershom Collingwood (q.v.), and Edith Mary "Dorothy" Collingwood (q.v.), and sister of Barbara Crystal Collingwood (q.v.), she was born at GILLHEAD, near WINDERMERE, and received her early tuition in art from her parents, and at Cope's Studio in London, subsequently becoming an accomplished amateur painter of portraits. Included among her portrait subjects was Arthur Ransome (q.v.), a friend of the Collingwood family from his early manhood, whose portrait is in the collection of the Abbot Hall Art Gallery, KENDAL. Ransome had a romantic attachment to Dora for many years, but she married Ernest Altounyan, son of an Armenian doctor. She later lived at Aleppo, Syria, with her husband. Represented: Abbot Hall A.G., Kendal; Ruskin Museum, Coniston.

*COLLINGWOOD (Gnosspelius), Barbara Crystal (1887-1961)

Sculptor and painter. The second daughter of William Gershom Collingwood (q.v.), and Edith Mary "Dorothy" Collingwood (q.v.), and younger sister of Dora Collingwood (q.v.), she was born at GILLHEAD, near WINDERMERE and received tuition in art from her parents, and at Cope's Studio in London, before becoming a successful portrait sculptor and painter. She showed her work at the Royal Academy on three occasions between 1915 and 1917, and at various provincial exhibitions throughout her life. Among the many famous heads which she modelled was that of John Ruskin (q.v.), examples of which are at the Ruskin Museum at CONISTON, and the Armitt Library, AMBLESIDE.* She also carved the War Memorial at HAWKSHEAD, to her father's design. She was President of the Lake Artists' Society 1932-1946 in succession to her father, with whom she lived until her marriage to Oscar Theodor Gnosspelius (1878-1953), surveyor, civil engineer and inventor. Represented: Armitt Library, Ambleside; Ruskin Museum, Coniston.

COLLINGWOOD, Mrs. Edith Mary "Dorothy" (*née* Isaac) (1857-1928)

Portrait, landscape, flower and miniature painter in oil and watercolour. The wife of William Gershom Collingwood (q.v.), and mother of Dora Collingwood (q.v.), and Barbara Crystal Collingwood (q.v.), she was born the elder daughter of Thomas Isaac, a corn merchant of Maldon, Essex. She began drawing at an early age, and when she was eighteen her parents allowed her to go to an art school in London. There she lived with relatives of her future husband, meeting him while they both attended the

Barbara Crystal Collingwood: John Ruskin.
Plaster bust. *The Armitt Trust, The Armitt Library, Ambleside.*

Slade. For several years she painted people and flowers, and decorated various domestic and personal objects with her paintings, but after her marriage in 1883, and her move with her husband to GILLHEAD, near WINDERMERE, soon afterwards, she began to specialise in painting flowers and miniatures. In 1901 she was elected to the society of Miniaturists, and began exhibiting in London.

Two of her works in portraiture were shown at the Royal Academy exhibitions of 1910 and 1911. She also exhibited in Cumbria, showing one of her flower paintings at Carlisle Art Gallery in 1896, and throughout her life at Lanehead, CONISTON, she locally exhibited and sold her work alongside that of her husband, and occasionally her daughters. Her work as a miniature painter took her all over the North of England, one of her commissions involving a visit to Wallington Hall, Northumberland, where she was asked to complete the panels of flower paintings in the Great Hall, to which John Ruskin (q.v.) had contributed work. She travelled widely abroad before the First World War, landscape sketching in the Tyrol, Venice and the Italian Lakes. Her health gradually failed in the post war years but she is said to have painted until her death. Many examples of her work were shown, alongside that of her husband, at a special exhibition at the Abbot Hall Art Gallery, KENDAL, in 1971.

*COLLINGWOOD, William Gershom (1854-1932)

Landscape and figure painter in oil and watercolour. The eldest son of William Collingwood, R.W.S., a Member of the Royal Society of Painters in Water Colours, he was born at Liverpool and studied initially under his father, who took him sketching all over Switzerland. He later attended University College, Oxford, where he met John Ruskin (q.v.), and following this studied at the Slade under Alphonse Legros. In 1880 he first began exhibiting his work in London, showing his watercolour: *In a Vaudois Village*, at the Suffolk Street Gallery. Ruskin then asked him to come to CONISTON, to act as his secretary, and to study geology, later taking him abroad, where Collingwood filled sketchbooks with Italian Sculpture, and geological studies in the Alps Savoy. In 1883 he married Edith Mary Isaac, whom he had met at the Slade, and shortly after moved to GILLHEAD, near WINDERMERE, where all four of his children (see Dora Collingwood, and Barbara Crystal Collingwood) were born. Ruskin found them a property: Lanehead, near his home at Brantwood, CONISTON, after the birth of the children, and here Collingwood and his wife remained for almost the rest of their lives.

During this period in Cumbria, Collingwood found his vocation as a painter, and began to paint Lake District scenery in all its moods, though not until 1902 with his *Winter at Coniston,* did he begin to show this type of work at the Royal Academy, having from 1885 concentrated on figure and flower studies and continental landscapes. Also in Cumbria he became even further interested in the geological aspects of the area introduced to him by Ruskin, and in many features of its ancient and more recent history. He became a member (and later President), of the Cumberland and Westmorland Antiquarian Society, and underlined his growing interest in landscape painting by becoming a founder member of the Lake Artists' Society in 1904, and President 1922-32.

Although the demands made upon him by Ruskin from

William Gershom Collingwood:
The Northern Gods Descending.
Watercolour 30×17. *Roy Miles Gallery.*

the time of his move to Lanehead in 1891 were considerable, Collingwood nevertheless found time to engage in many literary and artistic activities, including the writing of his books on the life and work of Ruskin, and various works of historical fact and fiction, the exhibition of archaeological studies at Carlisle Art Gallery in 1896, and a tour of Iceland in 1897 which produced a book illustrated with his own watercolours. After Ruskin's death he spent some years as Professor of Fine Art at University College, Reading, but resigned his chair in 1910 to return to CONISTON. Here, except for a period with Admiralty Intelligence during the First World War, he remained for the rest of his life. He showed one further work at the Royal Academy – his *Swallow Scar, Coniston,* of 1915 – but otherwise appears to have been content to exhibit either with the Lake Artists' Society, or at his home. His last great literary work was the revision of his 1902 edition of *The Lake Counties* (republished in 1932). Many interesting insights into the life of the Collingwood family are contained in the autobiography of

Arthur Ransome (q.v.), and the catalogue of the exhibition devoted to the work of husband and wife held at the Abbot Hall Art Gallery, KENDAL, in 1971. Represented: Abbot Hall A.G., Kendal; Carlisle A.G.; Keswick Museum; Preston A.G.; Ruskin Museum, Coniston.

COLLINS, Henry (1782-1824)
Marine painter. Little is known of this artist of WHITEHAVEN, except that one of his paintings of the Brocklebank ship *Princess Charlotte,* executed in 1816, was for thirty years the property of local carver and gilder James Martin. It was exhibited in WHITEHAVEN in 1885, and is said to have shown Collins as a "very mature artist". In the following year it was purchased by Harold Brocklebank. Collins may have been related to a MISS COLLINS, also of WHITEHAVEN, who painted in the middle of the 19th century. He died at PARTON, near WHITEHAVEN, his obituary in the *Whitehaven Gazette,* 16th August, 1824, stating: "... He was a man of very superior taste in his profession, and although inferior to the celebrated Salomon (Salmon)‡ was considered the first marine painter in the North of England".

‡ *Robert Salmon (q.v.).*

COLOMB, General George Thomas, Hon R.H.A. (1787-1874)
Landscape painter. Colomb was possibly born in Galloway in Scotland, and did not visit Cumbria until he had served in the British Army for many years, and had attained the rank of Major. He first arrived in the area in September 1827, taking lodgings at Armathwaite Castle on the banks of the River Eden, and remaining there until 1830. In the month following his arrival he became a subscriber to the Carlisle Academy, and by 1830 he was exhibiting at the latter, showing six landscapes, and had become elected President. He also in this year exhibited at the Dumfries Exhibition. During his stay at ARMATHWAITE he was described as "perhaps one of the cleverest amateur painters in the north". A lottery of his collection of paintings was held in Dumfries in 1833, when he was described as "a first rate painter, and in the opinion of many, rivals in some things, and surpasses in others, even the great Glover himself".‡ He appears to have settled at Knockbrex, in Galloway, after leaving Cumbria. He had a one-man exhibition in Dumfries in 1837, and is next recorded at Dublin, from which in 1841 he sent six landscapes and marine subjects to the Royal Hibernian Academy exhibition of that year. He exhibited at the Academy until 1868, becoming an honorary member in 1854. He died at Dalkey in Ireland.

‡ *John Glover Senior (q.v.)*

*COOPER, Alfred Heaton (1863-1929)
Landscape painter in oil and watercolour; book illustrator. Cooper was born in or near Bolton, Lancashire, and trained as an accountant until he was twenty-one. In 1884 he gained a scholarship to Westminster School of Art, where he was taught by George Clausen, and Frederick Walker, among others, and began to develop an interest in two themes in painting which were to dominate his work for the rest of his life: country people at work in their natural surroundings, and the effects of light on landscape.

After training in London he spent periods of time in Morocco (1888), Scotland and the Lake District (1889-90), and Norway (1891-92), where he met his future wife. During this period he also began exhibiting at the Royal Academy, a practice which he was to maintain until four years short of his death, showing many Cumbrian and Scottish landscapes. In 1894 he married at Balholm in Norway, moving subsequently to Bolton, where he spent three years. Here, and later at Southport in Lancashire, where his daughter Ellide was born, he found it difficult to make a living, and by 1900 the family had moved first to HAWKSHEAD in the Lake District, later to a cottage on Mines Beck. At CONISTON, his two sons Frithjof, and William Heaton (see below) were born, and with his family now considerably enlarged he welcomed the opportunity given to him in 1904, to provide seventy-five illustrations to a book: *The English Lakes.* This was to prove the beginning of a long and fruitful relationship with its publishers, and was to produce a dozen books covering various parts of Britain, and Scandinavia. In this period he built a Norwegian-style home at CONISTON (1905), and on the Sognefjord, Norway (1907), later moving to ULVERSTON to help with the schooling of his children. His second daughter, Una, was born at ULVERSTON, and the family remained there until about 1914, when they moved to AMBLESIDE.

Alfred Heaton Cooper: Ambleside; Lake Road in the snow. Watercolour 21½ × 14⅜. *Abbot Hall Art Gallery.*

From the publication of his first book until his death Cooper became increasingly popular, exhibiting his work both in Sweden and in Britain, where he continued to exhibit at the Royal Academy, the Royal Institute of Painters in Water Colours, and various other London and provincial establishments. His last home, at AMBLESIDE, was a 17th century cottage once occupied by the poet Sir William Watson, where he died of cancer in 1929. His son WILLIAM HEATON COOPER (b. 1903), has become one of Cumbria's best known professional artists: his grandson, JULIAN COOPER (b. 1947), is also an artist. Represented: Abbot Hall A.G., Kendal.

CORNILLON, A. (fl.1831-1845)
Landscape painter in oil; drawing teacher. Cornillon, a Frenchman by birth, is recorded as working in CARLISLE, between 1831 and 1839, as a teacher of drawing and French. During his stay at CARLISLE two of his lithographs of the city were published (1832).

CORSON, Joseph (1806- after 1858)
Painter of portrait miniatures; clockmaker. He was probably the son of James Corson, a shipwright at MARYPORT, and was baptised at the Wesleyan Church in the town. He appears to have been mainly a watchmaker, supplementing his income by portrait painting, and worked at KESWICK, MARYPORT and WHITEHAVEN. In the 1841 Census he was at MARYPORT; in 1847 he was listed in a directory as a "miniature painter" living at WHITEHAVEN, and in the 1851 Census he was at MARYPORT, and was described as a "watchmaker and portrait painter". He was at MARYPORT in 1858, and appears to have died in the 1860's. Joseph's brother James was also a clockmaker, but is not known to have painted.

Their work in clockmaking is described in *The Clockmakers of Cumberland*, by J. B. Penfold, in his chapter, "The Clockmakers of Maryport".

COURT, Salathiel (late 17th, early 18th cent.)
Inn-sign and landscape painter. Court was born at PAPCASTLE, near COCKERMOUTH, towards the close of the 17th century, and was left an orphan at an early age. He is best known in connection with the story of *The Lion That Ran Away* (recently retold in *Legends of the Lake Counties*). This story arose out of a commission he once received to paint a lion for an inn-sign. He asked if he might paint the lion chained, and when this request was refused, he decided to paint the animal in watercolour, which disappeared from the sign at the first rain fall. When accused of trickery he pointed out that as the lion had not been painted chained, it was hardly his fault that it had disappeared. He later reconciled his differences with the inn-keeper and painted the animal in oil. It is said that he became popular as a painter of the houses of neighbouring yeomen, and hunting scenes. Later he became a bellman at WHITEHAVEN. Following this he was imprisoned for an offence involving the production of false marriage lines, and was transported to the American Colonies, where he died seven years later. An interesting account of Court's life can be found in John Askew's *Guide to Cockermouth*, 2nd edition, 1872.

*COUTTS, Hubert – see TUCKER, Hubert.

COWPER (COWPER-ESSEX), Thomas, later Colonel (1863-1927)
Figure, flower and portrait painter. He was the elder son of Thomas Christopher Cowper-Essex, of HAWKSHEAD. He

Hubert Coutts (Tucker):
A Moorland Sheep Farm.
Watercolour 24×32.
The Rev. J. Breay.

was educated at Harrow and later became a painter, exhibiting his work as "Thomas Cowper" at the Royal Academy, the Royal Institute of Oil Painters, the Royal Society of Portrait Painters, the New Gallery and in the provinces between 1891 and 1906. He served in the South African War 1901-2, and in 1903 he assumed the additional name of "Essex", as his father had done before him. From 1906 to 1917 he was Lieutenant Colonel, 3rd Battalion, The Royal North Lancashire Regiment. In the First World War he was in command of the 3rd (reserve) Battalion of the Regiment, retiring as honorary colonel in 1917. He was killed in a road accident in France in 1927.

COX, Thomas J. (fl.1833-1850)
Architectural draughtsman. Cox practised as an architect in CARLISLE in the first half of the 19th century. He exhibited at the Carlisle Academy in 1833, showing his design for the *Carlisle Mechanics' Institute etc., about to be erected,* and at Carlisle Athenaeum in 1850 showed his *Design for the City and District Bank, English Street.* His design for the Mechanics' Institute was not successful in meeting the approval of the sponsors of the project.

*CRANKE, James, Senior (1707-1780)
Portrait painter in oil. Cranke was born at URSWICK in the FURNESS area of Cumbria, where he possibly received some encouragement to paint from itinerant artists visiting the locality. After some attempts to earn a living painting at his home village he went to London, where his "diligence and assiduity" in his application to painting are said to have earned him a position at the Old Academy of St. Martin's Lane. About 1744 he married the daughter of a prosperous family and moved to Bloomsbury, where at least four of his children, including James Cranke Junior (q.v.), were born. In 1752 Cranke, his wife and children had moved to FURNESS, and by 1755 to his birthplace, where he had built a large new house to accommodate his family. His some twenty-five years of remaining life saw him establish himself as a successful portrait painter at URSWICK, producing many portraits of North Country landowners, several family portraits, and at least one painting of fruit. Most of this work has now been lost, or has survived in a much deteriorated condition. It was still accessible and impressive enough in 1906, however, to enable Harper Gaythorpe, F.S.A. Scot., our principal source of information about Cranke Senior and Junior (*Two "Old Masters" – the Crankes of Urswick* – Cumberland and Westmorland Antiquarian and Archaeological Society's Transactions, Vol. VI, New Series, 1906) to comment: "In all, the faces are excellent, and must have been good likenesses". Surprisingly, Gaythorpe does not confirm, nor indeed refer to, the attribution of *The Last Supper,* in St. Mary's, URSWICK, to the hand of Cranke Senior. Perhaps this is because the subject matter was, in his view, more appropriate to the work of Cranke Junior. Represented: Barrow Museum and A.G.

CRANKE, James, Junior (1746-1826)
Portrait and fruit painter; copyist. Cranke was born in London, the second son of James Cranke Senior (q.v.), and came to the FURNESS area of Cumbria about 1751. When he was nine the family settled at URSWICK, his father's birthplace, where he is believed to have attended

James Cranke, Senior:
Portrait of a Lady in Rubens' costume. Oil 30×25.
On loan to the Abbot Hall Art Gallery from a private collection.

the local grammar school, and to have been introduced to painting by Cranke Senior. As a young man he spent some time studying at the galleries of Dresden and Antwerp, where he is said to have copied works by Leonardo da Vinci, and Rubens. Before the year 1773 he went to Warrington, Lancashire, with some introductions to the principal families of the area, and settled there for a time. While living in, or about, Warrington, he painted a copy of Andrea del Sarto's *Holy Family,* which now hangs above the altar of Trinity Church, in the town, and commenced exhibiting at the Royal Academy, giving a London address.

Some doubt exists from this point forward as to whether he lived exclusively in London for the next quarter century or merely used it as a base, as all his exhibits until 1800 are identified with addresses in the capital, while strong connections with Warrington during this period are also claimed. Also there is some suspicion that at least one of the twelve Royal Academy exhibits of Cranke Junior, may in fact have been sent by Cranke Senior. By the turn of the century, however, he had definitely moved north to Gainford, in County Durham, to join, and look after the affairs of, his clergyman brother John, who had suffered from fits following his appointment there in 1798. At Gainford he painted the Royal Arms for the vestry of the church, and a number of portraits and religious compositions, also finding time to help save the church from being washed away by floods, and establish a reputation as a man of "taste and genius".

On his brother's death Cranke Junior left Gainford and returned to URSWICK, living for the rest of his life with his nephew at Hawkfield in the village. During this period his portrait was painted by Daniel Gardner (q.v.). For some years before his death he was blind. Cranke Junior has frequently been described as the nephew of Cranke Senior, and not as he really was – the latter's son. Also Redgrave, Graves, and several others have confused one with the other, or treated both as the same person. For the information here presented we are indebted to the authority quoted in the entry for James Cranke Senior.

*CROSSLAND, James Henry ("Herbert") (1852-1939)

Landscape painter in oil. He was born at Sandal, near Wakefield, Yorkshire, and subsequently became a successful professional artist, practising mainly in the Lake District. He exhibited at the Royal Academy, the Royal Cambrian Academy, the Suffolk Street Gallery, the Royal Glasgow Institute of Fine Arts, and at various provincial art galleries. During this period he lived first at Belper, Derbyshire (1885), later at WINDERMERE (1889), BROUGHTON-IN-FURNESS (1903-c.1924), then at AMBLESIDE, at which he appears to have spent the remainder of his life. While living at BROUGHTON he became a founder member of the Lake Artists' Society (1904), and a regular exhibitor at its annual exhibitions. He painted mostly Cumbrian and Scottish landscapes. Represented: Abbot Hall A.G., Kendal; Keswick Museum; Ruskin Museum, Coniston.

CROSTHWAITE, Daniel (fl.1833-1851)

Portrait and landscape painter in oil. Crosthwaite was born at ULVERSTON, in the FURNESS area of Cumbria, and became a member of the School of Artists practising at COCKERMOUTH. He exhibited at the Royal Academy, the Society of Arts, and the Suffolk Street Gallery, between 1833 and 1845, showing portraits and landscapes, and receiving the Society of Arts Isis Gold Medal for the best portrait in its exhibition of 1833. The British Museum has an engraving of his portrait of the Rev. John Stonard of ULVERSTON, dated 1833. His view of ULVERSTON from the north west was engraved in 1842, and a view of Furness Abbey in 1844. In 1851 he was living at Benson Street, ULVERSTON, after which nothing is known of him. He was probably related to Samuel Crosthwaite (q.v.), and Thomas Crosthwaite (q.v.). Represented: British Museum.

CROSTHWAITE, Robert (d.1844)

Sculptor and stonemason. Crosthwaite practised as a sculptor and stonemason at ASPATRIA in the first half of the 19th century. His obituary records him as "... a first rate artist in his time of life ... his tombstones and monuments in the churchyards of the West evincing both talent in design and execution rarely to be rivalled in the country ...". He was possibly related to ISAAC, JOSEPH and THOMAS CROSTHWAITE, all three of whom practised as sculptors and stonemasons either at WIGTON or ASPATRIA in the 19th century, the last named taking over the former premises and quarrying facilities of Joseph Blain (q.v.) at CHALK, near DALSTON, in 1837.

*CROSTHWAITE, Samuel (1791-1868)

Portrait and landscape painter in oil; copyist and engraver. Born at COCKERMOUTH, the son of James Crosthwaite, he became associated with the Cockermouth School of Artists while working as a weaver, and possibly received tuition from Joseph Sutton (q.v.). Following this he travelled to London to further his studies, and in 1823 contributed two landscapes to the Royal Academy. From London he appears to have moved to KENDAL, from which in 1824, he sent some twenty portraits and landscapes to the second annual exhibition of the Carlisle Academy. One of these exhibits was a self portrait, of which no trace can be found at the present time. Crosthwaite remained at KENDAL for the rest of his life, sending six further works to the Carlisle Academy by 1826, and two works to the 1846 exhibition of Carlisle Athenaeum. During this period he worked briefly in Liverpool and may well have exhibited in that city.

One of his best known subjects in portraiture was William Wordsworth (1770-1850), of whom he painted no fewer than four portraits. His first was painted at the invitation of the poet, and was executed in 1833; his last,

James Henry (Herbert)
Crossland:
River Scene.
Oil 5½×9¼.
James Alder Ltd.

Samuel Crosthwaite: Dorothy Wordsworth, 1833.
Oil $21\frac{1}{2} \times 17\frac{1}{2}$. *Rydal Mount, Ambleside.*

only three weeks before Wordsworth died. One of these portraits was purchased by the Earl of Lonsdale soon after it was painted, and is now in Dove Cottage, GRASMERE. He also painted the only surviving portrait of Dorothy Wordsworth[#] (see F. Blanshard's *Portraits of Wordsworth*, 1959, for more details of his portraits of the family, and interesting insights into his work and character), now at Rydal Mount, AMBLESIDE. A view of COCKERMOUTH by the artist is on view at Wordsworth's birthplace, at COCKERMOUTH, and various of his portraits may be found in public and private collections throughout the area in which he worked. He engraved several portraits by George Sheffield, Senior (q.v.),[#] and eighteen of his coloured engravings after Old Masters were included in a sale of his work by public lottery which was held at KENDAL in 1850. He was possibly related to Daniel Crosthwaite (q.v.), and Thomas Crosthwaite (q.v.). He died at KENDAL. Represented: Keswick Museum; Whitehaven Museum.

CROSTHWAITE, Thomas (fl. 1842)
Portrait painter in oil. He was born at COCKERMOUTH, and was possibly the brother of Samuel Crosthwaite (q.v.). He appears to have practised mainly at WIGTON, and little more is known of him beyond what is contained in a description of his work which appeared in the *Cumberland Pacquet*, 14th June, 1842: "... we have seen some of Mr. Crosthwaite's latest productions in which the hand of no ordinary master is perceptible in almost every touch. His likeness' are inimitable and he not merely transfers the countenances to the canvas, but embodies in it the very life and character of the original. If we may be allowed to

hazard a conjecture we dare say that Mr. Crosthwaite will at no distant period take a very high stand among artists of the present day". This newspaper description referred to a visit by Crosthwaite, to KESWICK. His wife died at KESWICK two years later, so he may have remained there for an extended period. He was possibly related to Daniel Crosthwaite (q.v.).

CURWEN, John Flavel (1860-1932)
Architectural draughtsman and author. Curwen practised as an architect in KENDAL and produced many drawings of old buildings associated with the town, sometimes from memory, or from information given by others. He is best remembered for his *Kirkbie-Kendall* written and illustrated by himself, with some assistance from A. N. W. Hodgson (q.v.), and published by Titus Wilson in 1900. He also wrote several other antiquarian works associated with Cumbria. He was a Fellow of the Society of Antiquaries, and a Fellow of the Royal Institute of British Architects. His *Old Buildings of Kendal*, in pencil and watercolour, is in the collection of Kendal Public Library and shows buildings in the town's Stricklandgate taken down in 1822 and 1833. This work was shown in "The Artists' Kendal" exhibition at the Abbot Hall Art Gallery, KENDAL, Summer 1975.

DALTON, Richard (1715-1791)
Draughtsman and engraver. He was born at DEAN, the son of a Rector, and after first working as a coach painter in London, went to Rome to study art. Here he met Lord Charlemont, who in 1749 asked Dalton to accompany him to Sicily, Greece, Constantinople and Egypt. On his return to England he became librarian to the Prince of Wales, and in 1763 George III sent him back to Italy to make a collection of drawings, medals, etc. This led to his appointment as keeper of royal drawings and medals, and in 1778 to surveyor of royal paintings. He is said to have possessed "little powers as an artist", but his output was considerable. He drew and engraved a number of views to illustrate his travels, made some engravings of the Holbein drawings in the royal collection, and published two works containing his own etched and engraved illustrations: *A Selection from the Antiquities of Athens*, and *The Ceremonies and Manners of the Turks*. He also produced an etching from life of Sir Joshua Reynolds, when young. His only exhibited work was his drawing of *An Egyptian Dancing Girl*, shown at the Society of Artists, in 1766. He was a member of the Artists' Committee appointed in 1755 to establish a Royal Academy, and was treasurer and director of the Society of Artists in 1765. He died in London. His brother was John Dalton, poet and divine.

DANIEL, Henry Wilkinson (fl. 1908-1953)
Portrait painter and etcher. This artist practised in CARLISLE for several years in the middle of the present century. His first employment was as a surveyor, but he later took up art and studied at the Slade under Professor

Frederick Brown. He was living in London in 1908, and at Playden, Sussex in 1912, but by 1916 he was living at Cramond Bridge in Scotland, becoming art master at Trinity College, Glenalmond, and Governor of the Allen Fraser Art College, Arbroath. He exhibited widely, showing his work at the Royal Academy, the Royal Institute of Oil Painters, the Royal Scottish Academy and the Royal Scottish Society of Painters in Water Colours, and at various London and provincial galleries; a one-man exhibition of his work was staged at Carlisle Art Gallery in 1953, and his portrait of G. H. Routledge was illustrated in the *Cumberland News,* 17th May, 1952.

DAVIS, Joseph Barnard (1861-1943)

Landscape painter in oil and watercolour; illustrator. Barnard was born at BOWNESS-ON-WINDERMERE, and later lived in London, where he exhibited at the Royal Academy, the Royal Institute of Painters in Water Colours, the Suffolk Street Gallery, and various other art establishments between 1890 and 1911. He appears to have spent his entire professional life in London. The National Portrait Gallery has his pen and ink portrait of the artist Frederick Goodall (1822-1904).

DAWSON, Francis (fl.1791-1820)

Seal cutter and engraver. This artist worked in Dublin and London before opening a marble yard near WHITEHAVEN, specialising in "...all kinds of Plain and Ornamented CHIMNEYS, GRAVE STONES, MONUMENTS and various other Articles in the Marble Line...", according to his advertisement in the *Cumberland Pacquet,* 8th January, 1793. This publication also recorded in its 14th April, 1795 issue that "A few days ago, a very handsome monument was erected in St. Nicholas's churchyard in this town (WHITEHAVEN) to the memory of the late Henry Littledale, Esq., and his two daughters ... The whole was executed by Mr. Francis Dawson, marble cutter of this town, and does great credit to his taste and abilities...". A well-engraved bookplate dating from Dawson's Dublin days is also known.

DELL, A. S. (fl.1889-1901)

He was listed in a directory of 1901 as an artist living at 7 St. James Road, CARLISLE. He showed one work at the Walker Art Gallery, Liverpool, in 1889, while living at Liverpool.

DOBSON, John (1799-1867)

Portrait and genre painter in oil and watercolour. He was born at CARLISLE, and was apprenticed to a shoemaker at an early age. In this occupation he formed a friendship with the father of Samuel Bough (q.v.), who was also a shoemaker by trade, but was then working as a servant for Sir Joseph Gilpin, a patron of the arts. Sir Joseph encouraged Dobson in his painting, and he became one of the first students of the Carlisle Academy on its foundation in 1823, receiving tuition from Matthew Ellis Nutter (q.v.). Later he held his own drawing classes in CARLISLE, where one of his pupils was Samuel Bough. Although Dobson appears to have remained a shoemaker all his life, he not only taught drawing, but became an accomplished painter of portraits and genre subjects, showing his work at the Carlisle Academy from 1823-

1833, the Dumfries Exhibitions of 1828 and 1830, and Carlisle Athenaeum, in 1846 and 1850. Carlisle Art Gallery has his *Girl in a white satin dress,* dated 1833. This painting has featured in two of the gallery's major exhibitions since 1970: "Cumberland Artists 1700-1900", in 1971, and "The Carlisle Exhibitions 1823-1850", in 1973. Represented: Carlisle A.G.

DUCKETT, Thomas (1804-1878)

Sculptor. Born at Preston, Lancashire, Duckett was a self-taught artist, who after employment by a local plasterer changed his occupation to that of wood carver. Later he went to Liverpool where he was employed by Franceys, and showed a bust of the Rev. Dunn at the Liverpool Academy. From Liverpool he moved to KENDAL to join the firm of Francis Webster & Sons,‡ eventually becoming manager of their sculptural department. His first large work of note was his *St. George and the Dragon* in limestone, for the pediment of Kendal Roman Catholic Church. Another work was his monument to William Pearson (d. 1856), at St. Mary's Church, CROSTHWAITE, near KENDAL; a bust. On leaving KENDAL some time after 1857 Duckett returned to Preston, dying there in 1878. He was responsible for many sculptural works for clients in Preston, and North Lancashire before and after working in KENDAL, notable amongst which was his statue of Sir Robert Peel in Winckley Square, Preston. (1851). Represented: Kendal Museum; Preston A.G.

‡ *See Francis Webster (q.v.), and George Webster (q.v.).*

*DUNBAR, David, Senior (1782-1866)

Sculptor. Dunbar was born at Dumfries and is principally interesting in the context of this dictionary as one of the prime movers in the foundation of the Carlisle Academy, and as an artist who was later responsible for many important sculptural commissions in Cumbria. The son of a stonemason, he was apprenticed to his father, and by the age of seventeen had become so proficient as a sculptor that he was carrying out the carving of capitals and other decorative parts of Lowther Castle. Later he entered the studio of Sir Francis Chantrey in London, remaining there for nine years and beginning to exhibit at the Royal Academy. Moving to CARLISLE by 1822 he was employed by Paul Nixson (q.v.), and had a well established studio in the city. In 1822 he became one of the small group of local artists comprising Matthew Ellis Nutter (q.v.), Robert Carlyle Senior (q.v.), Paul Nixson (q.v.), and Joshua Anderson (q.v.), responsible for the foundation of a "Carlisle Academy for the Encouragement of Fine Arts in the North of England", and in 1823, together with his employer, mainly responsible for the erection of The Artists' Academy in the city. This led to one of his earliest important commissions: a figure for the niche above the archway of the building; a sculptor finishing the bust of a princess. Together with Nutter, Dunbar arranged the Academy's first exhibition, and held classes, having among the pupils in his own class Musgrave Lewthwaite Watson (q.v.). He showed twelve works at the opening exhibition of the Academy in 1823, and showed work regularly until exhibitions ceased in 1833.

In 1825 Nixson received an important statue commission requiring marble, and sent Dunbar to Carrara in Italy to make a selection of material. He was allowed to remain in Italy for more than a year, using the time to visit Rome, and meeting Joseph Gott, and Musgrave Lewthwaite Watson, his former pupil. On his return to CARLISLE he remained actively involved in the affairs of the Academy, and showed his work at Newcastle, Dumfries, Birmingham and Leeds. In 1830, however, he decided to move to Newcastle, basing himself there for the next decade and becoming one of the best known sculptors in the North East of England before deciding to move to London, shortly after resuming exhibiting at the Royal Academy in 1842. From London he is said to have travelled "the length and breadth of Britain to carry out commissions", before returning to Dumfries to die in 1866.

His Cumbrian work included his bust of Robert Anderson "The Bard of Cumberland", shown at the Carlisle Academy 1823, and the latter's memorial tablet erected in Carlisle Cathedral in 1834; also the recumbent figure of Katherine Losh#, for the mausoleum built by her sister Sarah Losh (q.v.), beside St. Mary's Church, WREAY. Pevsner's *Cumberland & Westmorland* identifies many other pieces by the sculptor in churches throughout Cumbria. He was the father of DAVID DUNBAR, JUNIOR (*c.*1817-*c.*1842), who practised at Newcastle upon Tyne and Manchester. Several previous dictionaries have confused the dates and work of Dunbar Senior, and Junior, possibly because of the former's long working life, and the fact that he discontinued exhibiting at the Royal Academy for many years in the middle of his career. Represented: National Portrait Gallery; Carlisle A.G.

DURDEN, James, R.O.I. (1878-1964)
Landscape and portrait painter in oil and watercolour. Durden was born at Manchester, and studied at the Manchester College of Art and at the Royal College of Art, before becoming a successful professional artist. He exhibited at the Royal Academy, the Royal Institute of Oil Painters, the Royal Society of Portrait Painters, the Royal Institute of Painters in Water Colours, the provinces and abroad. During this period he lived in London, and for several years at WHITEHAVEN and KESWICK. One of his two final contributions to the Royal Academy was his *Grasmere Sports, Westmorland*, shown 1937. Durden became a member of the Royal Institute of Oil Painters in 1927, and also in this year won a silver medal at the Paris Salon. Represented: Keswick Museum.

EDMONDS, E. M. (fl.1860-1905)
Landscape painter in watercolour; architectural draughtsman and lithographer. Little is known of Edmonds except that he was a competent landscape painter and draughtsman who practised in both KENDAL, and London. He contributed three works to the Suffolk Street Gallery from KENDAL in the period 1872-4, all of which featured South Country subjects, while from his

David Dunbar, Senior:
Katherine Losh statue
in the Losh Mausoleum,
St. Mary's, Wreay.

London address between 1889-1905, he contributed one work to the exhibitions of the Royal Society of Artists, Birmingham, and thirty-seven works to the New Gallery. Some of his work was executed in pencil on tinted paper, and later heightened with Chinese White, much in the style of the drawings of Thomas Allom (1804-1872). An example of Edmonds' Cumbrian work in the form of a lithograph of Kendal Castle, 1860, was shown in "The Artists' Kendal" exhibition at the Abbot Hall Art Gallery, KENDAL, Summer, 1975. Kendal Town Hall has an example of his work in watercolour depicting a street scene with figures c. 1860.

EVERSON, Richard (fl. c.1805-1885)
Portrait painter in oil. Everson was a portrait painter active in KENDAL in the 19th century. Kendal Town Hall has his portraits of William Pennington, Mayor of the town 1786-7, and 1803-4, and John Whitwell, M.P. for KENDAL 1868-1880, and Mayor on six occasions.

EWING, James A. (1843-1900)
Sculptor. He was born at CARLISLE, but practised mainly at Glasgow, showing his work at the Royal Scottish Academy and the Glasgow Institute of Fine Arts between 1880 and 1898. Glasgow Art Gallery has his bust of Sir Michael Connal; Paisley Art Gallery his bust of Peter Kerr. He was the brother of GEORGE EDWIN EWING (born Birmingham), and collaborated with him in several commissions.

EYRE-WALKER, Bernard, A.R.E., S.G.A. (1887-1972)
Landscape painter in watercolour; etcher and aquatinter. Eyre-Walker was born at Harlow in Essex, the son of William Eyre Walker R.W.S., a member of the Royal Society of Painters in Water Colours. His family was North Country in origin, and although he lived in other parts of the country before settling at AMBLESIDE in 1927, it was in the Lake District that he produced some of his most memorable work. Despite his lack of orthodox training, and the handicap of being colour blind, he became a successful watercolourist and aquatinter, though because of his handicap much of his early work had to be confined to etching. He exhibited at the Royal Academy, the Royal Society of Painter-Etchers, and for many years at the Manchester Academy. In 1950 his work was shown at Liverpool, Birkenhead and Bootle, in Lancashire. He was elected an associate member of the Royal Society of Painter-Etchers in 1912, and a member of the Society of Graphic Artists in 1922. A major exhibition of his watercolours, pencil and wash drawings, etchings, aquatints and colour aquatints was held at the Abbot Hall Art Gallery, KENDAL, in 1973. Represented: Abbot Hall A.G., Kendal.

FAIRLIE, William Jordan (1825-1875)
Amateur landscape painter in watercolour. He was born at CARLISLE, and possibly became a pupil of Matthew

Ellis Nutter (q.v.), while he was working in gingham manufacturing in the area. He exhibited four landscapes at the Royal Academy between 1853 and 1865, including his *Blea Tarn and the Langdale Pikes* (1857). He also showed work at Carlisle Athenaeum in 1846. He died at CARLISLE.

FARQUHAR, Sir Robert Townsend (1841-1924)
Landscape painter in watercolour. He was born at Goldings, and exhibited at the leading London galleries from 1873, including the Suffolk Street and the Dudley Gallery. He showed three landscapes in 1873/4 at the Suffolk Street Gallery while living at GRASMERE, including his *A Peep from Silver How, Grasmere*. He also exhibited at the Royal Scottish Academy, and the Walker Art Gallery, Liverpool. After leaving GRASMERE he lived at Brighton.

FAULDER (FALDER), Joseph (1730-1816)
Portrait and sign painter in oil; engraver. Generally regarded as "The Father of the Cockermouth School of Portrait Painters", and one of the first sign painters in Cumberland, he was born at COCKERMOUTH and became a largely self-taught artist. While working as a sign painter he made engravings, and later took up portraiture. Faulder was something of an intellectual, and had outstanding teaching ability in the fields of philosophy, mathematics and art. One of his pupils was Joseph Sutton (q.v.), who became strongly influenced by Faulder's teaching, and passed this influence on to his six apprentices; he also came into contact with Samuel Crosthwaite (q.v.), who was also influenced by Sutton's teachings. Faulder remained active as a sign painter into his eighties, one of his last commissions being his Coat of Arms for St. Mary's Church, HARRINGTON, executed 1812. Sutton published a mezzotint engraving portraying Faulder, in 1824, copies of which are held by the British Museum and Carlisle Library. None of Faulder's easel paintings have so far been identified.

FELL, C. (fl.1872)
Portrait painter. This artist contributed one work to the Royal Academy in 1872, while living at CLAPPERSGATE, near AMBLESIDE. The work was entitled: *René, son of Professor du Bois Reymond, Berlin.*

FERGUSON, Charles J. (1840-1904)
Architectural draughtsman. A pupil of Sir Giles Gilbert Scott, he was for some time County Architect for Cumberland. While living at CARLISLE in 1881-2 he contributed two works to the Royal Academy, later moving to London, where he continued to exhibit at the Academy until 1889. Whitehaven Museum has his pen and ink drawing of St. Nicholas Church, WHITEHAVEN. This drawing was lithographed by Ackermann. Ferguson was responsible for designing many buildings in Cumbria.

FERGUSON, Richard (fl.1879)
Portrait painter in oil. Nothing is known of this artist except that he painted a portrait of John Woodcock Graves (q.v.), signing and dating his work on the reverse: "Rich Ferguson, 1879". This work was noted in CARLISLE.

FERGUSON, William James (fl.1849-1886)
Landscape painter in watercolour. Ferguson worked at
KESWICK in the middle of the 19th century, producing
several landscapes in watercolour which he exhibited at
the Suffolk Street Gallery, the British Institution and
Carlisle Athenaeum between 1850 and 1853. Also while
living at KESWICK he was invited to contribute to the
exhibition of British Art at the Crystal Palace, the *Carlisle
Patriot*, 5th April, 1856, stating: "Mr. Ferguson, artist of
Keswick, having been invited to contribute to the
collection of native art now forming at the Crystal Palace,
Sydenham, is about to enrich that exhibition with two
pictures from his pencil, the one a very felicitous
representation of Falcon Crag, Derwentwater, from near
Lord's Island, and the other a very striking portraiture of a
Mountain Tarn in Cumberland". He also exhibited at the
Royal Academy, and at various exhibitions in London.

FIELDING, Frederick F. (fl.1808-1826)
Landscape painter in oil and watercolour. One of the five
artist sons of Nathan Theodore Fielding, he was possibly
born at Sowerby in Yorkshire, and was taken with his
brothers to live in the Lake District as a boy. The family
took a cottage first at AMBLESIDE, later at KESWICK.
Frederick later practised in CARLISLE, living in the Market
Place of the city in 1810-1811. He showed work featuring
Cumbrian subjects at the Royal Academy in 1810 and
1826, and contributed three landscapes to the Carlisle
Academy in 1824. Carlisle Art Gallery has his oil *Carlisle
from Stanwix*, painted in 1811, and a study for this work.
His brothers ANTHONY VANDYKE COPLEY
FIELDING (1787-1855), and THEODORE HENRY
ADOLPHUS FIELDING (1781-1851), also produced
much work associated with Cumbria. The Abbot Hall Art
Gallery, KENDAL, has the former's *Landscape near
Ullswater* (1813).#

FINLINSON, J. (fl.1824-1826)
Architectural draughtsman. He exhibited two works at the
Carlisle Academy in 1824 from a WIGTON address. He
also exhibited at the Whitehaven Exhibition of 1826, a
contemporary newspaper report commenting: "...102

Easton House, Cheshire, the seat of the Right Hon. Earl
Grosvenor – J. Finlinson. A very pretty architectural
drawing exhibiting considerable taste and judgement in the
execution".

FISHER, John (fl.1829)
Architectural draughtsman. Fisher was active in KENDAL
in the early 19th century, and may have been associated
with the family of Francis Webster (q.v.), the KENDAL
architect. Two of his pen and wash drawings of the town's
"White Hall", in 1829, are in Kendal Town Hall.

FISHER, Matthew (1828-c.1889)
Portrait painter in oil; photographer. Born at DALSTON
FORGE, near CARLISLE, Fisher appears to have become a
self-taught artist before specialising in portraiture. He was
married at CARLISLE in 1858, and appears to have
remained in the city for much of his life, later turning to
photography, and opening a photographic studio in 1861.
Among his portrait subjects in oil were Sir George Musgrave, Lieutenant-Colonel Salkeld, and W. N. Hodgson,
M.P.; his portrait of the latter was published as a
lithograph in 1867. After 1867 he moved to Gateshead,
Co. Durham, where he is said to have given up painting,
possibly in favour of photography. He died at Gateshead.

FLINTOFT (FLINTOFF), Joseph (fl.1827-1843)
Landscape painter in oil. Flintoft practised at KESWICK
between 1827 and 1843, painting landscapes in a somewhat primitive style. His oil *Woollen Mills at Millbeck*,
1831, is in a private collection, and is illustrated in
Cumberland Heritage, by Molly Lefebure, Victor
Gollancz, 1970. An engraving of his *St. John's Church
and Parsonage, Keswick*, was published by T. Bailey &
Son. He is best known for his relief model of the Lake
district, completed in 1842 and now in Keswick Museum.
Represented: Carlisle Library.

FORD, Rev. W. (fl.1833-1839)
Architectural and landscape draughtsman. He is best
known for his pen and ink drawings of churches in
Cumbria. His *Cappon Tree at Brampton* was engraved,
and published in 1833. Represented: Carlisle Library.

Anthony Vandyke Copley
Fielding: Landscape
near Ullswater, 1813.
Watercolour $4\frac{3}{4} \times 8\frac{1}{8}$.
Abbot Hall Art Gallery.

27

FOTHERGILL, John (fl. c.1798-1800)

Sign painter. Fothergill worked as a sign painter in KENDAL in the last quarter of the 18th century. His business was in the town's Elephant Yard, and it is here that he is said to have given tuition to Thomas Stewardson (q.v.) in the latter's early career.

FOTHERGILL, Robert (fl.1771)

Architectural draughtsman. His watercolour designs for Appleby Gaol, c.1771, are in the Library of the School of Fine Arts, University of Pennsylvania, U.S.A. Nothing more is known of this artist, and his connections with APPLEBY.

FRIER, Mr. (fl.1714-1715)

Portrait painter. A "Mr. Frier" was paid £6. 9s. for "dressing pictures and drawing the King's picture" in CARLISLE in the period 1714-15. On the accession of the King in question – George 1st – the picture was hung in the Town Hall at CARLISLE.

*GARDNER, Daniel (1750-1805)

Portrait painter in pastel, gouache and oil. Born at KENDAL the son of a baker, Gardner attended the town's grammar school and later studied art in the KENDAL studio of Christopher Steele (q.v.), where a fellow pupil was George Romney (q.v.). About 1767 or 1768 he left KENDAL for London, and is thought to have spent some time working with Romney before entering the Royal Academy Schools in 1770. There he spent two years receiving tuition from a variety of visiting professional artists, including Zoffany, R.A., Nathaniel Dance, R.A., and Francesco Bartolozzi, R.A. In 1771 he won a silver medal at the Schools for a drawing of Academy Figures, and in the same year his drawing *Portrait of an Old Man* was accepted and hung at the Royal Academy. This was to prove his only exhibited work, a circumstance which is usually explained by assuming that Romney advised him against exposing his work to the contentious juries presiding over the selection of works for hanging at the Academy at that time. After two years at the Schools, Sir Joshua Reynolds, then President of the Academy, offered to continue Gardner's tuition in return for help in his studio. He remained with Reynolds for only a short time, however, before setting up his own successful studio, specialising in small full-length and half-length portraits in watercolour and pastel.

About 1776 or 1777 Gardner married; a son George being born in 1778, and some three years later a second son, whose name is not recorded. Unfortunately both Gardner's wife and his second son died shortly after the birth, and he never fully recovered from the double blow. He sent his surviving son George to be looked after by his lifelong friend William Pennington at KENDAL, but while continuing to visit the boy regularly as he grew up, father

Daniel Gardner: Ellinor Bold, c.1780.
Gouache 9½×8. *On permanent loan to the Abbot Hall Art Gallery, from the Provincial Insurance Co. Ltd.*

and son did not become close again until in 1802, or 1803, when they visited Paris together. This was during the brief Peace of Amiens, and Gardner used the opportunity to fill sketch books with drawings of sculpture in the Louvre which had been looted from Italy. Their visit was abruptly terminated by the re-opening of hostilities in May 1803, and they only narrowly escaped being taken prisoners of war. A little over two years later Gardner died of a liver complaint in London.

His work has become increasingly appreciated in recent years, his habit of producing paintings very similar in composition to those of his much better known contemporary Romney, now being recognised as a merely superficial indebtness on his part to the latter's influence. His technique was entirely his own, and embraced a variety of media, frequently used in combinations which not only worked aesthetically, but have caused his work to deteriorate remarkably little since it was first produced. Interestingly, several of his portraits have at times been attributed to John Constable (1776-1837), with whom he had a close friendship in his later life. He has had several exhibitions devoted to his work in recent years, the most notable of which were staged at Kenwood in 1972, and at the Abbot Hall Art Gallery, KENDAL in 1962 and 1973. Represented: National Portrait Gallery; Tate Gallery; Abbot Hall A.G., Kendal.

GARSIDE, William G. (fl.1830)

Topographical and architectural draughtsman. Garside is recorded as an artist who painted two views of Cropper's Mills at BURNESIDE, near KENDAL while working at the

Daniel Gardner: The Wife and Children of John Moore, Archbishop of Canterbury. Pastel $24\frac{1}{2} \times 33\frac{1}{4}$. *Tate Gallery*.

latter. His work has been described as "primitive", but displaying "good line and colour". He is also said to have produced engravings and items of sculpture, and to have attended the same school as William Bowness (q.v.).

GAYTHORPE, William (1806-1841)
Landscape and miniature painter in watercolour. He came to WHITEHAVEN with his father in 1810, and subsequently became a land surveyor and draughtsman to the Earl of Lonsdale, and teacher of painting. He exhibited at the Carlisle Academy in 1824 and 1825, and in 1829 he executed the designs of the five and ten pound notes of the Whitehaven Joint Stock Bank. Both of his contributions to the Carlisle Academy are listed as portraying castles, and were sent from WHITEHAVEN. A self portrait is in a private collection, and was illustrated in Carlisle Art Gallery's "The Carlisle Exhibitions 1823-1850" exhibition, in 1973. He died at WHITEHAVEN, and was buried in the churchyard of St. Nicholas in the town.

GIBBINGS, Walter Phelp (1861-1936)
Architectural draughtsman. Gibbings was a native of North Tawton, Devon, and came to CARLISLE in 1883 as surveyor to Charles J. Ferguson (q.v.). He later designed a number of buildings in CARLISLE, including Lindisfarne Street (1896), for which Carlisle Art Gallery has his original watercolour design, and the Palace Theatre (1905), the drawings for which are in the Record Office, CARLISLE. After leaving Ferguson he began his own business as auctioneer and estate agent in the city, and was Mayor of CARLISLE 1915-16.

*GIBSON, Richard "The Dwarf" (1615-1690)
Portrait painter. Usually described in books on English painting as "probably" born in Cumberland, Richard Gibson "The Dwarf" would, if definitely born in Cumbria, qualify as its earliest recorded artist. The direct opposite in scale to the elephantine John Glover Senior (q.v.), Gibson stood only three feet ten inches tall, and had the remarkable good fortune not only to meet and marry a woman of his own size, but to father a brood of children, five of whom lived to maturity and grew to normal size.

His peculiarities aside, Gibson emerges as one of Britain's earliest painters of miniatures, and one upon whom *Dame Fortune* appears to have smiled benignly all his long life. At a tender age we find him a page to a lady at Mortlake, where his ability as a draughtsman attracted the interest of the manager of a local tapestry works. Following some tuition in these works he became interested in the work of Sir Peter Lely (who evidently not only befriended him, but painted a portrait of him together with his diminutive wife, and may even have given him some tuition), and having made something of a name for himself with his portrait work in watercolour, he was introduced to the Court of Charles I. Here he was quickly noticed by Queen Henrietta Maria, who found a bride for him, called Ann Shepherd. From this point forward his future was assured. He became drawing instructor to both Princess Ann and Princess Mary, and when the latter became the unwilling wife of William of Orange in 1677, we are told that he accompanied her to Holland.

Gibson evidently remained in Holland for some eleven years, returning to England when William and Mary came

to the throne. Little is known of his subsequent life, though he is known to have continued painting portrait miniatures, some in the style and manner of Lely. He is popularly believed to have painted several portraits of Cromwell, but the whereabouts of these is unknown. He died in London, and was buried at St. Paul's, Covent Garden. Gibson had several relatives who practised as painters of portrait miniatures; notable among these was his daughter SUSAN PENELOPE GIBSON (1652-1700). Represented: British Museum; Victoria and Albert Museum; Windsor Castle Collection.

GIBSON, Thomas (1810-1843)
Portrait and landscape painter in oil and watercolour. Gibson was born at North Shields, Northumberland, the third son of James Gibson, and became a professional artist practising in the North East of England and CARLISLE. He exhibited at the Suffolk Street Gallery in 1841, the Newcastle Exhibition of 1834, and Carlisle Athenaeum in 1843. Much of his later life was spent at CARLISLE, where he established a considerable reputation as a portrait painter. He died in London, where according to Carlisle newspaper reports of his death, he was "pursuing his professional studies". Seventy of his paintings were sold in CARLISLE in the year following his death.

GILCHRIST, Philip Thomson, R.B.A. (1865-1956)
Marine and landscape painter in oil. Born at STANWIX, near CARLISLE, Gilchrist was educated in Hampshire, and

Richard Gibson: Isabella Dormer, aged 8, in 1671. Miniature 3×2½. *Victoria and Albert Museum.*

spent some time in the calico printing business before he turned to art. He studied under Tom Mostyn, and subsequently exhibited at the Royal Academy, the Royal Scottish Academy, the Royal Society of British Artists and in the provinces. He was elected a member of the Royal Society of British Artists in 1906, and was also a member of Liverpool and Manchester Academies of Arts. He worked mainly in Lancashire, and lived at Sunderland Point near Lancaster.

GILPIN, Captain John Bernard (1701-1776)

Landscape painter, draughtsman and etcher; drawing master. He was born at Scaleby Castle, near IRTHINGTON, and received tuition in art from his father, William Gilpin (q.v.), and Matthias Read (q.v.), before deciding on a military career. He became a Lieutenant in 1721, and joined his regiment at Fort William. He was stationed at Windsor Forest for a short time, but in 1733 he was back in Scotland.

In 1738 he was made Captain of an "Independent Company of Invalids" garrisoning CARLISLE and settled at the Deanery in the city. In 1745 he helped defend CARLISLE against Bonnie Prince Charlie, but had to flee to WHITEHAVEN after the surrender. In 1749 he left for Plymouth, but within a year he had retired on full pay, and had to make only occasional visits to the port. During this period (1749-1755) he made many rough sketches in pencil and grey wash, which have survived in an album. Gilpin had a studio at the Deanery at which, from settling there in 1738 he produced a variety of landscape works in black-lead pencil, chalk, Indian ink, oil, and in the form of etchings. He also gave drawing lessons to a number of young local artists, including John "Warwick" Smith (q.v.), Robert Smirke (q.v.), Guy Head (q.v.), and Joseph Stephenson (q.v.). He also gave instruction to his sons Sawrey Gilpin (q.v.), and William Gilpin (q.v.), exercising considerable influence over their later artistic development. His own work came much under the influence of Alexander Cozens, particularly during his middle and later life. He died at Scaleby Castle.

His Plymouth sketches were exhibited at Kenwood in 1959, at the "William Gilpin & the Picturesque" exhibition, and at Carlisle Art Gallery in 1971, in the "Cumberland Artists 1700-1900" exhibition. An account of his life and work is contained in *William Gilpin, his drawing, teaching and theory of the Picturesque*, C. P. Barbier, Oxford at the Clarendon Press, 1963. Represented: Carlisle Library.

*GILPIN, Sawrey, R.A. (1733-1807)

Animal and sporting painter in oil and watercolour; etcher. Gilpin was born at CARLISLE, the son of Captain John Bernard Gilpin (q.v.), and the younger brother of the Rev. William Gilpin (q.v.), and was first taught drawing by his father. He decided to follow a career in business, however, and with this intention he travelled to London. Here he changed his mind in favour of art, and in 1749 became a pupil of Samuel Scott, the marine painter and follower of Canaletto. Scott's studio was at Covent Garden, and Gilpin's interest in animal painting was stimulated by the sight of horses bringing produce to the market.

In 1758 he left Scott and became a professional artist, finding as his earliest patron of note The Duke of Cumberland, under whom his father had served at Windsor Park, where the Duke was a Ranger. When the Duke died in 1765 Gilpin stayed on at Windsor for several years, and used the opportunity to paint the several species

Sawrey Gilpin:
Horse Trotting, 1782.
Oil 17×20½.
On loan to the Abbot Hall Art Gallery from a private collection.

31

Sawrey Gilpin: Grey Arab and a Mare. Oil 28×35⅞. *Fitzwilliam Museum.*

32

of animal that roamed the park. Horse painting was his speciality, however, and after exhibiting at the Incorporated Society of Artists' Rooms from 1762, and the Royal Academy from 1786, he became an associate of the latter in 1795, and a full member in 1797. His success in horse painting was somewhat eclipsed by that of George Stubbs (1724-1806), a few years his senior, and then in command of the market for such works. His work fell short of Stubbs' in excellence, being marred by anthropomorphism of the sort best illustrated by his *Election of Darius*, but he has been described by Stubbs' biographer Basil Taylor (*Stubbs*, Phaidon, 1971), as the only artist of Stubbs' period who was able to "claim a rival competence".

Gilpin also painted in conjunction with George Barret, R.A., and Zoffany, R.A. painted some figures into his pictures. His work also included etching, examples of which he used in a small book of horses, and for a set of drawings illustrating oxen. His *The Death of the Fox* was engraved by John Scott. One of his pupils was John "Warwick" Smith (q.v.). Gilpin lived for many years at Knightsbridge, London, but on the death of his wife he went to live with his friend Samuel Whitbread in Bedfordshire. His health later deteriorated and he returned to live in London with his daughters, dying there in 1807. His son WILLIAM SAWREY GILPIN (1762-1843) followed his father in becoming an artist. Represented: British Museum; Victoria and Albert Museum; Tate Gallery; Fitzwilliam Museum, Cambridge; Abbot Hall A.G., Kendal; Carlisle A.G., and various provincial art galleries.

GILPIN, William (1657-1724)

Landscape painter in oil and watercolour; copyist. The eldest son of Dr. Richard Gilpin, Rector of Greystoke Church, he was born at GREYSTOKE, near PENRITH, and later lived at Scaleby Castle, near IRTHINGTON, a property purchased by his father. He later became the Recorder of CARLISLE, and Steward to Sir John Lowther of WHITE-HAVEN. At the latter he made the acquaintance of Matthias Read (q.v.), who taught him the rudiments of painting. Under Read he painted several large landscapes in oil, and produced some small sepia washes, later developing into a talented gentleman painter, and sharing with Read the artistic tuition of his son John Bernard Gilpin (q.v.). He died at Scaleby Castle. None of his works have come to light except a painting of the Holy Family after Caracci in the Scaleby Castle sale of 1904.

*GILPIN, Rev. William, M.A. (1724-1804)

Landscape painter in watercolour; writer on aesthetics. He was born at Scaleby Castle, near IRTHINGTON, the son of Captain John Bernard Gilpin (q.v.), and elder brother of Sawrey Gilpin (q.v.). He studied at ST. BEES and at CARLISLE, learning drawing from his father, then entered Queen's College, Oxford, where he obtained his B.A. in 1744. In 1746 he returned to CARLISLE, and later in the year he was ordained curate at IRTHINGTON. He returned to Oxford and took his M.A. in 1748, following which he held several curacies in London before becoming master of Cheam School. He was master at Cheam for some thirty years, and during this period undertook a number of sketching tours of the British countryside, including Kent

Rev. William Gilpin: Solway Firth. Watercolour $4\frac{7}{8} \times 7$.
Tyne & Wear County Museums, Laing Art Gallery.

in 1768; Norfolk in 1769; South Wales in 1770; Cumberland and Westmorland in 1772; North Wales in 1773; the South Coast in 1774; the West of England in 1775, and the Highlands of Scotland in 1776. These tours lead to the publication of several books illustrated with his own engravings.

Shortly after his tour of the Highlands he retired as Vicar of Boldre, in the New Forest, publishing among several works: *Observations relative chiefly to picturesque beauty, made in the year 1772, on several parts of England, particularly the Mountains and Lakes of Cumberland and Westmorland* (Two Vols., 1786). With this latter work, one of his five treatises on the *Picturesque* in which he introduced the use of the "newly invented aquatinta" to illustrate his drawings, he won the admiration of George III, and found such a ready market for it that four editions were printed in about twenty years. Gilpin is said to have exercised considerable influence upon the taste of his day while Vicar of Boldre "by providing elegant rules for the amateur with a water-colour box, and a system for the aesthetic observer . . . By his publications . . . William Gilpin stirred in many an increased awareness of beauties to be found among the mountains and lakes . . ." (Martin Hardie: *Water-Colour Painting in Britain*, Vol. I, pp. 76-77). While at Boldre he also displayed his advanced educational theories by founding a model school for gipsies and day labourers working in the New Forest, using money received from the publication of his books, and the sale of his drawings. Many of these drawings were sold at Christie's in 1802 and 1804, raising a substantial sum towards the cost of building and running his schools. He died at Boldre and is buried in the churchyard there.

A large number of his drawings have survived, but taken out of context with his theory of the *picturesque* have little attractiveness. Some of the better examples are illustrated in : *William Gilpin: His drawing, teaching and theory of the Picturesque*, C. P. Barbier, Oxford at the Clarendon Press, 1963. Represented: British Museum; Victoria and Albert Museum; Fitzwilliam Museum, Cambridge; Laing A.G., Newcastle; Leeds A.G.; Sheffield A.G., and various provincial art galleries.

*GLOVER, John, Senior (1767-1849)

Landscape painter in oil and watercolour; etcher. He was born at Houghton-on-the-Hill, near Leicester, and showed an interest in drawing and calligraphy from an early age. At the age of nineteen he was appointed Writing Master of the Free School at APPLEBY, and here became an accomplished painter of landscapes in watercolour, producing many views of "gentlemen's seats" in the area during his seven-year stay. Also in this period he visited London to see picture exhibitions and to take art lessons, one of them being given by John "Warwick" Smith (q.v.).

He left APPLEBY in 1794 to become a drawing master at Lichfield, shortly after showing his first work at the Royal Academy. Glover retained a lifelong attachment to Cumbria, many of the several hundred works which he showed at the Royal Academy from 1795, the Old Watercolour Society from 1805, the British Institution from 1810, the Suffolk Street Gallery and the Carlisle Academy from 1824, depicting Lake District views. Before 1820 he bought a house at Ullswater to which he had intended to retire, but sold it for £1100 to buy a painting by Claude, an artist whom he had always admired, and whose work in oil he had attempted to imitate. In 1831 he went to Tasmania with his family, where despite his eighteen-stone bulk and club feet he hoped to succeed as a farmer. He continued to show work in London until his death at Launceston, Tasmania in 1849. Represented: British Museum; Victoria and Albert Museum; Fitzwilliam Museum, Cambridge; Laing A.G., Newcastle, and various provincial art galleries.

*GOLDSCHMIDT, Hilde (b.1897)

Portrait and landscape painter in oil and pastel. She was born at Leipzig and began her studies there in 1914. Between 1920 and 1923 she studied at the Dresden Academy, where she became one of the master pupils of Oscar Kokoschka. In 1923 she went to New York, where she exhibited at the New Gallery J. B. Neumann. On her

Hilde Goldschmidt: Olaf Stapledon, 1948. Pastel $20\frac{1}{4} \times 16$.
Abbot Hall Art Gallery.

return to Europe she had a studio in Paris 1926-7, and in 1928 she went to the south of France. In 1929 she extensively toured Italy, finally settling for a time in Capri. On returning to Germany she had her first one-man

John Glover, Senior:
Ullswater, 1827.
Oil 30×46.
Phillips.

34

exhibition in Munich in 1932. Later she went to Kitzbühel in Austria, where she lived until moving to London in 1939. Three years later she settled in the Lake District, living there until 1950 on the Langdale Estate near AMBLESIDE. Here she initially earned her living sewing fur gloves (sometimes travelling to London and Glasgow to handle painting commissions). This eventually led to work at a social centre on the estate as a teacher of leather crafts, and evening classes in neighbouring towns and villages.

During her Langdale period she produced some of her most important early paintings, most of them executed in a lyrical Expressionist style, and featuring portraits, and landscapes with figures. She also met Kurt Schwitters (q.v.), who was working in the area at that time. Her painting was not taken seriously by local people, and she sold little work. Her work of the period was later shown at Manchester, however, and since returning to Kitzbühel she has exhibited widely throughout Europe. A major exhibition of her work was held at the Abbot Hall Art Gallery, KENDAL, and three other provincial galleries, in 1973. The catalogue contains a detailed account of her Lake District period by Dr. J. P. Hodin. Represented: Abbot Hall A.G., Kendal, and various Austrian art galleries.

GOUGH, Charles (d.1805)

Landscape painter in watercolour; copyist. Gough is said to have been a Manchester artist, and a friend of William Green (q.v.). Green gave him some copying work to do at AMBLESIDE in the autumn of 1804, and in the following year he died while climbing Helvellyn to sketch. Gough was accompanied by his dog, and the animal remained with his body for three months until it was discovered. This action on the part of the dog inspired both Sir Walter Scott (1771-1832), and William Wordsworth (1770-1850) to write lines about its devotion. Gough was buried at TIRRIL, near PENRITH. A monument to the memory of the dog was erected on Helvellyn in 1891.

GOULD, David (fl.1885-1930)

Landscape and flower painter in watercolour. It was at Gould's home at AMBLESIDE that the inaugural meeting of the Lake Artists' Society was held on 12th October, 1904. He is first recorded as living at AMBLESIDE (1885), from which in 1896 he sent four landscapes to Carlisle Art Gallery's exhibition of that year. Just before the formation of the Society, however, he was working in Belfast, and he subsequently worked in Ireland in 1918, and 1928. In addition to showing his work in Cumbria, he exhibited at the Royal Academy, the Royal Hibernian Academy, the Royal Glasgow Institute of Fine Arts, and at various galleries in the provinces, until 1930. Represented: Abbot Hall A.G., Kendal.

GRAVES, John Woodcock (1795-1886)

Naive portrait and landscape painter. Graves is best remembered as the writer of the song "D'ye ken John Peel?" which immortalised the famous Cumbrian huntsman John Peel, but he was also a naive artist who seems to have had something of an obsession with Peel as a subject for his portraits. His first successful portrait of the huntsman was painted in Tasmania in 1865, thirty-two years after Graves had emigrated to that country, and eleven years after the death of its subject. To paint the picture he is said to have had to rely entirely on his memory, and manufacture his own brushes and colours. Five unfinished pictures of Peel were stolen by Tasmanian natives before he finally completed one, and this he sent home to a Cumbrian publisher in 1867, asking that copies of it be made and circulated to every local home. His wish was not immediately fulfilled, but the picture has since become well known by other means. In 1904 it was bought by an hotelier in CARLISLE, who used it as the basis for the bottle label design of the "John Peel" blend of whisky. In 1966 it was purchased by S. Redmayne and Sons, the tailors, of WIGTON, who reproduced it in their booklet about John Peel. Graves died in Hobart, Tasmania in 1886, after a long and colourful life on the island, during which he became widely known for his mechanical inventions, writing, "Ballad-making", and painting. Graves' portrait of Peel, and his *View of Ruthwaite*, were shown at the Abbot Hall Art Gallery, KENDAL, in its "Cumbrian Characters" exhibition, in 1968.

*GREEN, William (1760-1823)

Landscape painter in oil and watercolour; engraver. He was born at Manchester, and was first employed as a surveyor before turning to art. In 1778 he was involved in a survey of "Lancashire – north-of-the-sands", and while at ULVERSTON made the acquaintance of historian and topographer Thomas West. West encouraged Green to think of becoming an artist, and shortly after returning to Manchester he took a course in painting, becoming so proficient that he began to offer instruction. He visited the Lake District several times between 1791 and 1794 and in 1795 he published his first work illustrating the area: *Forty-Eight Views of the Lake District, and Four Views of Wales*, a collection of drawings in aquatint. This was followed by his *Series of Picturesque Views of the North of England*, of 1796. Green left Manchester for London in the latter year and studied under John Landseer, the engraver father of Sir Edwin Landseer. Here he married, and after the birth of his two daughters, he decided to move with his family to AMBLESIDE.

Settled at AMBLESIDE by 1800, Green quickly became a friend of William Wordsworth (1770-1850) and his circle of poet friends, and established an exhibition of drawings and engravings for sale to tourists. He also began to draw and paint widely throughout the neighbourhood, later producing among several works, his *Seventy Eight Studies from Nature (Lake District)*, 1809; *A Description of Sixty Studies from Nature; etched in the soft ground*, by William Green of Ambleside, 1810; *A Description of a Series of Sixty small prints etched by William Green from drawings made by himself*, 1814, and in 1819, *The Tourist's New Guide*. His last works consisted of twelve coloured views of the Lakes, with forty views of AMBLESIDE and KESWICK, published in 1821.

Green's work as a painter has frequently been dismissed as repetitive but it won the warm admiration of men like Wordsworth, with whom Green shared some responsibility for the popularisation of the Lake District in the first half of the 19th century. He showed four examples of his Lake District landscape work at the Royal Academy between 1797 and 1811, but otherwise preferred

William Green:
Raven Crag, Thirlmere.
Watercolour 9×12.
Private collection.

to exhibit locally. He died at AMBLESIDE, but is buried in St. Oswald's Churchyard, GRASMERE. His epitaph was composed by Wordsworth, part of it reading: "... by his skill and industry as an artist he produced faithfully representations of this country ...". Represented: British Museum; Victoria and Albert Museum; Abbot Hall A.G., Kendal; Laing A.G., Newcastle, and various provincial art galleries.

GUNNING, Robert Bell (*c*.1830-1907)

Portrait and landscape painter in oil. He was born at Dumfries, but later moved to WHITEHAVEN, where he taught art for more than forty years, and painted many local subjects. He died at Dumfries but is interred at WHITEHAVEN. Represented: Whitehaven Museum.

HALL, H. R. (fl.1875-1902)

Landscape painter in oil and watercolour. Hall was born at BROUGHTON-IN-FURNESS, and later practised as a professional artist at Blackpool, and at his birthplace. He exhibited at the Royal Academy in 1902, and also showed work at the Royal Scottish Academy, and the Royal Society of Artists, Birmingham.

*HALL, Oliver, R.A., R.W.S., R.E. (1869-1957)

Landscape painter in oil and watercolour; etcher. Born in London, Hall first displayed an interest in art by copying illustrations from *Harpers Magazine*. These were shown to a tutor at the Royal College of Art, who obtained a place for him at the College. He later attended evening

classes at Lambeth and Westminster Schools of Art. Hall was much influenced by the work of Daniel Alexander Williamson (q.v.) and spent a lengthy period with the latter at his home at BROUGHTON-IN-FURNESS. His early work was in watercolour, and he produced some etchings, but he later preferred to work in oil. Much of his work portrayed North Country landscape subjects, and included his *Shap Moors*, purchased for the Tate Gallery by the Chantrey Bequest in 1920,[#] but he also painted in many other parts of England and Wales, and travelled in Spain, Italy and France.

He exhibited at the Royal Academy from 1890, showing 108 works, and also showed his work at the Royal Scottish Academy, the Royal Water Colour Society, the Royal Society of British Artists, the Royal Society of Painter-Etchers, and many London and provincial galleries, including the Dowdeswell Gallery, at which he held his first one-man exhibition in 1898. He was elected an associate of the Royal Academy in 1920, and become a full member in 1927, and Senior Academician in 1945. He became a member of the Royal Water Colour Society in 1919, and a member of the Royal Society of Painter-Etchers in 1895 and 1926. Much of his early life was spent in Sussex, but he later lived at ULVERSTON, dying there in 1957. His son CLAUDE MUNCASTER (b. 1903) is a well known professional artist. Represented: Tate Gallery; Laing A.G., Newcastle, and various provincial and overseas art galleries.

HALLIFAX, Samuel (d.1898)

Sculptor. The eldest son of Joseph Hallifax, Headmaster of the Free Grammar School, WIGTON, and subsequently Rector of KIRKBRIDE, he showed a talent for sculpture at an early age. His father wished him to study for the Church, but he was determined to become a sculptor, and while there is little evidence that he succeeded in his chosen profession his name is associated with several pieces of sculpture. According to T. W. Carrick, *History of Wigton,*

1949, he was responsible for two lions at his home for some years – Longthwaite House, also sculpture plinths on each side of the front door to the latter, representing Queen Victoria and the Prince Consort. At the Rectory at KIRKBRIDE he was responsible for "some finely wrought corbels" supporting the roof spouting, and at the Old Rectory, SEBERGHAM, where he spent his final years, two greyhounds which have since been destroyed. Hallifax was a distant relative of Samuel Bough (q.v.), and a close friend of William Henry Hoodless (q.v.), and was responsible for introducing the two artists to each other in Edinburgh when Bough was living in the city.

HAMILTON, Lieutenant Thomas Richard (1758-1839)

Amateur landscape and plant painter in watercolour. Hamilton was a Lieutenant in the 76th Regiment of Infantry, and made landscape sketches and plant studies while serving in the Army. He retired to HESKET-NEW-MARKET, dying there in 1839. His watercolour *Caldbeck Church*, of 1801, from a private collection, was shown at Carlisle Art Gallery's "Cumberland Artists 1700-1900" exhibition, in 1971.

*HARDEN, John (1772-1847)

Amateur landscape, portrait and genre painter in oil and watercolour. Harden was born at Borrisoleigh, Co. Tipperary, the son of a well-to-do landowner, and appears to have drawn from his earliest years. Later he toured widely, making sketches while visiting Wales and England (1795), South West Ireland (1797), the Lake District (1798), the Isle of Wight (1799), and the Lakes in 1802 and 1803. The last of his trips to the Lake District was made in the company of his second wife "JESSY" (JANET) HARDEN, and after a short spell together in Edinburgh with her newspaper proprietor father Robert Allan, the couple decided to make their home at Brathay Hall, a farmhouse at the head of Lake Windermere. Here they lived for more than thirty years, Harden spending much of his spare time making drawings of everything of interest in the area, the family entertaining a succession of well known writers and artists, including no lesser giants in their respective fields than John Constable (1776-1837), and William Wordsworth (1770-1850).

None of Harden's work was exhibited despite its high quality, and the praise which it received from many visiting artists. He evidently preferred to draw and paint purely for pleasure, or merely to illustrate the journals which he kept throughout his life. In much of his artistic activity he was joined by his wife, who had studied under Alexander Nasmyth, and was herself a talented painter, mainly in oil. Although much of the Hardens' time was spent at Brathay Hall they remained frequent visitors to Edinburgh, and, indeed, the family went to live there for two years from 1809 while Harden worked for his father-in-law. The family also went abroad on at least one occasion, making a Grand Tour of the Low Countries, Germany, Switzerland, Italy and France in 1829. Harden also visited Ireland throughout most of his life, paying his final visit in 1840. In 1834 the Hardens sold Brathay Hall and moved to Field Head House, OUTGATE, near HAWKSHEAD. "Jessy" Harden died three years later, and Harden spent the remainder of his life partly in Edinburgh, and partly in the Lake District with his daughter Jane, where he continued to live at Field Head House for some years; later at Miller Bridge near AMBLESIDE. He died at Miller Bridge, and is buried at St. Anne's Churchyard, AMBLESIDE.

Oliver Hall:
Shap Moors, 1919.
Oil 40×50.
Tate Gallery.

John Harden:
The Quill Winder.
Watercolour 10⅜×13⅛.
*A.S. Clay Collection,
Abbot Hall Art Gallery.*

Although Harden's work has had to wait a long time to become discovered it has now received its due recognition. It has recently featured in a number of important exhibitions, including "An Exhibition of Water-colours and Drawings by John Harden", Arts Council of Great Britain, Bristol, 1951, and "Eminent Amateurs, 18th and 19th Century Painters", the Abbot Hall Art Gallery, KENDAL, 1964. Perhaps the most important single factor in bringing about his recent recognition, however, has been the publication by the Abbot Hall Gallery of a monograph on Harden's life and work. Written by Daphne Foskett, the well known authority on miniature painting, it contains five colour plates, and 109 black and white illustrations, and represents a fitting tribute to this, one of Cumbria's

most talented amateur artists. Represented: British Museum; National Gallery of Scotland; Abbot Hall A.G., Kendal; Armitt Library, Ambleside; Carlisle A.G., and various provincial art galleries.

*HARRINGTON, Robert (1805-1884)

Animal and sporting painter in oil. He was born at CARLETON, CARLISLE, and was apprenticed to his uncle's calico printing works near the city. He studied at the Carlisle Academy in the evenings under Matthew Ellis Nutter (q.v.), and painted in his spare time. His work came to the attention of local M.P. and art patron Major Aglionby, who paid for him to study in London, where he first studied under John Zeitter, and later under Abraham

Robert Harrington: Roan and White Shorthorn Bull.
Oil 31½×41½. *Simon Carter Gallery.*

38

Cooper, R.A. On leaving London he returned to CARLETON, where he became a successful animal and sporting painter. He exhibited at the Carlisle Academy in 1828, 1830 and 1833, at the Dumfries Exhibitions of 1828 and 1830, and Carlisle Athenaeum in 1846 and 1850. His output of paintings was evidently prodigious, and included horses, greyhounds and stock.[#] He also painted animals for the works of Samuel Bough (q.v.), and Jacob Thompson (q.v.). Many of his paintings were published as engravings in London and CARLISLE. One of his pupils was William Brown (q.v.), who also painted his portrait. This portrait portrayed Harrington in the beaver hat with which he is said to have returned from London. Another of his portraitists was Thomas Heathfield Carrick (q.v.). Harrington died at CARLETON, his obituary stating that he was: "one of the cleverest delineators of animal and still life Cumberland has produced". Represented: Carlisle A.G.

*HAUGH, George (1756-1827)

Portrait, landscape, genre and religious subject painter. Haugh was born at CARLISLE, and after some tuition from Captain John Bernard Gilpin (q.v.) he was encouraged to enter the Royal Academy Schools. He entered the Schools in 1772, and eight years later settled at Doncaster, where he appears to have spent most of his professional life. He first began exhibiting at the Royal Academy in 1777, while living in Cumbria, subsequently sending ten works from both London and Doncaster addresses until 1807. During this period he also began exhibiting at the British Institution, sending nine works from his Doncaster address between 1808 and 1818. Most of the work which he exhibited at the Royal Academy and the British Institution consisted of landscapes and historical subjects, though it is believed that he made his living mainly from portrait painting. While living at Doncaster he also exhibited at the Carlisle Academy, showing fourteen landscapes between 1824 and 1826. One of his portrait subjects was *The Countess of Effingham with her dogs*, painted in 1787.[#] This painting is in the collection of Mr. and Mrs. Paul Mellon.

*HAVELL, William (1782-1857)

Landscape painter in oil and watercolour. Havell first visited Cumbria in 1807, accompanied by Ramsay Richard Reinagle (1775-1812), and meeting John Harden (q.v.). He subsequently spent almost two years at AMBLESIDE (1807-9), producing many studies in oil and watercolour of local scenery. Some twenty works featuring Cumbrian subjects were sent by him to the Royal Academy, the British Institution, and the Suffolk Street Gallery, during the remainder of his life. One of the most frequently reproduced of these works is his *Skelwith Force, Westmorland, Langdale Pikes in the distance*, shown at the British Institution in 1810 (see plate 75, *Britain Observed*, Geoffrey Grigson, Phaidon, 1975). His view of Lodore is illustrated at the front of this volume.

*HEAD, Guy (1760-1800)

Portrait, landscape and figure painter in oil; copyist. Head was born at CARLISLE the son of a butcher, and received his first lessons in art from Captain John Bernard Gilpin (q.v.), in association with several other young local artists. Encouraged by the Captain he went to London and

entered the Royal Academy Schools, where his work was admired by Sir Joshua Reynolds. Following this he is believed to have been assisted by a wealthy friend to travel on the continent, visiting Holland, Germany and Italy, and making copies of works by the Old Masters.

Back in CARLISLE by 1783 he married Jane Lewthwaite, remaining in the city until the birth of his first daughter in 1785. After this he travelled with his family, first to Rome where he spent several years as a portrait painter and copyist; later to Naples where he also maintained a studio. When Naples was threatened by Napoleon in 1799 the artist and his family were allowed to take refuge on Nelson's flagship, and to bring with them many of Head's paintings. The family were then conveyed back to London, a son – Horatio Nelson Head – being born on the voyage. Nelson was the child's Godfather – hence the name (and possibly the portrait referred to below). Once in London Head rented a small gallery in which to show his paintings, subsequently despatching them to STANDINGSTONES, near WIGTON, where lived his sister. He was back in CARLISLE for the baptism of his second daughter in 1799, but his health deteriorated soon after, and returning to London he died there at the age of forty.

Head's more important work consisted of a large number of highly competent copies of works by the Old Masters, a number of accomplished portraits, and a few landscapes. His work as a copyist included his *Elevation of the Cross*, after Rubens, which was purchased after his death by the Royal Academy for £420; that of portrait painter: John Flaxman, the sculptor, and the Duke of Sussex, painted in Rome in 1792 and 1798; and Horatio

George Haugh:
The Countess of Effiingham with Gun and Shooting Dogs, 1787.
Collection of Mr. and Mrs. Paul Mellon.

39

Guy Head: Nelson receiving the French Admiral's sword after the Battle of the Nile, 1798.
Oil 87¾×66½. *National Portrait Gallery, London.*

Nelson, painted in 1798 (this work was purchased by the National Portrait Gallery for £8,580 in 1976). He also produced a number of landscapes in oil, and in the form of sketches. He exhibited his work sparingly throughout his career, showing at the Spring Gardens Exhibition of 1780, and the Society of Artists, the Free Society of Artists, and the Royal Academy between 1779 and 1800. Several of his works were shown posthumously at the Carlisle Academy between 1823 and 1825, and at the Dumfries Exhibition of 1830. Represented: National Portrait Gallery; Victoria and Albert Museum.

HEARD, Isaac (d.1859)
Portrait painter in oil. He was born at WHITEHAVEN, and was probably the brother of Joseph Heard (q.v.). He exhibited at the Whitehaven Exhibition of 1826, the *Cumberland Pacquet,* 5th September, 1826, recording: "No. 5 Portrait of a Gentleman – I. Heard. Whoever has once seen the original of this portrait cannot for a moment hesitate about the resemblance. It is painted by a native artist, now in London, and is highly creditable to his abilities". Pigot's *Directory of Liverpool* for 1834 identifies "Heard Joseph & Isaac (portrait and marine) 11, Norfolk Street", indicating the presence of the two brothers in Liverpool at that time, and it is assumed that like Joseph, Isaac remained there until his death.

*HEARD, Joseph (c.1799-1859)
Marine painter in oil. Born at EGREMONT, he was probably the brother of Isaac Heard (q.v.), and became a member of the school of marine painters at WHITEHAVEN. He exhibited at the Carlisle Academy in 1827, and may also have exhibited at Liverpool between his arrival there about 1834, and his death there some twenty-five years later. He appears to have left WHITEHAVEN in 1826, and to have spent some time in London before moving to Liverpool. His work consisted almost entirely of marine paintings, many of them featuring Liverpool and its shipping. This last circumstance has often led to him having been claimed as a Liverpool artist, but his origins and early life were entirely Cumbrian. His work has been reproduced in *A Dictionary of British Marine Painters,* Arnold Wilson, 1967, *British 19th Century Marine Painting*, Denys Brook-Hart, 1974, and Tomlinson's *History of the Bibby*

Joseph Heard:
The Shuttle.
Oil 20×30.
Gomshall Gallery.

Line, 1970. His painting *The Shuttle* has been reproduced as a limited edition colour print courtesy of the Gomshall Gallery,# and his *Cumberland: A Storm in the Solway* has featured in two of the exhibitions of Carlisle Art Gallery since 1970. Represented: National Maritime Museum; Carlisle A.G.; Whitehaven Museum; Walker A.G., Liverpool.

HEATHCOTE, Miss or Mrs. MARGARET (fl.1867-1913)

Landscape painter in watercolour. Little is known of this artist except that she is believed to have lived at KESWICK from 1867 until the late 1880's, showing her work at various exhibitions in London during this period. From 1887 until 1913 she evidently lived in London, exhibiting at the Alpine Club, the Dudley Gallery and the New Dudley Gallery, and the Society of Women Artists. Her speciality was mountain scenery.

HERD, Richard (c.1835-1910)

Marine and landscape painter in oil. He was born at SEDBERGH, and later became a solicitor's clerk and Registrar of Marriages at WHITEHAVEN, painting in his spare time. By 1883, however, he was describing himself in a local directory as a professional artist, and Registrar of Marriages at WHITEHAVEN, and in a directory of 1897 he is listed as an artist only, practising at Victoria Road in the town. He died at Huddersfield. His oil of the brig *Village Girl*, from the collection of Whitehaven Museum, was included in the "Marine Paintings & Models" exhibition at Whitehaven Public Library, in 1971.

HINDE, Joseph (1747-1762)

Portrait painter in oil; copyist. The nephew of Matthias Read (q.v.), Hinde was probably born at WHITEHAVEN. The only works of his which have survived are his copies of portraits in the Lowther collection.

HINDSON, R. G. (fl.1825-1850)

Portrait and genre painter. Hindson practised as a portrait and genre painter at PENRITH in the second quarter of the 19th century, contributing genre works to the 1825 exhibition of the Carlisle Academy, and the 1850 exhibition of Carlisle Athenaeum.

*HINDSON, William (fl.1842)

Sculptor and stonemason. The son of a local stonemason, Hindson was engaged by Sarah Losh (q.v.) to carry out much of the carving in the church which she built at WREAY in memory of her sister Katherine. He evidently worked closely under her direction, providing competent interpretations of her novel designs for the treatment of various features of the church. These included gargoyles treated as snakes, tortoises and alligators, and the use of floral, fern and pine cone forms as decoration on the surrounds of windows and doors.# It is said that Sarah wanted all who had co-operated in the building and decoration of the church (see also William S. Losh and John Scott) to remain anonymous, but that Hindson cunningly carved his name on the underside of the font bowl. His work on the windows of the church is illustrated in Pevsner's *Cumberland & Westmorland*, plate 65. Other views of the church were published in *Country Life*, 4th

William Hindson:
Part of carved surround to main door, St. Mary's, Wreay.

Edward George Hobley: A Shaft of Light, 1897.
Oil 36⅛×28. *Walker Art Gallery.*

November, 1971, pp. 1230-1, in "A memorial to two sisters", by M. A. Wood.

HIRD, Robert (late 18th, early 19th century)

Portrait painter. He was possibly born at COCKERMOUTH, where he became one of the six apprentices of Joseph Sutton (q.v.). Little further is known of this artist or his work.

*HOBLEY, Edward George (1866-1916)

Landscape, genre and animal painter in oil; art master. Hobley practised as a professional artist at Bradford, and at Farsley near Leeds, before taking up a position as art master at PENRITH by 1899. He exhibited at the Royal Academy from 1893, and also showed work at the Royal Cambrian Academy, the Royal Society of Artists, Birmingham, and at various provincial art galleries. Represented: Walker A.G., Liverpool.

HODGSON, Christopher (1785-1849)
Architectural draughtsman. Hodgson was an architect who was responsible for designing many buildings in CARLISLE, his principal work being the County Gaol, 1824-27, for which his original watercolour drawings are in Carlisle Library. A notebook illustrated with his drawings is in the collection of the Society of Antiquaries of Newcastle upon Tyne. His brother John Hodgson, was also an architect.

HODGSON, A. N. W. (fl.1900)
Architectural draughtsman. Hodgson is known only by the pen and ink drawings of old KENDAL which he contributed to *Kirkbie Kendall*, by John Flavel Curwen (q.v.). His pen drawing *Blackhall Croft*, is in the collection of Kendal Public Library, and was executed in 1900. This work was shown in "The Artists' Kendal" exhibition, at the Abbot Hall Art Gallery, KENDAL, Summer, 1975.

*HODGSON, John James (1871-1906)
Landscape and architectural painter in watercolour; book illustrator. He was born at CARLISLE and first became a pupil teacher before deciding on a career in art. His earliest tuition was received from Herbert Lees (q.v.) at the Old Art School in the Mechanics' Hall, and here he subsequently became a teacher before attending Windsor and Slade Schools of Art, and winning the Queen's Prize for architectural drawing. After receiving his Art Master Certificate he returned to CARLISLE, where he took up a position at Carlisle School of Art. Hodgson's life was dogged by ill-health but he became a successful art teacher, a prolific spare-time painter, and an able book illustrator. One of his earliest commissions in the latter

John James Hodgson: Plover and Snipe.
Illustration from "A History of Fowling".

field was his illustrative work for *A History of Fowling*,# by R. A. Macpherson, M.A., published by David Douglas, 1897, and undertaken jointly with pupil and friend Joseph W. Simpson (q.v.). Hodgson's watercolours mainly featured well known landscape and architectural subjects and were painted in CARLISLE, the Lake District, and various other parts of Britain, and abroad.

He showed his work at the Carlisle Art Gallery exhibition of 1896, and was a regular exhibitor at the city's Art and Crafts Exhibitions. He also exhibited at the Royal Scottish Society of Painters in Water Colour, but his reputation did not become fully established until he had shared an exhibition at Scott & Son's Gallery, CARLISLE, in 1904, with friends Paul Greville Hudson (q.v.), and Will Tyler (q.v.). In 1905 he showed his work at an exhibition of modern art at the Walker Art Gallery, Liverpool, two of his exhibits later being requested for showing at Leeds. He was invited to take part in an exhibition of living British Artists at the Tate Gallery, but unfortunately died before he could participate. He died at CARLISLE. An exhibition of 140 of his paintings and other studies was held at Carlisle Art Gallery in 1970. His younger brother FREDERICK W. HODGSON (1884-1967) was also artistically talented. Represented: Carlisle A.G.

HODGSON, Oliver Ussinon (1810-1878)
Marine painter in oil. Hodgson was born at WHITEHAVEN, and is said to have become a pupil, and later an apprentice, of John Clementson (q.v.). His work is very similar stylistically to that of his master, and of Robert Salmon (q.v.). Whitehaven Museum has several of his works including his painting of the brig *Favourite*, painted in 1832, and he is known from local directories to have been working at WHITEHAVEN as late as 1847. He died at WHITEHAVEN. His oil of *Parton from the sea*, from the collection of Whitehaven Museum, and the work referred to earlier, were included in the "Marine Paintings & Models" exhibition at Whitehaven Public Library, in 1971.

HOGG, Arthur H. (fl.1865-1929)
Portrait painter; topographical draughtsman and etcher. He was born at KENDAL, and studied art at South Kensington and later in Paris. One of his early works in portraiture was his portrait *c*. 1885 of the Rev. John Cooper, M.A. 1815-1896, Vicar of KENDAL, Canon of CARLISLE, Archdeacon of Westmorland. He also produced a number of pen and wash drawings described as *Bits of Old Kendal*, in 1891. He exhibited his work at the Royal Academy, the London Salon, and at various London galleries between 1913 and 1929, while living in the capital. His *Bits of Old Kendal* was included in "The Artists' Kendal" exhibition at the Abbot Hall Art Gallery, KENDAL, Summer, 1975.

HOGGARTH, Arthur Henry Graham, R.B.A. (1882-1964)
Landscape painter in watercolour. He was born the second son of Arthur Hoggarth of KENDAL, and after education at the local grammar school went to Keble College, Oxford, where he obtained a degree in modern

William Henry Hoodless:
Caldbeck Mill.
Watercolour 12×16.
B. & R. Moss.

history. Hoggarth drew from his extreme youth and as a young man had cartoons published in *Punch* and other leading magazines. He exhibited throughout his subsequent career as an academic, showing his work at the Royal Academy, the Royal Institute of Painters in Water Colours, the Walker Art Gallery, Liverpool, the Lake Artists' Society, and various other provincial art societies, and also became a member of the Royal Society of British Artists. During this period he taught at schools at Sandwich, Kent, and at York, later becoming a tutor at Churcher's College, Petersfield, Hants (1911), and subsequently Headmaster (1927). Following his retirement he lived at STAVELEY, near WINDERMERE, dying there in 1964. Hoggarth was descended from an old TROUTBECK, near AMBLESIDE, family. One of its members, Richard Hoggarth (later Hogarth), was the father of the celebrated William Hogarth. Represented: Abbot Hall A.G., Kendal, and various overseas art galleries.

*HOODLESS, William Henry (1841-1902)

Landscape painter in oil and watercolour. He was born at WIGTON, the son of a stationer, and became interested in art as a young man. He visited fellow Cumbrian Samuel Bough (q.v.), in Edinburgh, and Bough advised him to enter Edinburgh School of Art, where he twice won prizes as a student. On learning that his father's health was failing, Hoodless returned to WIGTON, taking over the family business on the latter's death. He remained passionately interested in painting, however, often filling the windows of his stationer's shop with his pictures. He worked mainly in the Lake District, and is said to have walked sometimes twenty miles in a day to make a sketch. He exhibited his work at Manchester from 1865 to 1871, the Royal Scottish Academy and Liverpool in 1865, and Carlisle Art Gallery in 1896. He is said to have died following a journey to CALDBECK on foot through deep snow, and three days spent sketching in the open air. He died at WIGTON. Represented: Carlisle A.G.

HOLYOAKE, P. W. (fl.1910)

Landscape painter in oil. He exhibited one work at the Royal Academy in 1910, while at the School of Art in KENDAL. His *Nether Bridge* (private collection) was included in "The Artists' Kendal" exhibition at the Abbot Hall Art Gallery, KENDAL, Summer, 1975.

HOUSEMAN, John (fl. c.1800)

Landscape draughtsman. He was born in Cumberland, and published a tour of the Lakes using his own illustrations.

*HOWARD, George, 9th Earl of Carlisle, H.R.W.S. (1843-1911)

Landscape and portrait painter in oil, watercolour and pastel; etcher. He was the son of the Hon. Charles Howard (a son of the 6th Earl of Carlisle) and Mary Parke, a former pupil of Peter De Wint. He was educated at Eton, and studied at Trinity College, Cambridge, drawing and painting while at both. In 1864 he married, commissioning Philip Webb to design his London home, and later asking William Morris and Burne Jones to decorate it. The following year he went to South Kensington School of Art, studying under Da Costa and Legros, and making the acquaintance of many professional artists, including Rossetti. He found himself greatly attracted to the Pre-Raphaelite style of painting and thereafter followed it closely himself. He first began exhibiting his work in 1868, showing some sixty works at the Royal Academy, the Royal Society of Painters in Water Colours, the Grosvenor Gallery, the New Gallery, and various other London galleries between that date and his death in 1911.

In 1874 he commissioned Burne Jones to design windows for St. Martin's, BRAMPTON, and in 1884 a bas relief for the library at Naworth Castle, near BRAMPTON, seat of the Earls of Carlisle, and part of the estates which he had inherited in 1878. During his residence at the latter, both before and after becoming 9th Earl in 1889, in

43

succession to his uncle, he entertained many famous writers and artists, frequently drawing or painting their portraits. He travelled widely throughout his life, visiting many parts of Europe, and travelling to Africa, Egypt, India and the West Indies. Wherever he travelled he produced sketches or finished works. He was Liberal M.P. for East Cumberland 1879-80, and chairman of the National Gallery for thirty years. He was also an honorary member of the Royal Society of Painters in Water Colours. He died at Hindhead, Surrey, and is buried at Lanercost Priory, near BRAMPTON. His daughter CECILIA MAUDE (b. 1869) was a talented amateur artist; her daughter is Winifred Nicholson (q.v.). Major exhibitions of his work have been held at Leighton House, London (1954), and Carlisle Art Gallery (1968 and 1978). Represented: British Museum; National Portrait Gallery; Carlisle A.G.

Paul Greville Hudson: Portrait of Will. Tyler (q.v.).
Oil 30×36. *Carlisle Museum & Art Gallery.*

*HUDSON, Paul Greville (1876-1960)

Landscape and portrait painter in oil; illustrator and decorative artist. Born in London of Anglo-French extraction, Hudson studied at the London College of Art, exhibiting at the Royal Academy when he was only eighteen. He began his career as a professional artist by illustrating for the London dailies, and after a short period of work at Bolton, Lancashire, went to CARLISLE at the age of twenty-five to work as a commercial artist for Hudson Scott and Sons, now the Metal Box Company. Here he worked at designing the decorations for boxes, also painting in his spare time. In 1904, along with friends John James Hodgson (q.v.), and Will Tyler (q.v.), he held his first exhibition at Scott & Son's Gallery, CARLISLE, later exhibiting at the London Salon, and at various galleries in Paris. He also while working at CARLISLE travelled widely abroad, painting in Germany, France and Holland. After his retirement to Scotland in 1939 he exhibited at the Royal Scottish Academy, and at Hawick and Galashiels Art Clubs. He also assisted the Art Department of Hawick High School during World War Two. In 1961 a retrospective exhibition of his work was shown at Carlisle Art Gallery. Represented: Carlisle A.G.; Carlisle Library; Wilton House Museum, Hawick.

HULL, William (1820-1880)

Landscape, fruit and flower painter in watercolour; illustrator. Hull was born at Graffham, Huntingdonshire, the son of a farmer, and only settled in Cumbria after a varied career in which he trained to enter the Moravian church as a minister, spent several years as an assistant at its settlements in Yorkshire and Ireland, worked as a printer's clerk, and travelled on the continent as a tutor. His earliest tuition in art came from the Germans Petersen and Halle, and while it is evident that he painted from an early age, he did not begin to exhibit his work until he was thirty-eight, showing his *Greenhead Ghyll, Grasmere,* at the Royal Academy exhibition of 1858. By this time he had apparently become a full-time professional artist, and was living at Manchester, his home from 1845 until he moved to RYDAL in 1870. While living at Manchester he also began exhibiting at the Suffolk Street Gallery, and at other galleries in London, mainly showing Welsh and South of England landscapes, but from 1871, with his move to RYDAL, he almost exclusively showed Cumbrian landscapes, exhibiting five works at the Royal Academy and two works at the Suffolk Street Gallery, between that date and 1877.

Hull suffered a stroke in 1850 which left him deaf and lame, and this could well explain why he so long delayed becoming a professional artist; prior to this date he was able to follow the various other professions mentioned. He has been identified in other dictionaries of artists as the "W. Hull" referred to by Martin Hardie as a fruit and flower painter who sometimes closely followed the work of Hunt. (*Water Colour Painting in Britain*, Vol. III). He died at RYDAL, and is buried at GRASMERE. Represented: Victoria and Albert Museum; Abbot Hall A.G., Kendal.

*IBBETSON, Julius Caesar (1759-1817)

Landscape and genre painter in oil and watercolour; etcher. Ibbetson was born at Farnely Moor, near Leeds, and led a chequered life as an artist before deciding to settle in the Lake District. He first visited the area in 1798, four years after the death of his wife, and decided to make his home there. He moved to the shores of Rydal Water in the spring of 1799, remaining there for several years before moving to CLAPPERSGATE, near AMBLESIDE, and subsequently to nearby TROUTBECK. A detailed and well illustrated account of his five years in Cumbria is contained in Rotha Mary Clay's biography of the artist: *Julius Caesar Ibbetson*, published by Country Life, 1948.‡ In it she refers to the several fine landscapes which he produced during his stay, including a view of Lake Windermere showing Brathay Hall, later to become the

Julius Caesar Ibbetson:
Castle Crag, Borrowdale.
Oil 31×40.
Abbot Hall Art Gallery.

Julius Caesar Ibbetson:
Ambleside:
The Market Place, 1801.
Oil 17½×23½.
*Art Gallery, and Temple
Newsam House, Leeds.*

45

William Irving: Fighting Fifth leaving Newcastle. Pen and ink 9×14. *Dean Gallery.*

William Irving: The Eden near Armathwaite. Watercolour 15×19¼. *Carlisle Museum & Art Gallery.*

home of her great grandfather, John Harden (q.v.). Harden met Ibbetson, and his new young wife Bella Thompson, on a visit to the area in 1803.

Ibbetson's years in Cumbria were among the most productive in his career, and at least half of the some thirty-six works which he showed at the Royal Academy from his arrival there until his death featured local subjects. Indeed the last picture painted by the artist fell into this category. Painted in 1817 it portrayed *The Market Place of Ambleside with the old buildings as they stood in 1801*.[‡] Finally, his stay in the area produced his *Accidence, or Gamut of Painting in Oil and Water Colour*, published 1803. After leaving Cumbria he moved to Masham in North Yorkshire, where he died in 1817. His son JULIUS IBBETSON (1783-1825), was a successful artist and drawing master. Represented: British Museum; National Portrait Gallery; Victoria and Albert Museum; Tate Gallery; National Gallery of Ireland; Abbot Hall A.G., Kendal; Carlisle A.G.; Laing A.G., Newcastle, and various provincial art galleries.

‡ *Curiously, this account has, on page 102, a story regarding Ibbetson and an inn-sign said to have been painted by him at TROUTBECK, which is identical with that recounted of Salathiel Court (q.v.), in John Askew's Guide to Cockermouth, 2nd. Edition 1872.*

*IRVING, William (fl.1818-1824)
Portrait painter in oil. He was probably born at LONGTOWN, his earliest recorded work being his portrait in 1818 of David Lang, the so-called "priest" at Gretna in Dumfriesshire.[‡] He exhibited four portraits at the Carlisle Academy in 1824, giving addresses in LONGTOWN and London, so may have moved to the capital about this date. Conflicting reports as to the quality of his work appeared in the local press of his day; one paper said it was "outrageously coloured", while another described it as the product of "considerable ability". Carlisle Art Gallery has his portrait of Lang.

*IRVING, William (1866-1943)
Portrait, landscape and genre painter in oil and watercolour; illustrator. Born at AINSTABLE the son of a farmer, William Irving moved with his parents to Tyneside in his infancy and later attended the Newcastle School of Art under William Cosens Way. At the end of his tuition he was recommended by Cosens Way for a position with the *Newcastle Weekly Chronicle* as an illustrator, and he remained in this occupation for many years while building up a reputation as a portrait painter. He also in this period became a member of the Bewick Club of Newcastle, and showed at one of its exhibitions his first important landscape with figures: *The End of the Season*, 1891. Later he began showing his work at the Royal Academy, exhibiting his *Ducks and Darlings* in 1898, and his *Happy Days* in 1901. These were followed in 1903 by his *Blaydon Races – a study from life*, now one of the North East of England's most popular and famous paintings. It is said that when it was exhibited in the window of a Newcastle art dealer's shop it attracted the attention of such a large crowd that the police asked the manager to draw the blinds. The painting now hangs in the city's County Hotel, opposite Newcastle Central Station.

While employed by the *Chronicle*, and a local magazine called: *Monthly Chronicle of North Country Lore and Legend* (later reprinted in 5 volumes, covering its life from

William Irving: David Lang – the Gretna "Priest". Oil 14×12. *Carlisle Museum & Art Gallery.*

1887-1891), Irving was frequently called upon to prepare portraits of local celebrities as pen and ink drawings, for line reproduction. Many of these assignments subsequently led to portrait commissions in oil, by either the sitters, or other interested parties. Shortly after painting his *Blaydon Races* he was commissioned to paint two portraits of Newcastle M.P. and newspaper proprietor Joseph Cowen (one for the *Chronicle*, and one for Cowen's family). On receiving payment for this commission he decided that he would increasingly look to portraiture for his living, and to further enhance his reputation in this field he would study in Paris. About 1905 he left Newcastle and enrolled as a pupil in the Academie Julian, where he had amongst his tutors some of the leading French painters of the day. Returning to Tyneside about 1908, he resumed his profession with renewed vigour and, according to contemporary accounts, with a marked improvement in his skill.

Irving painted portraits until close to his death, but with the growing competition of photography found it increasingly difficult to find sitters. In his final years he frequently turned to picture restoration as a source of income, and was responsible for extensive work on the painting by Luca Giordano in St. Andrew's Church, Newcastle. He remained a frequent visitor to his birthplace throughout his life, producing many landscapes along the banks of the River Eden in the area of ARMATHWAITE.[‡] Most of these landscapes were executed in watercolour, and invariably included figures and animals. He died at Newcastle at his home and workplace for many years, in the Jesmond area of the city. His son STANLEY ROLLINGS IRVING was a keen amateur painter in oil and watercolour. Represented: Carlisle A.G.; Laing A.G., Newcastle.

Charles Jenour: Portrait of Margaret Gibson, 1844.
Watercolour 11×8¾. *Whitehaven Museum.*

William Jackson: Monument to the Rev. Fawcett.
St. Cuthbert's, Carlisle.

*JACKSON, William (b.1820- after 1875)

Sculptor. Jackson was probably born at COCKERMOUTH, where he practised as a sculptor most of his life. He attended the Royal Academy Schools as a young man, and returning to COCKERMOUTH became a successful sculptor of statues and funeral monuments. The *Carlisle Journal,* 10th December, 1852, reported: "We understand that Mr. Jackson has had two medals awarded him by the Royal Academy. He was for several years employed in the studio of Weeks, the successor of Chantry", but it is not clear whether these circumstances pre-dated his return to COCKERMOUTH, or occurred at subsequent dates. His principal works are his monument to the Reverend Fawcett (1852),# in St. Cuthbert's, CARLISLE, and a statue of Sir Robert Clifton, for Nottingham.

JAMESON, T. (fl.1809)

This AMBLESIDE artist is known to us via the diaries of Joseph Farington (1747-1821). Farington says that John Constable (1776-1837) informed him that John Harden (q.v.) had helped Jameson in his financial difficulties, and found him lodgings in London so that he could follow the profession of drawing master, or take up other activity connected with art. Nothing is known of him subsequently. Represented: British Museum.

Edward Jeffrey: The Stables, Ravenstonedale, Kirkby Stephen.
Pen and ink 2¾×4. *Cumbria Magazine.*

48

*JEFFREY, Edward (1898-1978)
Painter in watercolour; illustrator. Jeffrey was educated in
Newcastle upon Tyne, later studying art at Armstrong
College (later King's College, now Newcastle University).
He exhibited at the Royal Institute of Painters in Water
Colours, the Royal Scottish Academy, the Royal Society
of British Artists, the National Society of Painters,
Sculptors and Gravers, and widely in the provinces. He
was a member of the Lake Artists' Society, and Kendal
Art Society, and lived at KIRKBY STEPHEN for a number
of years. Many of his illustrations have appeared in
Cumbria Magazine.◊

JENKINSON, J. P. (fl. c.1800-1830)
Marine painter in oil. Jenkinson produced several views of
shipping at MARYPORT and WHITEHAVEN in the first
quarter of the 19th century. He may have been a pupil or
friend of William Brown (q.v.), as at least one example of
his work, *A View of Maryport,* dated 1819, is almost
identical with a painting by Brown of the same title and
date in the Walker Art Gallery, Liverpool.◊ His later
connections seem to have been with Liverpool.

*JENOUR, Charles (d.1851)
Portrait painter in pastel. Jenour practised as an artist in
WHITEHAVEN in the second quarter of the 19th century,
mainly as a visiting professional portrait painter based in
London. He exhibited at the Royal Academy between
1825 and 1832, mainly showing portraits. His obituary in
the *Carlisle Journal,* 11th April, 1851, remarks that he
was "... well and favourably known in Whitehaven".
Represented: Carlisle A.G.; Whitehaven Museum.

JOHNSON, George (J. ?) Holdon (fl.1825-1829)
Profile painter. Johnson practised as a profile painter in
WHITEHAVEN in 1825, and KENDAL in 1829. He may
identify with the J. H. JOHNSON (fl.1825-1830), who
sent works to the Carlisle Academy in 1825 and 1828
from Newcastle and Dumfries addresses, and who also
sent works to the Dumfries Exhibitions of 1828 and 1830
while working as a drawing master in the town. His works
were mainly landscapes, however, some with historical
connections.

JONES, Austin (fl. c.1890-1910)
Landscape painter in oil. Jones practised as an artist in
KENDAL at the beginning of the 19th century, living in the
town's Highgate. His *Nether Bridge, Kendal,* of 1909, is in
Kendal Town Hall.

KENDALL, Richard (fl.1851)
Portrait painter. He is recorded as a portrait painter
practising at AMBLESIDE in 1851.

KENNEDY, James (fl.1791-92)
Engraver. He came from London to CARLISLE to work for
F. Jollie, the printer, and was responsible for engraving
many of the illustrations for Hutchinson's *History of
Cumberland,* 1794.

John Dalzell Kenworthy: Self Portrait. Oil 19×15.
Whitehaven Museum.

***KENWORTHY, John Dalzell, A.R.Cam.A.
(1858-1954)**
Portrait and rustic painter in oil and watercolour; book
illustrator. Kenworthy was born at WHITEHAVEN, and
later practised as a professional artist, showing his work at
the Royal Academy, the Royal Cambrian Academy,
Carlisle Art Gallery, and in Liverpool. He also wrote, and
illustrated with his watercolour drawings *A Fisherman's
Philosophy,* published by the *Whitehaven News* in 1933.
Whitehaven Museum has several examples of his work,
including a self portrait.◊ He lived at both WHITEHAVEN,
and nearby ST. BEES for most of his professional life, and
was elected an associate of the Royal Cambrian Academy
in 1914. He died at WHITEHAVEN.

KING, William (fl.1787-1790)
Wood carver, gilder and looking-glass manufacturer. He
started in business at WHITEHAVEN in 1787. In the period
1788-1790 he executed carvings for the interior of
Workington Hall "in a style greatly superior to anything
ever attempted, or perhaps ever seen in this part of the
Kingdom", according to one commentator. He was
possibly the father of William Atkin King (q.v.).

KING, William Atkin (fl.1825-1864)
Landscape painter. He is recorded as a landscape painter
living at WHITEHAVEN in the middle of the 19th century.
He was possibly the son of William King (q.v.), and

carried on the latter's business as a carver and gilder. He exhibited one work at the Carlisle Academy in 1825, and two works at the Whitehaven Exhibition of 1826.

*KIRKBRIDE, John (1786-1854)
Sculptor; marble and stone mason. Kirkbride was probably born at CARLISLE, and worked from his youth at the marble works of Nixson and Denton in the city's Finkle Street, eventually rising to foreman, and taking over his employers' business in 1838. Here he was joined by sons JAMES (b. 1813), and ISAAC (b. 1815), and carried on a highly successful business until his death in 1854. Among his many commissions were his monuments to Robert Ferguson (d. 1816),# at St. Michael's, STANWIX, William Thurnam (d. 1823), at Carlisle Cathedral, and John Steward (d. 1848), at St. John's Evangelist, HENSINGHAM. He was also responsible for the carving in the arcade erected in Lowther Street, CARLISLE, for butchers, in 1844, by Thomas Nelson (q.v.). Pevsner's *Cumberland & Westmorland* mentions several works by "Kirkbride of Carlisle". His sons carried on the business after his death.

KIRKPATRICK, James (fl.1820-1845)
Portrait painter in oil. He was a friend of Samuel Bough (q.v.) while the latter practised at CARLISLE. In 1845, however, he left CARLISLE for Newcastle upon Tyne. Bough wrote a letter of introduction for Kirkpatrick to John Wilson Carmichael stating: "I beg to introduce you to Mr James Kirkpatrick, portrait painter, of this place, a kindly, quiet decent body, as ever lived; and beg that you will show him some of your pictures, and to introduce him to the Messrs Richardson. Mr. James Kirkpatrick has been obliged to leave Carlisle on account of the difficulty of finding employment in his particular walk . . .". Bough himself was to leave CARLISLE shortly afterwards for much the same reasons, remarking in his letter to Carmichael: "There is little chance of growing fat by landscape painting in Carlisle . . .". Nothing is known of Kirkpatrick after he moved to Tyneside, though he is known to have remained in contact with Bough. His portrait of Bough's father is in Carlisle Art Gallery.

KNOX, T. (fl.1849)
Landscape painter. He exhibited at the Royal Academy, and at various other exhibitions, in 1849, from KESWICK. His contribution to the Royal Academy was entitled: *View of Derwent water, from Watendlath Road.*

LAMBERT, Miss (fl.1824)
Genre painter. She contributed five works to the 1824 exhibition of the Carlisle Academy from an address at KENDAL. "Miss Lambert, the mistress of a respectable seminary for the education of young ladies at Kendal – and, as such, her pictures are certainly worthy of attention, though not remarkable as specimens of art", commented the *Carlisle Patriot*, 9th October, 1824.

John Kirkbride: Monument to Robert Ferguson, St. Michael's, Stanwix.

LAW, Thomas (fl.1824-1829)
Amateur landscape painter in watercolour; animal painter in oil; copyist. Law exhibited two works at the Carlisle Academy in 1824, while living at PENRITH. One of these works was: *Portrait of Marmion, a Horse. The property of the Right Hon. the Earl of Lonsdale*; the other was entitled: *Landscape with Figures, after Berghem.* He painted two views of Lowther Castle, which were published by James Brown of PENRITH, in 1829. Carlisle Art Gallery has copies of these engravings, but no other works of the artist are known. The works described suggest that he may have been patronised by the Earl of Lonsdale.

LEES, Herbert, A.R.C.A. (1831-1907)
Landscape painter in oil; art teacher and illustrator. Lees was born at Hanley, Staffordshire, and attended the art school at South Kensington before taking up a position there as head figure draughtsman. After teaching at South Kensington for some years he became an associate of the Royal College of Art, and in December, 1853, he was admitted as a student at the Royal Academy Schools. Five years later he came to CARLISLE as Headmaster of the School of Art in the city, remaining there for three years before taking up a similar appointment at Sunderland, Co. Durham. In the following year he returned to CARLISLE, once again taking up the position of Headmaster of the School of Art, and remaining there in this capacity until his retirement in 1898. During his period as Headmaster many of Cumbria's most talented young

artists received tuition at the School; these included John Scott (q.v.), William Smallwood Winder (q.v.), John James Hodgson (q.v.), Henry Herbert Bulman (q.v.), and Joseph W. Simpson (q.v.). He also painted, and prepared illustrations, in his spare time, showing five landscape works at the Carlisle Art Gallery exhibition of 1896, and for the visit of H.R.H. the Princess Louise, to CARLISLE in 1877, submitting illustrations to the *London Illustrated News*. On his retirement, Lees acted as a consulting master to the Carlisle School of Art, and gave private tuition. He died at CARLISLE. Represented: Carlisle Library.

Le FLEMING, Miss Mildred (fl. 1884-1891)

Landscape painter in watercolour. A member of a well known family at Rydal Hall, AMBLESIDE, she exhibited three works at the New Water-Colour Society and three works at its successor, the Royal Institute of Painters in Water Colours, between 1884 and 1891.

LEWTHWAITE, John (fl. c.1830-1866)

Portrait painter in oil. Lewthwaite was born at COCKERMOUTH, where he became one of the six pupils of Joseph Sutton (q.v.). In 1866 his portraits of Robert Benson, John Richardson, the Rev. Edward Fawcett, John Steel M.P., the Duke of Wellington, and Sir Robert Peel, were shown at Cockermouth Mechanics' Institute. Nothing further is known of this artist.

LILLEY, John (fl. 1853)

The *Carlisle Journal*, 17th June, 1853, recorded in its marriage announcements: "At Bolton last week Mr J. Lilley, artist, to Miss Mary Ann Bulger, both of Bolton Low Houses". This may be the same John Lilley who exhibited portraits at the Royal Academy, the British Institution, and the Suffolk Street Gallery between 1832 and 1846 from London addresses. BOLTON LOW HOUSES is near WIGTON.

*LINTON, William James (1812-1898)

Engraver; landscape painter in watercolour; writer. One of Britain's most remarkable wood engravers, Linton was born in London, and after an apprenticeship with G. W. Bonner soon became a popular engraver of illustrations for books and periodicals. At the age of twenty-one he was invited to contribute to Martin and Westall's *Pictorial Illustrations of the Bible*, and the *Illustrated London News* used him from its foundation in 1842. From an early age he also became interested in politics, and involved in the publication of a number of books and periodicals with political objectives, including a weekly called *The Leader,* which advocated Republican principles. In 1852 he moved to CONISTON, living there for fifteen years before eventually disposing of his home – Brantwood – to John Ruskin (q.v.). At Brantwood, Linton continued his work in wood engraving, and was responsible for a further number of publications, including a volume of his poems: *The Plaint of Freedom* (1852); a periodical called the *English Republic*, and a Tyneside magazine: *The Northern Tribune*. He also continued to exhibit at the Royal Academy, his first work after moving to CONISTON being shown in 1855, and entitled: *The Ivory Carver*, after E. H. Wehnert; his last work, *Dead Ripe*, was shown in 1864.

Linton had brought an invalid wife with him to Brantwood, and she was nursed by Elizabeth Lynn, daughter of Vicar Lynn of CROSTHWAITE, near KESWICK. His wife died in 1857, and he married Elizabeth in 1859. His second wife was a gifted writer, and wrote *The Lake Country* (1864), with 100 illustrations by Linton.* He was never successful while living at Brantwood, however, and in 1867 he decided to move to America, leaving his children by his first marriage at boarding schools under the care of Elizabeth. The family followed Linton to America in 1868, and here he became one of the most distinguished wood engravers of his day. He was elected a member of the National Academy of America in 1882, and became a member of the Society of Painters in Water Colours. He was also responsible for writing several books on the history, theory and practice of wood

William James Linton:
Sharrow Bay, Ullswater.
Illustration from
"The Lake Country".

engraving, including: *Practical Hints on Wood Engraving*, 1879; *A History of Wood Engraving in America*, 1882, and *Wood Engraving, a Manual of Instruction*, 1884. His greatest work, however, was his *The Masters of Wood Engraving*, published in 1889. He continued to publish his poetry while in America, and wrote his *Memories* in 1896. He died at New Haven, Connecticut. A detailed account of the Linton family's stay at Brantwood is contained in V. Jackson's "Life with the Lintons", *Cumbria Magazine*, April 1970, pp. 24-26.

LISHMAN, James (d.1850)

Landscape painter in watercolour; drawing master. Lishman practised as a painter and drawing master at ULVERSTON and KENDAL in the second quarter of the 19th century. He was described as "Mr James Lishman of Ulverston, dancing and drawing master", when he married in KENDAL in 1829, and was listed in a local directory of 1834 as a "Landscape painter, Castle Street, Kendal". The Abbot Hall Art Gallery, KENDAL has his *Abbot Hall and the Parish Church*, 1825.

*LONGMIRE, William Taylor (1841-1914)

Landscape, animal and genre painter in oil and watercolour. A member of a well known family at TROUTBECK, near AMBLESIDE, Longmire was born the son of a farmer and butcher and was intended to follow in his father's footsteps. He was much attracted to drawing, however, and while living as a child at STAVELEY, near WINDERMERE, he came to the attention of the vicar, who encouraged him to his ambition to become a painter. Later at BOWNESS-ON-WINDERMERE he studied under a Mr. Howe, but here fell into the lake, and went to school without first changing his clothing. He contracted a fever as a result of which he remained stone-deaf for the rest of his life. By the early 1870's he had settled at AMBLESIDE and was practising as a full-time professional artist. He did not make a satisfactory living from his work, however, and is said to have tried to economise by sometimes working

on up to twenty pictures concurrently, painting one colour at a time. Longmire's deafness did not apparently impede his social life and he became one of the town's most colourful and popular characters during his many years of life there. His work varied considerably in quality and it was not exhibited outside the Lake District. Some of his better work involved animal portraiture, examples of which are at Townend, the National Trust property at TROUTBECK. Represented: Abbot Hall A.G., Kendal.

*LOSH, Sarah (1785-1853)

Amateur architect and sculptor. She was the eldest daughter of John Losh, who had settled at Woodside, near WREAY, after amassing a fortune from the manufacture of chemicals on Tyneside. Sarah was passionately interested in architecture, and after schooling with her sister Katherine, in London and Bath, travelled Italy and France seeing everything of interest. When Katherine died in 1835, Sarah was overcome with grief and in memory of her sister began setting up drinking troughs for horses, restoring wells and beautifying churches in the area around WREAY. Her finest tribute to the memory of her sister was the church of St. Mary, which she designed and built at WREAY in the style of a

Sarah Losh:
Carved stone serpentine form, exterior of St. Mary's, Wreay, based on clay moulding by Sarah Losh, and executed by William Hindson.

William Taylor Longmire:
River Brathay.
Oil 12×18.
Northgate Gallery.

Roman basilica, and a nearby mausoleum. As her principal sculptor she engaged William Hindson (q.v.), son of a local stonemason, first producing her own mouldings in clay to serve as models for his work, which included the gargoyle illustrated in this volume; additional work was carried out by John Scott (q.v.), from nearby DALSTON, her cousin William S. Losh (q.v.), and herself. Her work consisted of the alabaster candlesticks for the altar, and part of the font. She also designed the statue of her sister in the mausoleum executed by David Dunbar Senior (q.v.), providing the sculptor with a sketch of Katherine taken at Naples in 1817, from which to work. Lonsdale in his: *The Worthies of Cumberland,* Vol. 4, 1873, which contains much interesting information about the Losh family, comments of Sarah's contribution to Dunbar's statute: "She aided him so materially that the portrait statue became very much her own design".‡ Pevsner's *Cumberland & Westmorland* contains a detailed description of St. Mary's Church, and the mausoleum; the church interior is illustrated plate 64, and a window, plate 65. An account of the building of the church and mausoleum, together with photographs, appeared in *Country Life,* 4th November, 1971, pp. 1230-1, in "A memorial to two sisters," by M. A. Wood.

‡ *See illustration in connection with entry for David Dunbar Senior (q.v.).*

LOSH, William S. (fl.1842)

Sculptor. The cousin of Sarah Losh (q.v.), he collaborated with the latter and William Hindson (q.v.) in the carving of the alabaster font in St. Mary's, WREAY, the church erected by Sarah in memory of her sister Katherine. He is said to have been responsible for the cover of the font.

LOWES, James (1774-1834)

Architectural draughtsman and engraver. Born at CARLISLE, Lowes showed an aptitude for drawing and engraving from an early age. He was engaged by Hutchinson to engrave the works of Robert Carlyle Senior (q.v.) for a *History of Cumberland,* published 1794, and himself contributed work to this publication, including his *Queen Mary's Tower and Lady's Walk,* illustrated Vol. II, p. 593. Lowes was evidently taught landscape painting by Carlyle, but remained an engraver all his life, securing a position in this capacity on the staff of the *Carlisle Journal,* and staying there throughout his career.

*LOWRY, Strickland (1737-c.1785)

Portrait and landscape painter in oil. Born at WHITEHAVEN, Lowry practised as a painter in the town until after 1762, following which he worked in Ireland. He returned to WHITEHAVEN from Ireland after several years, again practising as a painter in the town before working in Worcestershire, Shropshire and Staffordshire. While working in England he was patronised by Lord Pigot, and produced thirteen views of churches for Philip's *History and Antiquities of Shrewsbury,* published in 1779. Some of his most interesting work was produced in Ireland, however, though his movements during the periods in which he is believed to have been working there are obscure. Pictures by him are said to occur in and around Dublin, and in the east of Ireland as far north as Co. Down. In a manuscript account book at Newbridge,

Strickland Lowry: Portrait of Mrs. Sarah Holmes, 1780. Oil 36½×28½. *Ulster Museum.*

Donabate, Co. Dublin, there are entries which state: "To Lowry for the picture of the children £9.2.0", and "To Lowry the painter £4.11.0". His style is said to resemble that of Joseph Wilson, the Belfast born painter who was working in the 1770's, and Lowry is known to have painted a portrait of Mrs. Wilson. His *Portrait of a Lady,* 1780[#] – Sarah Holmes, wife of Robert Holmes of Dublin – would appear to have been painted in the Irish capital, while a companion picture of the same date, *Lurgan Volunteers,* apparently refers to Lurgan in Co. Armagh. After his final visit to Ireland, Lowry settled at Worcester, where he died in the middle 1780's. His *Portrait of a Lady* was included in the "Irish Portraits 1660-1860" exhibition, held at the National Gallery of Ireland, Dublin, in 1969, and at the National Portrait Gallery, London, and Ulster Museum, Belfast, in 1970. Lowry's son, Wilson Lowry (q.v.), became a well known engraver. Represented: Ulster Museum, Belfast.

LOWRY, Wilson (1760-1824)

Engraver. The son of Strickland Lowry (q.v.), he was born at WHITEHAVEN, and accompanied his father to Ireland some time after 1762. He later returned to WHITEHAVEN with his father, then went to Worcester, where he endeavoured to obtain employment as a house painter. He then tried house painting in London for a time, but decided to return to Worcester, where he obtained some elementary instruction in engraving from an engraver called Ross. At the age of about seventeen he obtained a place at the Royal Academy Schools and once more moved to London. On leaving the Schools he soon became a much sought after professional engraver. His early plates did not bear his name, however, as they were executed for other artists. He engraved most of the plates of mechanical subjects in Ree's *Encyclopaedia*, Crabbe's *Technological Dictionary,* and the *Philosophical Magazine,* for this and other types of work inventing several special types of engraving instrument. These instruments were described and highly praised by John Landseer (the engraver father of Sir Edwin Landseer) in his lectures at the Royal Institution. He was also the first engraver to use diamond points for ruling, and is said to have discovered the secret of biting in steel successfully.

Some of his finest work was in the field of architectural engraving, and included the illustrations for Murphy's *Batalha*, and Nicholson's *Architecture.* He regarded one of his engravings for the latter – *From the Doric Portico at Athens* – his best work, and once said that if he were to have received a thousand pounds for the attempt he could not do a single line better. Worcester Record Office has his wash drawing of Elmley Castle, Worcester, dating from the late 18th century, but no other examples of his work outside engraving have come to light. He died in London after a "lingering illness", leaving a son JOSEPH WILSON LOWRY (1803-1879), to follow in his footsteps as an engraver, and a daughter MATILDA LOWRY (Mrs. Heming), to practise as a landscape and portrait painter in watercolour. Matilda's portrait of her father, now in the collection of the National Portrait Gallery, was published as an engraving in London in the year following his death.

LOWTHER, T. (fl. *c.*1800)
Portrait painter in oil. Lowther practised in CARLISLE about the year 1800. His only known work is an oil painting in a primitive style, of the hiring fair at Carlisle Cross *c.* 1800, showing Margery Jackson the "Carlisle Miser" hiring her servant "Croglin Wattie". Represented: Carlisle A.G.

LOWTHIAN, David (fl. *c.*1800)
Portrait painter in oil. He practised at KENDAL about the year 1800. Kendal Museum has his *Portrait of Ann Mount,* the country milk woman, painted in a primitive style.

LOWTHIAN, Jaby (b.1813)
He was listed as an "artist (painting)" living at CARLISLE, in the Census returns for the city in 1861. He was born at RENWICK, and lived at Sale in Cheshire, and PENRITH, before moving to CARLISLE.

MACHELL, Colonel Christopher (1747-1827)
Amateur landscape painter in pen and wash. He was descended from an ancient Westmorland family who were Lords of the Manor of CRACKENTHORPE, near APPLEBY. He himself was not born there, but at ASBY, where his father was rector. He went as a young man to America to fight in the War of American Independence, where he lost an arm in the Battle of New York, and on his return was much annoyed to find that Crackenthorpe Hall had been sold by his brothers without first giving him an opportunity to purchase it. He eventually married and settled at Beverley, Yorkshire, where he became a friend and patron of Francis Nicholson (1753-1844), and began to draw and paint seriously, producing drawings in pen and wash wherever he travelled. He was Deputy Lieutenant for the East Riding, and was a skilful musician and botanist. A large collection of his drawings was presented by Lady Valda Machell to the Victoria and Albert Museum in 1951, which in its turn presented them to other art museums. Several examples of his work were included in the "Eminent Amateurs" exhibition at the Abbot Hall Art Gallery, KENDAL, in 1965. Represented: Victoria and Albert Museum; Abbot Hall A.G., Kendal; Wakefield A.G.; Walker A.G. Liverpool, and various provincial art galleries.

MACHELL, Rev. Thomas (1647-1698)
Architectural draughtsman; antiquarian. Machell was descended from an ancient Westmorland family who were Lords of the Manor of CRACKENTHORPE, near APPLEBY. He may have been educated at Appleby Grammar School before attending Queen's College, Oxford, where he graduated B.A. in 1668, and proceeded to M.A. in 1672. He also became a Fellow of the College in the latter year. In 1677 he was presented by the 3rd Earl of Thanet with the rectory of KIRKBY THORE, near APPLEBY, remaining parson there until his death twenty-one years later. During this period he took a keen interest in antiquarian and architectural matters, producing a manuscript account of his antiquarian researches in Cumbria, illustrated with his sketches, and becoming involved in the introduction of classical architecture into the area, in collaboration with Edward Addison of KIRKBY THORE. His illustrated manuscript is in the possession of the Dean and Chapter of CARLISLE. One of his drawings from this manuscript: *Kendal Castle,* is reproduced in *Prelates and People,* by C. M. L. Bouche, and was illustrated in "The Artists' Kendal" exhibition at the Abbot Hall Art Gallery, KENDAL, Summer, 1975.

MACMILLAN, James (d.1863)
Landscape painter and engraver. He practised in CARLISLE in the first half of the 19th century, where he became a close friend of Samuel Bough (q.v.), and did some engraving of the work of the latter, and members of the Nutter family, in addition to painting landscapes. His obituary stated that "as a landscape painter he was no mean hand; but his taste in this respect far exceeded his power of execution". His collection of paintings sold for £100 following his death.

*MAILE, Alfred – see TUCKER, Alfred Robert

MANNERS, William, R.B.A. (fl.1888-1920)
Landscape, street scene and genre painter in oil and watercolour. He was born at Bradford and practised mainly in Yorkshire until after the turn of the century, showing his work at the Royal Academy, the Royal Scottish Academy, the Royal Society of British Artists (of

Alfred Robert Maile (Tucker): The Galilee Chapel, Durham Cathedral. Pen and ink 4×7. *Dean & Chapter of Durham Cathedral.*

which he was elected a member in 1893), and in the provinces. After 1904 he appears to have worked in the Lake District and the FURNESS area, using KENDAL as his base.

McCLELLAN, James (fl.1823-1869)
Copyist. He began in business as a painter and glazier in EGREMONT in 1823, painting copies in his spare time. He exhibited a copy after Wilkie at the Carlisle Academy in 1825, and two copies at the Whitehaven Exhibition of 1826. He was still in business at EGREMONT in 1869.

*McEUNE, Robert Ernest (1876-1952)
Portrait, figure, landscape and still-life painter in oil, watercolour and pastel. He was born at Gateshead, Co. Durham, and studied figure-drawing and painting at Gateshead School of Art, and at Armstrong College (later King's College; now Newcastle University), Newcastle upon Tyne. He later took up employment as an executive in a local coal company, but continued to take an interest in art in his spare time, producing many paintings and drawings, and preparing book illustrations. At the beginning of the Second World War he was forced due to ill-health to resign his coal company position and retired to PENRITH. Here he taught art as a member of Newcastle's Royal Grammar School while its pupils were evacuated to the town, and continued to draw and paint, showing his work at the Royal Academy, the Royal Institute of Painters in Water Colours, the London Pastel Society and in the provinces. His work was exhibited at Carlisle Art Gallery in 1952, and at the Shipley Art Gallery, Gateshead, in 1971, following this gallery's acquisition of a large selection of his oils, watercolours and pastels. Represented: Laing A.G., Newcastle; Shipley A.G., Gateshead.

MEEKLEY, Frederick George (1896-1951)
Landscape painter in oil and watercolour; commercial designer. Born at CARLISLE, Meekley attended the Carlisle School of Art under James Atherton (q.v.), before becoming an apprentice in the studio of Hudson Scott and

Sons, now the Metal Box Company, in 1912. With the exception of a period of service in the First World War, and two years spent working for printing firms in London and Leeds, he remained with the firm until his death. While working as a designer for the company he produced many landscapes and other works in his spare time, exhibiting at the Royal Academy, the Royal Scottish Academy, and in the provinces between 1927 and 1938. He also produced poster designs for the L.M.S. Railway Company, and the Carlisle Pageant, as well as designs for a miscellany of publications. Several of his landscape works were purchased by Carlisle Art Gallery in his lifetime, and a large memorial exhibition of his oils, watercolours and commercial work was staged at this gallery in 1952. Represented: Carlisle A.G.

MITCHELL, C. (fl.1794)
Drawing master and profile painter. Mitchell was working as a drawing master at WORKINGTON in 1794. One of his

Robert Ernest McEune: Rosthwaite. Watercolour 8×11. *Tyne & Wear County Museums, Shipley Art Gallery.*

55

advertisements (*Cumberland Pacquet*, 29th April, 1794) stated: "Drawing School, Workington: C. Mitchell, Drawing Master . . . intends opening a school 8 May 1794 for three days each week. Drawing will be taught in all its branches; also painting in watercolours, crayons, Indian ink etc. Profile shades done as usual". Nothing more is known of him.

*MITCHELL, William (*c.*1806-1900)

Marine and landscape painter in oil; cartoonist. One of Cumbria's most talented latter-day marine painters, Mitchell was born at MARYPORT, and was possibly a pupil of William Brown (q.v.) before becoming a professional artist in the town. His early work is little known, and it is possible that he did not work exclusively as a painter for many years. The earliest record of his use of the title "painter" dates to 1866, when he bought a grave plot at St. Mary's Church, MARYPORT. His earliest dated work to come to light, however, is his *The Tea Clipper Abbey Holme*,# of 1873. Bulmer's *Directory of West Cumberland*, 1883, listed him as an artist living at 147 King Street, MARYPORT, but he spent the final years of his life at High Street in the town, from which in 1896 he sent two marine paintings and two landscapes to the Carlisle Art Gallery exhibition of that year. He painted flower and bird studies while living at King Street, and frequently drew cartoons of local people for whom he had formed a dislike. It is possible that he also drew maps, as there is a map of MARYPORT dated 1834, which is signed "W.M.". He painted until close to his death, two of his latest works being his pair of oils *Old Maryport, in 1837*, dated 1898. He painted two self portraits which survive in the hands of his descendants. He died at MARYPORT. Represented: Carlisle A.G.; Maryport Maritime Museum; Whitehaven Museum.

MONINS, Captain W. C. G. (fl.1846-1852)

Amateur landscape painter. He showed seven works at Carlisle Athenaeum between 1846 and 1850 while living at CARLISLE, and took an active interest in the Mechanics' Institute in CARLISLE, and the formation of Carlisle Athenaeum. The *Carlisle Journal*, 4th July, 1846, report-

ing on the Carlisle Academy exhibition of that year, said of his exhibits: "Among the local artists and amateurs to whose work we would particularly point attention . . . and though last not least, Capt. Monins, an amateur who can fairly claim a place amongst professional artists for the skill and taste with which he handles the pencil". He was promoted to Major in 1853, and possibly as a result of this left the area.

MOORHOUSE, Mrs. Adelina Blanche (née Ellis) (b. 1885)

Landscape painter in watercolour, and pastel. The wife of George Mortram Moorhouse (q.v.), she studied at Leeds School of Art, and later lived with her husband at MORLAND, near PENRITH, where from 1923 she exhibited at the Royal Scottish Academy, the Royal Hibernian Academy, the Royal Cambrian Academy and in the provinces. She was a member of the Lake Artists' Society, and for many years lived at HELSINGTON, near KENDAL. Her pastel, *Westmorland Chimneys*, is in the collection of the Abbot Hall Art Gallery, KENDAL.

MOORHOUSE, George Mortram (1882-1960)

Figure painter in oil, watercolour and pastel; etcher. He was born near PENRITH, and studied at Lancaster School of Art under Sir W. Orpen, Augustus John, and John M. Swan, before becoming a professional artist. He exhibited at the Royal Academy, the Royal Scottish Academy, the Royal Hibernian Academy, the Royal West of England Academy and in the provinces, from 1908, living at MORLAND, near PENRITH, and HELSINGTON, near KENDAL. His *The Weir at Stramongate Bridge* (private collection), was included in "The Artists' Kendal" exhibition, at the Abbot Hall Art Gallery, KENDAL, Summer, 1975. He was the husband of Adelina Blanche Moorhouse (q.v.).

MORISON, C. W. M. S. (fl.1833)

Marine painter. He contributed eight works to the 1833 exhibition of the Carlisle Academy from an address at CARLISLE. Commenting on one of his exhibits – *Sea-piece, with the pleasure yacht of D. Morison Esq., and*

William Mitchell:
The Tea Clipper,
Abbey Holme, 1873.
Oil 37×60.
N. R. Omell Gallery.

Dutch fishing boats to windward, the *Carlisle Journal*, 2nd November, 1833, said: "A little more practice in his art, and a strict observation of nature, will enable Mr. Morison to become a successful painter of marine scenery. His pictures possess considerable merit and hold out much promise of future excellence".

*MURPHY, Denis Brownell (d.1842)

Painter of portrait miniatures in watercolour and enamel. Murphy was born in Dublin, and studied at the Dublin Society's Schools. He later practised as an artist in Dublin, where he exhibited miniatures in 1765 and 1768. About the latter year he went to London, but returned to Dublin in 1792. In 1798 he was living with his family at Lancaster, where he was visited by John Harden (q.v.), subsequently accompanying the latter on a sketching trip of the Lake District. He worked for a period in WHITEHAVEN in 1798, following which he worked at Newcastle upon Tyne, Edinburgh and London. He exhibited at the Royal Academy, and the British Institution, between 1800 and 1827, mainly showing portrait miniatures by his own hand, or after others, and in 1810 he was appointed Painter in Ordinary to The Princess Charlotte.

Many well known personalities of his day were included among his sitters, William Wordsworth (1770-1850),[#] and Thomas Bewick (1753-1828), to name only two. He also produced a copy of a portrait of Harden after Comerford, and an original work portraying Harden. Some of his work was later engraved. His portrait of Wordsworth (an unfinished work), was included in the "Irish Portraits 1660-1860" exhibition, held at the National Gallery of Ireland, Dublin, in 1969, and at the National Portrait Gallery, London, and the Ulster Museum, Belfast, in 1970. Represented: National Portrait Gallery; National Gallery of Ireland; Natural History Society, Newcastle upon Tyne.

Denis Brownell Murphy: William Wordsworth. Miniature (unfinished) $5 \times 3\frac{3}{4}$. *National Gallery of Ireland.*

George Nelson: Monument to Thomas Sheffield, Carlisle Cathedral. *Dean & Chapter of Carlisle Cathedral.*

NANSON, Thomas (fl.1823-1850)

Landscape painter. He contributed three works to the exhibitions of the Carlisle Academy between 1823 and 1833, from addresses at CARLISLE and London.

*NELSON, George (1810-1888)

Sculptor. He was possibly born at CARLISLE, and is said to have been encouraged to become a sculptor by Thomas Nelson (q.v.). He may have received tuition at the classes held by David Dunbar Senior (q.v.) at the Carlisle Academy, and probably met Musgrave Lewthwaite Watson (q.v.) there, before the latter's departure for London in 1824. He exhibited one piece of sculpture at the Carlisle Academy in 1833, following which he moved to London to take employment with a Mr. Coad, who had a terra cotta works at Lambeth. While in London he began exhibiting at the Royal Academy, showing fourteen sculptural works and sketches between 1837 and 1869. He also exhibited at Carlisle Athenaeum, showing work in 1846 and 1850. Among his Royal Academy exhibits were his portrait statue of Thomas Sheffield in alto relievo[#] (now

IN MEMORY OF THOMAS SHEFFIELD, OF CARLISLE, WHO DEPARTED THIS LIFE APRIL 4TH 1853. AGED 78 YEARS.

THIS MONUMENT IS ERECTED AS A TRIBUTE OF AFFECTION BY HIS WIDOW AND FAMILY.

Frederick Clive Newcome
(Suker):
The Gates of Borrowdale.
Oil 42×66.
*Fitz Park Museum &
Art Gallery.*

in Carlisle Cathedral), and his medallion portrait of Musgrave Lewthwaite Watson (also in Carlisle Cathedral). His principal work, however, was his *Musidora*, versions of which were shown at the Academy in 1847 and 1861.

When Watson died in 1847, Nelson executed in marble a number of works for which the former had prepared models in clay. These included Watson's composition for a monument to the 50th Regiment, now in Canterbury Cathedral. A plaster cast of his medallion of Watson was included in Carlisle Art Gallery's "Cumberland Artists 1700-1900" exhibition in 1971, and in this gallery's "The Carlisle Exhibitions 1823-1850" exhibition, 1973.

NELSON, George, Senior (fl.19th cent.)
Marine painter in oil. He was a sea captain of WHITEHAVEN who practised as a painter following his retirement. He was the father of George Nelson Junior (q.v.). Represented: Whitehaven Museum.

NELSON, George, Junior (d.1921)
Marine and landscape painter in oil and watercolour. He was the son of George Nelson Senior (q.v.), and possibly received tuition from his father before attending Liverpool School of Art from 1891 until 1894. He subsequently attended the Slade, where he received a gold medal for his work, then returned to WHITEHAVEN. He later took up a position as an art master at nearby ST. BEES, remaining there from 1906 until 1918. It is said that he qualified as an architect. Nelson favoured small canvases for his work, in contrast to the larger canvases favoured by his father, and exhibited at the Royal Society of British Artists, and at the Royal Institute of Painters in Water Colours. He died at WHITEHAVEN. Whitehaven Museum has several examples of his work.

NELSON, John (1726-1812)
Sculptor and architect. He was born at PENRITH, and later practised in Shropshire, where he became well known for "his eminent abilities in statuary". Among the works

which he produced while living at Shrewsbury for some fifty years were his two lions for the Lion Hotel, Wyle Cop, Shrewsbury, 1777; a statue of Sir Rowland Hill for Hawkstone Park, Salop, 1795, and a statue of Roger de Montgomery for Shrewsbury Castle, 1796. Shrewsbury School Library has one of his account books giving details of some of his many other works for the Shropshire and neighbouring counties. He died at Shrewsbury.

NELSON, Richard (c.1836-c.1920)
Sculptor. Nelson was born at MARYPORT, and possibly studied at the Carlisle School of Art before practising in the city, as a Richard Nelson won a bronze medal for human figure drawing at the School in 1858. He is supposed to have done sculptural work for the Houses of Parliament in London, and Carlisle Library has a book of drawings of sculpture signed "Richard Nelson" which may have been his work.

NELSON, Thomas (1807-1890)
Sculptor and architect. A member of a well known family of builders and stonemasons of CARLISLE, he was possibly related to George Nelson (q.v.), and may have been responsible for introducing the latter to Musgrave Lewthwaite Watson (q.v.). He is said to have "spent some time in an architect's office in London, gaining experience in plan-drawing and the working out of details and specifications" before practising as a sculptor and architect at CARLISLE, some time after 1838, and would appear to have been the Thomas Marsh Nelson who exhibited at the Royal Academy from 1830 until 1837, and at the Carlisle Academy in 1830. He designed two of his own homes, and was responsible for designing many structures in Cumbria in addition to producing works of sculpture, and a wide range of marble mantel-pieces. Much of this work in sculpture was executed in conjunction with his brother, JAMES NELSON, with whom he was joint owner of the Carlisle marble works. They sign tablets to John Dixon, of KNELLS, near

HOUGHTON (d. 1857), at St. John Evangelist, HOUGHTON; John Canning (d. 1830), at Ilmington, Warwick, and to the Rev. Christopher Hodgson, 1849, at Marholm, in the Isle of Ely. In 1857 they carved various decorative details for the mausoleum built by Lord Lonsdale at LOWTHER.

*NEWCOME (SUKER), Frederick Clive (1847-1894)

Landscape painter in watercolour. He was born at Penketh, near Warrington, Lancashire, the son of John Suker, later changing his name to that of Newcome so as not to be confused with his father, and brothers Arthur and John, all of whom also practised as artists. Shortly after his birth the family moved to Birkenhead, and then to Liverpool, where he attended evening classes at Liverpool School of Art and studied under John Finnie. He was exhibiting at the Liverpool Academy by the age of twenty, and had already made a sketching trip to Bettws-y-Coed in Wales, meeting there many leading artists of the day. He later worked in Warwickshire, Scotland, Devonshire and the Lake District before deciding to live at KESWICK in 1880. He exhibited at the Royal Academy from 1875 until 1887, and also showed his work at the Royal Scottish Academy and in the provinces. His first contribution to the Royal Academy, *Head of a Highland Glen,* attracted the praise of John Ruskin (q.v.), who said it was "the best study of torrent, including distant and near water, that I find in the room". Two of his patrons were the Earl of Derby, and the Duke of Hamilton, the latter commissioning him to paint a number of views in Arran which have never been exhibited.

Newcome left KESWICK for several winters to live at CARLISLE, and in addition to visiting Arran carried out several other commissions in various parts of the British Isles. For several years before his death he lived in the South of England, but at the end of 1893 he decided to move to CONISTON, where he died in the following year. His daughter MAY NEWCOME also practised as an artist, sending two landscapes to Carlisle Art Gallery's 1896 exhibition while living at FRIZINGTON. A special commemorative exhibition of his work was held at Carlisle Art Gallery in 1894, and examples were also included in this gallery's "Cumberland Artists 1700-1900" exhibition, in 1971. Represented: Blackburn A.G.; Carlisle A.G.; Keswick Museum.

*NICHOLSON, Isaac (1789-1848)

Wood engraver. Born at MELMERBY, Nicholson moved at the age of fifteen to Newcastle upon Tyne to become a pupil of Thomas Bewick (1753-1828). He remained with Bewick until 1811, and subsequently followed Bewick's style very closely in his wood engraving without ever equalling his former master's ability in practising the art. Bewick had to take Nicholson to task for copying his work while the latter practised at Newcastle, but despite this circumstance his master was generous enough in his autobiographical *Memoir,* published posthumously in 1862, to describe Nicholson as ". . . a good Apprentice & a good artist — his engravings on wood are clearly or honestly cut, as well as being accurately done from his patterns . . .". Much of his work is to be seen in the tailpieces which he engraved for Charnley's *Select Fables,* 1820, many of these later appearing in Charnley's *Fisher's Garlands* for various years.# Because so many of these

Isaac Nicholson: Angling scene from title page of Charnley's "Fishers Garland", 1828. Wood Engraving $2\frac{1}{2} \times 3\frac{1}{2}$.

portrayed riverside scenes they are commonly but inaccurately attributed to Bewick. His best known work consisted of his wood engravings for Sharp's *History of the Rebellion.* He also did work for Flower's *Heraldic Visitation of the County of Durham,* Watt's *Hymns,* and Defoe's *Robinson Crusoe.* Several examples of his work were included in the "Thomas Bewick" exhibition, Laing Art Gallery, Newcastle, Summer, 1978.

Winifred Nicholson: Amaryllis, 1967. Oil $23\frac{7}{8} \times 23\frac{7}{8}$.
Abbot Hall Art Gallery.

*NICHOLSON, Winifred, N.E.A.C. (b.1893)

Landscape and flower painter in oil and watercolour. She was born at Oxford, the daughter of Charles Roberts, and granddaughter of George Howard, 9th Earl of Carlisle (q.v.). She studied at the Byam Shaw School of Art, and later worked in Paris, Lugano, India and the Hebrides. In 1920 she married Ben Nicholson (b.1894), with whom she later became a member of the 7 & 5 Group, together with

Ivon Hitchens and Christopher Wood. She also became a member of the New English Art Club, this membership lasting from 1937 until 1943. Nicholson has lived at BRAMPTON for many years, during which time she has exhibited at the Beaux Art Gallery, the Lefevre Gallery, the Leicester Gallery, the New English Art Club, the Redfern Gallery, the Royal Scottish Academy, and latterly in the provinces, at the Abbot Hall Art Gallery, KENDAL, Carlisle Art Gallery, and the LYC Museum, BRAMPTON. The last named establishment recently published a book of her work entitled *Flower Tales*. Her daughter KATE NICHOLSON (b.1929), is also an artist. Represented: Tate Gallery; Abbot Hall A.G., Kendal; Bradford A.G.; Bristol A.G.; Carlisle A.G.; Manchester A.G., and various overseas art galleries.

NIXSON, Paul (1768-1850)

Architect and sculptor. Nixson practised as an architect at CARLISLE, and may also have been responsible for some work in sculpture, though as a one-time employer of David Dunbar Senior (q.v.) it is possible that these works have been wrongly attributed to him. Pevsner's *Cumberland & Westmorland* identifies several works which may fall into this category including the monuments to William Giles and his wife at St. Cuthbert's, CARLISLE, and Walter Vane, at St. Bega's Church, BASSENTHWAITE. Whatever his involvement in the production of these and other works to which his name has been given, Nixson undoubtedly exercised a considerable influence over the artistic affairs of CARLISLE during the early part of the 19th century. He was responsible for the design and erection of "The Artists Academy", in the city's Finkle Street in 1823, and the encouragement of Dunbar and his pupil Musgrave Lewthwaite Watson (q.v.) to visit Rome, apart from designing several fine buildings at CARLISLE. On his retirement as an architect he settled at DENT, dying there in 1850. A portrait of him by George Sheffield, Senior

(q.v.), is in the collection of Sir Henry Studholme. His drawing for St. Cuthbert's Parsonage House, of 1814, is in the Record Office, Carlisle.

NUTTER, Henry (1758-1808)

Portrait painter in oil. Nutter was born at WHITEHAVEN, but moved to CARLISLE when he was twenty to set up in business as a house painter. He later took up coach painting, then portraiture, but began drinking excessively and his business was only rescued from bankruptcy with the help of his wife and two sons, one of whom was Matthew Ellis Nutter (q.v.). One of his portraits, was shown posthumously at the Carlisle Academy in 1823, and there is a portrait of Matthew Wilkinson, the poet, at the one-time home of William Wordsworth (1770-1850), at Dove Cottage, GRASMERE, signed "Nutter", which is probably his work. No other examples are known.

*NUTTER, Matthew Ellis (1795-1862)

Portrait, landscape and sporting painter in oil and watercolour; drawing master. He was born at CARLISLE, one of the two sons of Henry Nutter (q.v.), and first received tuition in art from his father. He later attended the classes of Robert Carlyle Senior (q.v.), learning architectural drawing and landscape painting. On the death of his father he was obliged to help in the running of the family house and coach painting business, painting portraits in his spare time, but by 1819 he had started to receive his first commissions for landscapes, and later sporting pictures. With the death of his mother in 1821 he decided to give up the family business altogether and to draw and paint as a career. He became the secretary and drawing master at the Carlisle Academy on its opening in 1823, moving to 1, Academy Row, which had a studio attached, and later took up a position as drawing master at Green Row Academy, owned by his friend Joseph Saul.

Nutter became one of the most frequent exhibitors at the Carlisle Academy, and subsequently Carlisle

Matthew Ellis Nutter: Wetheral Viaduct. Watercolour $5\frac{3}{8} \times 8\frac{1}{2}$. *Carlisle Museum & Art Gallery.*

William Henry Nutter:
The News Room and
Library, Carlisle.
Sepia 6¾×9.
*Carlisle Museum &
Art Gallery.*

Athenaeum, showing seventy-nine works at the former between 1823 and 1833, and five at the latter in 1846 and 1850. Essentially a shy man, however, he did not choose to show his work outside his native city, nor was he tempted to work elsewhere, despite the encouraging remark of one painter from London, who, seeing one of Nutter's animal paintings, remarked: "There are but two men in the metropolis who could have painted it – Cooper and Ward . . .". He was content to paint and draw in the area of his birth throughout his professional career, from his earliest years displaying a strong interest in the ancient buildings of the city. Seventeen of his drawings of old buildings shown at the Carlisle Academy in 1833 proved so popular that they were lithographed and published with a text by Charles Thurnam in 1835, under the title: *Carlisle in the Olden Time.* Many of these drawings were based on those of his former teacher Robert Carlyle, Senior. He continued to paint landscapes, and occasionally sporting pictures, until his death, spending his final years at SKINBURNESS, on the Solway, where he died in 1862. He was the father of William Henry Nutter (q.v.). A large and varied selection of his work was shown as part of Carlisle Art Gallery's "The Nutter Family and their Friends" exhibition, Winter, 1971-72, including the work illustrated in this volume. Represented: Carlisle A.G.

*NUTTER, William Henry (1819-1872)

Architectural, landscape and sporting painter in watercolour; drawing master. He was born at CARLISLE, the son of Matthew Ellis Nutter (q.v.), and grandson of Henry Nutter (q.v.), and became a pupil of his father. By the age of eleven he was exhibiting at the Carlisle Academy, and by 1838 he had received his first commission – the task of illustrating Jefferson's *The History and Antiquities of Carlisle.* He joined his father as a drawing master in CARLISLE at an early age, later

opening a drawing school himself, and giving lessons at Annan Academy. His illustrations for local publications continued to be in demand, and appeared in *Carlisle in 1745,* by George Gill Mounsey, and Steel's *Guide to the Lancaster and Carlisle Railway*; an engraving of his *The Fire at Naworth Castle* (1844), appeared in a pamphlet on the fire. He also illustrated for other publications, his sepia sketch of the cutting of the first sod for the Silloth Railway being used in the *London Illustrated News,* in 1855.

He exhibited at the Carlisle Academy in 1830 and 1833, and Carlisle Athenaeum in 1846 and 1850, mainly showing landscape views, some of which were taken on visits to Edinburgh, Dumfriesshire and the Lake District. He remained firmly based at CARLISLE, however, until ill-health forced him to seek a warmer climate. In the summer of 1871 he toured Belgium and France, sending a number of his continental views back to CARLISLE for exhibition in the autumn, before settling at Malaga, Spain, for the winter. He died at Malaga in the following year, and is buried in the British Cemetery there. Many examples of his work were shown in Carlisle Art Gallery's "The Nutter Family and their Friends" exhibition, Winter, 1971-72, including the work illustrated in this volume. Represented: Carlisle A.G.

ODDIE, J. W. (fl.1882-1886)

This artist showed one work at the Walker Art Gallery, Liverpool, and one work at Manchester City Art Gallery, while living at Syzwick Hall, KESWICK, in the period 1882-86.

OLIVER, George Dale (1851-1928)
Architectural draughtsman. He was the son of Thomas Oliver, the well known Newcastle upon Tyne architect and architectural draughtsman, and went to London as a pupil of George Street R.A., before working as an architect at Birkenhead, Cheshire, and later at CARLISLE. He went to CARLISLE about 1878 to assist Mr. Corby Hetherington, and later became his partner. While working with Hetherington he contributed three works to the Royal Academy, these comprising his *Residence, Chatsworth Square, Carlisle*; *Carlisle Grammar School*, and *Carlisle Markets*, shown in 1885 and 1887. His design for the last named project was unsuccessful, but his Grammar School design was accepted, and he designed many other schools at CARLISLE in addition to his work for other types of project. He became County Architect for Cumberland. Carlisle Art Gallery has prints of his designs for Carlisle Market, and Carlisle Grammar School.

PARKER, Amy (fl.1903-8)
She showed two works at the Royal Society of Artists, Birmingham, and nine works at the Royal Cambrian Academy, while living at PENRITH, in the period 1903-8.

PARKINSON, Isabel (fl.1897)
She showed one work at the Walker Art Gallery, Liverpool, while living at GRANGE-OVER-SANDS in 1897.

PARKYN, Jem (fl. early 19th cent.)
He was responsible for painting the Royal Mail leaving the Bush Hotel at CARLISLE, in the early 19th century. His painting originally hung in the Howard Arms at BRAMPTON, and depicted many local celebrities, including the artist, a Mr. Ramshay (agent to the Earl of Carlisle), Mr. Orridge of the County Gaol, and Mr. Jackson of the Bush Hotel. Parkyn was apparently a local coaching hero as well as an amateur artist.

PARKYN, John Herbert, R.W.A., A.R.C.A. (1864-1939)
Genre and flower painter in oil, pastel and watercolour. He was born in Cumberland, the son of John Parkyn, a surveyor, and later studied at Clifton School of Art, the Royal College of Art, and at the Academie Julian, Paris. On returning to England he lived for some time at Bristol, where he began exhibiting at the Royal Academy, showing his first work: *A Study*, in 1884. By the turn of the century he had received the Prix de Rome on two occasions for his work (1891 and 1893), and had taken up an appointment as Head of Kingston upon Hull School of Art, and Curator of the Municipal Art Gallery, Hull. He remained at Hull for eleven years, founding the Hull Art Circle and Sketching club in 1901, and taking an active interest in all the various artistic activities of the town throughout his stay. On leaving Hull he took up an appointment as Headmaster of Ayr Art Academy, in Scotland, and lived at Dalry in Galloway for many years. He was a member of the Royal West of England Academy from 1886, and an

associate of the Royal College of Art. In addition to showing his work at the Royal Academy he exhibited at the Royal Institute of Painters in Water Colours, and widely in the provinces. Represented: Hull A.G.

PATTINSON, Captain Joseph (1782-1828)
Marine painter in watercolour. He was a sea captain of MARYPORT who painted in his spare time. His painting of the *H.M.S. Spartiate, 80 guns*, is in a Cumbrian private collection, and a painting of the *The Frances* leaving HARRINGTON, 1819, is said to be in the National Maritime Museum. He died in Quebec, Canada.

PEARSON, Wilson (1802-1854)
Portrait and figure painter in oil. Pearson was born at BROUGHTON CROSS, near COCKERMOUTH, where he became a self-taught artist before moving to Liverpool at the age of thirty. His obituary in the *Cumberland Pacquet*, 5th December, 1854, stated: "He was at one time a successful teacher of mathematics but for several years he enjoyed an extensive practise in portrait painting amongst the leading families in both Liverpool and his own native county". He died in Liverpool at the house of his nephew James Renny, a draper.

PETHER, William, F.S.A. (1731 – after 1794)
Engraver; painter of portraits and landscapes in oil and crayons. He was born at CARLISLE, and later moved to London, where he received a premium from the Society of Arts in 1756. He subsequently became a painter of portraits, and a mezzotint engraver, showing his work at the Society of Artists from 1761, the Free Society of Artists from 1764, and the Royal Academy from 1781. Although he produced many portraits, and several landscapes in his lifetime, Pether is best known for his work in mezzotint engraving, initially studying under Thomas Frye, and later producing among his many works, portraits of the three Smiths of Chichester, and engravings after Rembrandt, Dow, Teniers, and Wright of Derby. J. Herbert Slater, in his *Engravings and their value*, 1929, comments: "Many of this artist's plates, particularly those after Rembrandt, are highly esteemed, but there is inequality in his work. He was at best when engraving subjects disclosing great gradations of light and shade such as moonlight scenes and interiors illuminated by candle light", while Redgrave in his *Dictionary of Artists of the English School*, 1878, states of Pether's work outside of engraving: "His portraits in oil are rare; they are firmly and powerfully painted. His miniatures are spirited works . . .". He became a member of the Free Society of Artists in 1763, and appears to have spent his entire professional life in London, dying there some time after 1794. He was the cousin of ABRAHAM PETHER, (1756-1812), sometimes called "Moonlight Pether", the landscape painter.

POSTLETHWAITE, Miss Elinor (b.1866)
Genre and flower painter in oil and watercolour; wood engraver. Born at HALLTHWAITES, Postlethwaite studied at Frank Calderon's school, and at Westminster. She subsequently showed work at the Royal Academy, and the Suffolk Street Gallery. These works featured either flower studies or genre subjects. One of her contributions

to the Royal Academy (1903) was entitled: *The busy mother*. It is believed that she also produced colour woodcuts, and that she painted mainly in London and South Devon.

POSTLETHWAITE, Miss Mary Emily (fl.1882-1903)

Genre painter in watercolour. The sister of Elinor Postlethwaite (q.v.), she exhibited at the Royal Academy, the Suffolk Street Gallery, the Royal Glasgow Institute of Fine Arts, and in the provinces, while living at BROUGHTON-IN-FURNESS, and London.‡

‡ *Some compilers of artists' dictionaries have identified "Miss Elinor Postlethwaite", and the subject of the present entry, as one and the same person, this because the two women shared the same address in London during the period in which they each exhibited at the Royal Academy and the Suffolk Street Gallery. Both Graves, and Johnson and Greutzner, however (see bibliography), support the existence of two artists, named as above.*

*POTTER (Heelis), Helen Beatrix (1866-1943)

Author and illustrator of children's books; painter of landscapes, street scenes, flowers, fungi, etc., in watercolour. She was born at Kensington, London, the daughter of wealthy amateur photographer Rupert Potter, and granddaughter of one-time Liberal M.P. for CARLISLE, Edmund Potter, and began to show a talent for drawing from an early age. She later became an almost entirely self-taught artist, her earliest work consisting of detailed animal, insect and flower studies, interiors, landscapes with buildings, and drawings of fungi. Later she began to illustrate many of her letters to friends with small sketches of animals with which she was familiar, frequently indulging in pictorial fantasies regarding their activities. Several of these "picture-letters" later became the bases of books she was to write and illustrate. Meanwhile she had already successfully sold drawings for greetings cards to a London publisher (1890), and shown three of her watercolours at the Society of Women Artists' exhibition of 1896.

Her twenty books for children were all produced within the brief space of thirteen years. The first of these books was *The Tale of Peter Rabbit*, 1902. This was quickly followed by *The Tale of Squirrel Nutkin*, and *The Tailor of Gloucester*,* 1903, and *The Tale of Benjamin Bunny*, and *The Tale of Two Bad Mice*, 1904. Soon after the publication of the last named book she bought Hill Top Farm, NEAR SAWREY, near WINDERMERE, following this with the purchase of Castle Farm nearby. Here she became a successful farmer, as well as writer and illustrator of children's books, until the age of fifty, when failing eyesight ruled out the meticulous drawing required for her work. Her last book comparable with her best work was *The Tale of Johnny Town-Mouse*, published in 1918.

Many of the books by Beatrix Potter – the name she used as an author, even after marrying APPLEBY solicitor William Heelis, in 1913 – owed their inspiration to the scenery of the Lake District (with which family holidays had made her familiar from the age of sixteen, when she first stayed at Wray Castle, on the shore of Lake Windermere). "The coloured drawings for Peter Rabbit were done in a garden near Keswick, Cumberland", she once said, "and several others were painted in the Lake District. Squirrel Nutkin sailed on Derwent Water; Mrs. Tiggy-Winkle lived in the Vale of Newlands. Later books

Beatrix Potter: The Tailor of Gloucester at work. Watercolour, pen and ink $4\frac{3}{8} \times 3\frac{5}{8}$. *Tate Gallery.*

such as 'Jemima Puddleduck', 'Ginger and Pickles', 'The Pie and the Patty Pan', etc., were done at Sawrey in the southern end of the Lake District ...".

On her death Beatrix Potter bequeathed Hill Top Farm, Castle Farm, and various other properties to the National Trust, enabling visitors to see for themselves just how much her environment at SAWREY influenced her writing and her art. Her life and work are admirably documented and illustrated in *The Tale of Beatrix Potter*, 1946, *The Art of Beatrix Potter, 1955*, and *The Magic Years of Beatrix Potter*, 1978 – all published by Frederick Warne & Co. Ltd. The Abbot Hall Art Gallery, KENDAL, held a comprehensive exhibition of her work in 1966 to celebrate the centenary of her birth. Represented: British Museum; Tate Gallery; Armitt Library, Ambleside.

POWER, Leo Clement (b.1889)

Genre painter in oil. He was born at CARLISLE, the son of a railway official, and was educated at St. Patrick's School in the city. He subsequently moved to GRANGE-OVER-SANDS, showing his work at the Royal Society of British Artists, and various other art establishments.

PRESTON, Edward (fl. early 20th cent.)

Costume and figure painter in watercolour; decorative designer. Preston worked as a designer at Hudson Scott & Sons, now the Metal Box Company, CARLISLE, during the same period as Paul Greville Hudson (q.v.), and also became acquainted with John James Hodgson (q.v.). His portrait of Hudson in 18th century costume, from a private collection, was shown at the "John James Hodgson" exhibition, at Carlisle Art Gallery in 1970.

QUARRIE, Miss J. McG. (fl.1913-14)

She exhibited three works at the Dudley Gallery, London, and two works at the Society of Women Artists, between 1913 and 1914, while living at HENSINGHAM.

RAE, Colin, A.R.C.A. (d.1953)

Landscape and portrait painter in oil and watercolour; wood carver. He was born at Hereford, and later attended the Royal College of Art. After becoming an associate of the Royal College of Art, he took up an appointment as assistant art master at Carlisle School of Art, remaining there all his working life. He was appointed Principal of the School in 1943, on the death of Mr. Pickles, and retired in 1947. A one-man show of his work was held at Carlisle Art Gallery in 1950. He died at CARLISLE. His wife, Margaret Rae (q.v.), was also a talented artist. Represented: Carlisle Art Gallery.

RAE, Mrs. Margaret (fl.1914-1921)

The wife of Colin Rae (q.v.), she attended the Royal Academy Schools, and later became assistant mistress at Bath Art School 1914-16, and acting Head, 1916-18. She exhibited her work at the Royal Academy, and the Walker Art Gallery, Liverpool.

RAINBECK, Miss (fl.1830)

Amateur portrait painter in watercolour. She produced a portrait of Dora Wordsworth (q.v.) as a bridesmaid at the marriage of her brother John Wordsworth, to Isabella Curwen in 1830. It was included in the "Wordsworth Bicentenary Exhibition" organised by the Arts Council in 1970, and shown at the Abbot Hall Art Gallery, KENDAL, and various other galleries in Britain. The work remains in the possession of the Wordsworth family and may be seen at Rydal Mount, AMBLESIDE; a colour illustration appears in the guide to Rydal Mount.

*RANSOME, Arthur (1884-1967)

Author and book illustrator. Although best known as one of the most popular authors of children's books this century, Ransome was a talented artist, and one who showed a lifelong attachment to Cumbria. Born at Leeds, the son of a college professor, and an artistically gifted mother, Ransome, indeed, only narrowly missed being born in the Lake District; his childhood holidays were spent in the area, he received part of his education there, and the first friends of his mature life were members of one of its most popular and artistically talented families

Arthur Ransome:
Leading Lights, illustration from "Swallows and Amazons".
Pen and ink 4×3. *Abbot Hall Art Gallery.*

– William Gershom Collingwood (q.v.), his wife, son, and daughters. Only after years spent in London, Paris, Russia, Latvia and Esthonia, as author and journalist, however, was he able to take up residence in the area he loved best, and to do the type of writing for which he is most famous. Early in 1925 he settled at LOW LUDDER-BURN, near WINDERMERE, and though still a much sought-after writer for newspapers and magazines, he gradually resolved to devote the rest of his life to writing books.

In 1929 he gave up journalism altogether, and started to write his first major work for children: *Swallows and Amazons,* published in 1930. This was based on his boyhood adventures in the Lake District, but while he was confident enough to translate his youthful experiences into a book, he felt that someone else should handle its illustration. This same feeling applied to *Swallowdale,* published in 1931. The results did not please him, however, and when he came to write *Peter Duck,* published in 1932, he decided to illustrate this book himself, subsequently re-illustrating his first two books, and illustrating the nine other children's books which he published between 1933 and 1947. In 1940, and after a period in East Anglia, he returned to the Lake District, living on the shores of Coniston Water until the end of the Second World War. Later he moved to London, spending part of his time in the capital, and part in the Lake District.

The last house he occupied was an old farmhouse near

the foot of Lake Windermere. After a fall and the resulting severe illness in 1959, he never fully regained his health. He died 3rd June, 1967, and is buried in the churchyard of St. Paul's, RUSLAND. The Museum of Lakeland Life and Industry, KENDAL, has a large collection of his books, original book illustrations for *Swallows and Amazons*,# and personalia, presented by his widow; the Abbot Hall Art Gallery, nearby, has a portrait of Ransome painted by Dora Collingwood (q.v.). His autobiography, with Prologue and Epilogue by Rupert Hart-Davis, was published by Jonathan Cape in 1976.

RAWNSLEY, Mrs. H. D. (Edith – née Fletcher) (d.1916)
Landscape painter in watercolour. She was the daughter of John Fletcher, of The Croft, CLAPPERSGATE, AMBLESIDE, and in 1878 became the first wife of the Rev. H. D. Rawnsley, Residentiary Canon of CARLISLE, Vicar of WRAY, WINDERMERE (1878-1883), and later Vicar of CROSTHWAITE, near KESWICK (1883-1917).‡ As "Edith Fletcher", she showed one work in London in 1876, while as "Mrs. H. D. Rawnsley" she showed one work at the Royal Academy while living at WRAY, and two works at the New Watercolour Society (later the Royal Institute of Painters in Water Colours), while living at CROSTHWAITE. Her Royal Academy contribution was entitled: *A bit of Helvellyn, Wythburn*. She died at CROSTHWAITE, and is buried in the churchyard of St. Kentigern.

‡ *Canon Rawnsley (1851-1920) was one of the founders of the National Trust in 1895, and chaplain to Queen Victoria, and the next two sovereigns. He was an acquaintance of Beatrix Potter (q.v.), and a portrait subject of Frederic Yates (q.v.).*

RAY, Irving (1816-1906)
Sculptor. Ray was born at WIGTON, the son of a stonemason, and worked with his father from an early age. While still a young man he decided with his brother to visit Italy, but they got no further than London, for here they met a stonemason who was so impressed by their work that he offered them employment as long as they would remain there. After working in London for some time the brothers returned to WIGTON, where one of their early commissions was to carve a frieze for the banqueting hall of Brougham Hall, near PENRITH. Irving was responsible for many of the carvings at Highmoor House, near WIGTON, but his best known work was the pediment above the entrance of the Mechanics' Institute at WIGTON, completed in 1851.‡ This work represented the Goddess of Wisdom receiving homage from Learning and Knowledge "– quite a bit of a problem of characterisation to make such closely related allegories recognizable", Pevsner observes in his *Cumberland & Westmorland*. Ray's brother remained in partnership with him for many years but no independent works of his have yet been identified.

‡ *This building has now been demolished.*

*READ, Matthias (1669-1747)
Landscape, altar-piece, and portrait painter in oil; copyist. It is conjectured that Read was born in London, and that he first came to Cumbria as a pupil of Jan Wyck (1640-1702), having spent some time with the latter in Ireland. Certainly the two artists arrived in WHITEHAVEN about the same time, and both are known to have served the same patron: Sir John Lowther. Wyck was commissioned to paint a portrait of William III, at the Battle of the

Matthias Read: A prospect of Whitehaven from Brackenthwaite, *c.* 1730. *Sotheby's.*

Boyne, and a picture of WHITEHAVEN; Read to paint copies of some of the fine works by the Dutch Masters at Sir John's mansion. William Gilpin (q.v.), Sir John's steward, and Rector of CARLISLE, encouraged Read, allowing him access to the pictures at his home, Scaleby Castle, near IRTHINGTON, and engaging him as tutor in art to both himself and his children.

Writing of the events which followed Read's engagement by Gilpin, the latter's son the Rev. William Gilpin (q.v.), has said: "His productions there (WHITEHAVEN) excited a strong desire in the principal inhabitants to have his pencil employed in some suitable ornament for their new chapel, and in the end he was employed to finish it with an altar-piece which he executed to their satisfaction". This altar-piece for St. Nicholas Church in 1713, was followed by an altar-piece for Holy Trinity Church, WHITEHAVEN, and in 1722 he painted an altar-piece for St. Andrew's Church at PENRITH. Read had meanwhile settled permanently at WHITEHAVEN, building himself a substantial mansion on a plot acquired in 1701, and marrying a local girl, Elizabeth Hinde, by whom he eventually had one son and two daughters.

From all available evidence it would appear that he was popular not only as a painter of altar-pieces, but of landscapes and other subjects. According to the Rev. William Gilpin his work was much in demand for room decoration: "There was hardly a house in Whitehaven whose master could afford it, which had not a picture or two painted in panels over doors or chimneys by his hand", he commented. Sadly, all Read's altar-pieces have gone, along with many of his other works, and his fame must rest mainly on his work in landscape. He painted several views of WHITEHAVEN, his most famous being entitled: *A bird's eye view of Whitehaven,* painted in 1738. This view was engraved by Richard Parr. An earlier view of the town: *Whitehaven from Brackenthwaite c.1720,* was shown as one of three paintings attributed to Read in Carlisle Art Gallery's "Cumberland Artists 1700-1900"

exhibition, in 1971, and a similar view dated *c.* 1730 was offered for sale at Sotheby's in 1974.# Read is generally regarded as the "father of painting in Cumberland", his influence having been exercised mainly through members of the Gilpin family. He died at WHITEHAVEN, and was buried in the churchyard of Holy Trinity Church. Represented: Carlisle A.G.; Whitehaven Museum.

*REISS, George Francis, R.Cam.A. (1893-1973)
Amateur wood engraver of landscape and architectural subjects; etcher. Reiss was born at KENDAL, and subsequently joined the family pork butcher's business in the town, engraving in his spare time. He was a largely self-taught artist, but by patient application to his hobby he achieved an outstanding level of ability, showing his work at the Royal Academy, the Royal Scottish Academy, the Royal Cambrian Academy, the provinces, and the Paris Salon. He was elected an associate of the Royal Cambrian Academy in 1955, and a member in 1958. He was also for some time chairman of the Kendal Art Society, and a member of the Lake Artists' Society, the Grange and District Art Society, and the Lancaster Art Group. He died at KENDAL, his widow bequeathing a large collection of his wood engravings and tools to the Abbot Hall Art Gallery, KENDAL.

REYNOLDS, Miss M. E. (fl.1852)
Animal painter. She contributed one work to the Royal Academy in 1852 while living at AMBLESIDE. Her contribution was entitled: *Scene in Westmorland – girl and pony.*

RICHARDSON, John (1774-1864)
Architectural draughtsman in watercolour. Richardson practised as an architect at KENDAL, where he made a number of studies of local buildings in watercolour. One of these studies was entitled: *The New Biggin,* and is inscribed: "North East View of the New Biggin which

George Francis Reiss: Miscellaneous studies of buildings, landscapes, animals and plants. Wood Engravings. *Abbot Hall Art Gallery.*

Thomas Robinson: The Battle of Ballinahinch, 1798. Oil 54¼×84. On loan to the National Gallery of Ireland, from *Arus an Uachtaráin.*

stood in the middle of Highgate till 1803, when it was taken down. Drawn from memory in 1845 by the undersigned John Richardson". This work is in the collection of the Abbot Hall Art Gallery, KENDAL, and was included in this gallery's "The Artists' Kendal" exhibition, Summer, 1975. He was responsible for designing several buildings in KENDAL, including Town View and the Shakespeare Theatre. The Cumbria Record Office, KENDAL, has several of his drawings.

RIGBY, Cuthbert, A.R.W.S. (1850-1935)

Landscape painter in watercolour; author. He was born at Liverpool, and in 1865 became apprenticed to an architect in the city, spending much of his spare time painting, sketching and writing. In 1872 he received some tuition from W. J. Bishop, A.R.W.S., soon after abandoning his career in architecture and setting off on his first sketching tour of Cumberland. In 1875 he showed his first work at the Royal Academy: *Larch Firs, Randal How, Cumberland,* subsequently becoming a regular exhibitor at the Academy, the Royal Society of Painters in Water Colours, and various London and provincial galleries. Many of these works portrayed Cumbrian subjects and were contributed while he lived at Southport, Lancashire (1874 and 1882) BROUGHTON-IN-FURNESS (1880), SEASCALE (1884), KENDAL (1900), WINDERMERE (1901), and AMBLESIDE from 1906. Rigby also wrote considerably from 1888, in 1891 publishing *From Midsummer to Martinmas – a West Cumberland Idyll.* He was an associate of the Royal Society of Painters in Water Colours from 1877, and a member of the Lake Artists'

Society from its foundation in 1904, later serving as treasurer. His *Kendal Hiring Fair, Whitsuntide 1891,* and his *Greenside* (painted from his home at KENDAL in 1895), in the collection of the Abbot Hall Art Gallery, KENDAL, were included in this gallery's "The Artists' Kendal" exhibition, Summer, 1975. Represented: Victoria and Albert Museum; Abbot Hall A.G., Kendal; Maidstone Museum; Norwich Castle Collection.

RITCHIE, Robert (d.1822)

Nothing is known of this ULVERSTON artist except what was stated in his obituary notice in the *Carlisle Patriot,* 2nd November, 1822: "Mr Robert Ritchie of Ulverston, painter – a youth whose drawing merit was of the highest stamp and full of promise."

*ROBINSON, Thomas, *of Windermere,* (d.1810)

Portrait painter in oil. Robinson was born in a cottage on the banks of Lake Windermere and showed a talent for painting from an early age. On the recommendation of John Christian Curwen, M.P. for CARLISLE, he was placed as a pupil under George Romney (q.v.) about 1784, shortly afterwards moving to Dublin, where in 1790 he painted a portrait of *Chief Baron Barry Yelverton,* later Lord Avonmore. By 1793 he had settled in Northern Ireland, first at Lawrencetown, Co. Down, later at Lisburn, Co. Antrim. At Lisburn by 1798, Robinson painted what has since become one of his best known works: *The Battle of Ballinahinch,*⁕ advertising his painting in the *Belfast News-Letter* on the 6th November 1798, with the words: "Picture contains many original Portraits, and is a faithful representation of the Field of Battle and its events". The painting was exhibited in the Exchange Rooms, Belfast, at an admittance of "one British Shilling". A second advertisement referring to *The Battle* gave his prices for portraits, stating: "A three quarter portrait 5 guineas/Kit-Cat 7/Half length 12".

In 1801 he settled at Belfast, remaining there until 1808, when he moved to Dublin "leaving everywhere behind him many excellent portraits and other productions in which he displayed a great skill and taste . . ." (*Gentleman's Magazine*, September 1810, p. 288). He died in Dublin two years later, leaving a son, Thomas Romney Robinson (1792-1882), who became a well known astronomer, physicist and poet. One of the latter's works in poetry was his elegy to George Romney, written when he was aged ten, and later published with his portrait in Hayley's life of the artist (1809). *The Battle of Ballinahinch* was included in the "Irish Portraits 1660-1860" exhibition, held at the National Gallery, Ireland, Dublin in 1969, and at the National Portrait Gallery, London, and Ulster Museum, Belfast, in 1970. Represented: National Gallery of Ireland; Abbot Hall A.G., Kendal; National Trust, Castle Ward, Co. Down.

ROBINSON, Thomas (fl. late 19th cent.)
Amateur landscape and architectural painter in oil and watercolour. Robinson was a house-sign and ornamental painter, gilder and glazier in KENDAL, who painted in his spare time. The Abbot Hall Art Gallery, KENDAL, included several examples of his work in its "The Artists' Kendal" exhibition, Summer, 1975, including his watercolour: *Stramongate during the flood of 1898*.

*ROE, Clarence H. (d.1909)
Landscape painter in oil. Roe was born, and worked much of his life, in Cumbria, where a strong connection with WHITEHAVEN is claimed. He specialised in vigorously painted mountain, river and lake scenes using a somewhat restricted pallette. He also painted extensively in Scotland, and is known to have produced a number of coastal views somewhat similar in style to those of William Thornely. Most of his work was in oil, and he appears to have exhibited only at the Royal Hibernian Academy in 1887 while living in London. He is believed to have been one of the artist sons of ROBERT HENRY ROE (1793-1880). Kendal Town Hall has an example of his work: *On the Mint*, 1886.

*ROMNEY, George (1734-1802)
Portrait and history painter in oil. Romney was born at Beckside, a small farm near DALTON-IN-FURNESS, the son of a joiner and cabinet-maker, and subsequently received schooling at the neighbouring village of DENDRON. At the age of eleven he was apprenticed in his father's business at UPPER COCKEN (to which the family had removed in 1742), and spent the next ten years carving and gilding furniture, making flutes and violins, and copying prints from a monthly magazine in his spare time. His talent for portraiture is said to have been evident from an early age, and attracted the attention of the mother of Daniel Gardner (q.v.), a member of whose family occasionally shared his upholsterer's workshop with Romney's father. She asked George to paint her portrait, and later persuaded his father to let him take up portrait painting rather than cabinet making. A tutor was needed, and as the only portrait painter then known to the family locally was Christopher Steele (q.v.), he was apprenticed to Steele on 20th March, 1755.

Steele, an itinerant painter whose dandyism had already earned him the nickname "Count", was engaged to teach Romney for four years, but the apprenticeship was to prove something of a disaster for the young artist. Shortly after they had set up business temporarily in KENDAL his master eloped to Gretna with a lady pupil. Left to placate the girl's parents, deal with Steele's numerous creditors, and finish off several of his portraits, Romney fell ill with a fever, and while being nursed by his land-

Clarence H. Roe:
A Lakeland Torrent.
Oil 24 × 36.
Donald Hails.

George Romney: The Gower Family, *c*.1776. Oil 80×91¼. *Abbot Hall Art Gallery.*

lady's daughter formed a liaison with her as a result of which they had to marry. His master had meanwhile gone to York, and Romney joined him there immediately after his marriage, not returning to KENDAL with Steele for several months after the birth of his son John Romney, on 6th April 1757. The two artists found little work in KENDAL, however, and hardly had they returned to York when Steele suggested they move to Lancaster. Commissions proved even more scarce in Lancaster, and when Steele again suggested moving – this time to Ireland – Romney bought himself out of his apprenticeship and returned to KENDAL.

In the next five years before his departure to London, Romney painted a substantial number of portraits in KENDAL, and paid professional visits to York, Lancaster, Manchester and Cheshire. For part of this time he had as his pupil his younger brother Peter Romney (q.v.). In March, 1762, he left KENDAL for London, first disposing by lottery of some twenty of his paintings accumulated

since being released from his apprenticeship. Among these was his *King Lear in the Tempest tearing off his robes*. This was his first "historical picture" of note, and a type of work to which he was to return again and again throughout his career as a portrait painter, without ever achieving his ambition to become famous by it. Hardly had he settled in London, indeed, when he tried to establish a reputation for imaginative historical compositions with his *The Death of Rizzio* (1762), and *Samson and Delilah* (1764), and within two years he had set off to Paris to familiarise himself with some of the finest works of this sort in France. But portraiture was to remain his main source of income throughout his life, and thanks to introductions effected for him through an old friend from Dendron School, and others, he was soon making a name for himself. In 1768 he exhibited a large portrait of the Leigh family at the Free Society of Artists; in the following year, *The Warren Family*. By 1770, however, and exhibiting at the Society of Artists, Spring Gardens, he

Peter Romney: Portrait of Miss Scales. Pastel 24×21. *Private Collection*.

George Romney: The Four Friends: William Hayley with his son, Thomas, William Meyer and the artist, 1796. Oil $45\frac{7}{8} \times 39\frac{1}{4}$. *Abbot Hall Art Gallery.*

George Romney: Peter Romney (the artist's brother). Miniature $4\frac{1}{2} \times 4$. *National Portrait Gallery, London.*

was again striving for effect with his *Mirth and Melancholy* – each portraying a female intended to personify a theme from Milton.

In 1773 he took the serious step of abandoning his London practice to go to Rome. Here he became even further attracted to the "Grand Style" in painting, remaining in Italy for two years before returning to London. Much of his remaining life was spent in making sketches for large historical pieces as an antidote to the tedium of painting portraits. He had by now ceased to exhibit at the Society of Artists, and the Free Society of Artists (Romney never exhibited at the Royal Academy), and was not to exhibit again. He is perhaps, best known for his pictures of Lady Hamilton, whom he met in 1781. A romantic liaison between the two has long been suspected, and may well have been true in view of Romney's long estrangement from his wife.

His later life was far from happy, and when his health began to fail in 1796 he retired to Hampstead. In 1799 he returned to KENDAL to be nursed by his wife, dying there on 15th November, 1802. He was buried at DALTON-IN-FURNESS, in the churchyard of St Michael, where a monument marks his grave. "Accepted by common accord today as next after Reynolds and Gainsborough of the portrait painters before the age of Lawrence (Professor Ellis Waterhouse, *Painting in Britain 1580-1790*, p. 306), Romney's work has attracted more studies than that of any other artist of Cumbria. It has also been the subject of several important exhibitions, among the more recent: "George Romney, Paintings and Drawings", the Iveagh Bequest, Kenwood, 1961, and "Drawings from the Fitzwilliam Museum, Cambridge",

which toured Britain in 1978. The Abbot Hall Art Gallery, KENDAL, also mounted an important showing of his work as part of its "Four Kendal Portrait Painters" exhibition, Summer, 1973. This gallery has in its collection what is believed to be one of Romney's finest works: *The Gower Family.*# Represented: National Gallery, London; National Gallery of Scotland, Edinburgh; National Portrait Gallery; Tate Gallery; Wallace Collection; Abbot Hall A.G., Kendal; Carlisle A.G., and various provincial and overseas art galleries.

*ROMNEY, Peter (1743-1777)

Portrait painter in oil, watercolour, pastel and crayon. The younger brother of George Romney (q.v.), he was born at UPPER COCKEN near DALTON-IN-FURNESS, where his father John Romney worked as a joiner and cabinet-maker. He began to show a talent for drawing at an early age, and was apprenticed, or at least placed as a pupil, with his brother at KENDAL in the spring of 1759. The two brothers worked well together, George rapidly developing the skill in portrait painting in oil for which he was later to become famous; Peter (like Daniel Gardener (q.v.), who followed him as one of Romney's pupils), discovering that he had a particular facility in pastel painting. When George left KENDAL in 1762, Peter tried to establish himself as a portrait painter in the town, but once deprived of his brother's guidance he soon adopted "irregular habits" and failed in his ambition. All his later attempts to establish himself as a portrait painter were similarly doomed to failure, although he found several notable sitters.

71

In 1765, and after a short stay with his family at UPPER COCKEN, he followed his brother to London, but by the following year he had returned to UPPER COCKEN, shortly after moving to ULVERSTON, Lancaster and Manchester. In 1769 he paid a second visit to London, but again stayed only briefly, this time to move on to Liverpool. He was at Bradford in 1772; Ipswich in 1773, and Cambridge in 1774. He returned to Ipswich in 1775, where he was imprisoned for debt. His brother paid his debt, and he later moved to Stockport, Cheshire, where he died in 1777. Peter Romney's work has long been overshadowed by that of his famous brother, and there have been few attempts to present it in its proper light. One such attempt was that of René R. Meyer See, in the *Connoisseur*, February 1919. While perhaps over-enthusing about Peter's claim to greater appreciation, See presented the reader with a rare opportunity to study illustrations of his work. The works illustrated were all portraits, and would not have disgraced George Romney. Unfortunately few of his works can now be located, or indeed, confidently attributed to him, though he was invariably at pains to sign his work at a time when other artists were more careless, and used a variety of signatures, and sometimes the name "Peter Romeney", to ensure that his work could not be confused with that of his brother. The National Portrait Gallery, London, has a portrait of him by his brother; a quarter length in miniature.# An account of his life forms a supplement to the "Memoirs of the Life and Works of George Romney", 1830, by the Rev. John Romney (son of George Romney).

ROOK(E), John (1807-1872)

Landscape and marine painter in oil; natural history illustrator. He was probably born at WHITEHAVEN, where by 1847 he was describing himself as a "Painter, Landscape and Marine". In 1854 he took up a position as professor of drawing at the grammar school at nearby ST. BEES. Between 1853 and 1870 he completed a large series of fish and shell studies which were sold at Christie's on February 4th, 1975. His best known work, however, is his *Whitehaven Races,* painted in 1852, and reproduced as an engraving. Other engraved works were his *View of Whitehaven,* published by Callander & Dixon, 1848, and his *Flimby Lodge,* etched by James Macmillan (q.v.). Represented: Whitehaven Museum.

ROY, John (fl. 1834-1884)

Engraver. He was a pupil of James Macmillan (q.v.), and produced some of the engravings for Jefferson's *History and Antiquities of Carlisle,* 1838. His name appears on engravings of the work of William Henry Nutter (q.v.), and he appears to have been working at CARLISLE in 1884-5, as his name was included under the heading: "Engravers", in a local directory for that period.

RULE, Robert (b.1892)

Amateur landscape painter in watercolour. Rule was born at CARLISLE, and after education at Fawcett's School, joined his father's business in the city. Later he went into business on his own account at Perth in Scotland. During the First World War he served in minesweepers in the Royal Navy, returning to CARLISLE at the end of the war.

John Ruskin: Fisher Street, Carlisle, 1837.
Pencil $10\frac{3}{4} \times 7\frac{3}{4}$.
The Ruskin Galleries, Bembridge School, Isle of Wight.

He became a member of the Dumfries and Galloway Art Society in 1924, and has remained a member ever since. In the period 1928-1959 he spent four periods in the U.S.A. The first and last were spent visiting and sketching; the other two were business stays. He became a founder member and first chairman of the Carlisle and Border Art Society in 1949, and has exhibited his work on several occasions at the Royal Scottish Academy, and the Royal Scottish Society of Painters in Water Colours. He has frequently exhibited his work at Carlisle Art Gallery since 1910, and a major retrospective exhibition of his work was held at this gallery in 1962. Represented: Carlisle A.G.

*RUSKIN, John, H.R.W.S. (1819-1900)

Art critic; professor of fine art; landscape and architectural painter and draughtsman. The outstanding figure of art criticism of the 19th century, and himself an artist of no small accomplishment, Ruskin's associations with Cumbria extended from his earliest childhood until his death seventy-six years later. His earliest recollection was that of being taken to Friar's Crag on Lake Windermere; his last resting place is a tiny churchyard on the shores of Coniston Water. The son of affluent parents who early encouraged his evidently precocious artistic and literary abilities, Ruskin was born in London, and from the age of fourteen until many years later, travelled Europe familiarising himself with the subject matter and achievements of Western Art. Out of this experience, and his own highly developed sensibilities as an artist emerged a personal aesthetic which he expressed compellingly in dozens of books and articles, and in hundreds of watercolours and sketches.

Most of these watercolours and sketches were produced merely as records of things which had caught his fancy, or which he wished to capture on paper for later study, so may not be judged as finished works of art. Some of his earliest drawings were a series of maps done at the age of eight. But by 1831 he was filling sketch books with studies from nature – his first and eventually all consuming love as an artist. He took his earliest lessons in art from Charles Runciman, and two years later came under the tuition of Anthony Vandyke Copley Fielding (q.v.). His early style is said to have been influenced by Turner, and Samuel Prout; later by David Roberts. After 1840, however, he began to draw straight from nature, remaining devoted to this practice for the remainder of his life.

Ruskin was first taken to the Lake District in 1824, when he was five. His first important visit, however, was in 1837, for as a direct result he wrote his first book: *The Study of Architecture*. Writing of this tour, and an earlier tour of the continent with his parents, in his autobiography, *Praeterita*, he states: "Of the journey of 1837, when I was eighteen, I felt, for the first time, the pure childish love of nature which Wordsworth . . . takes for an intimation of immortality . . . No boy could possibly have been more excited than I was by seeing Italy and the Alps; neither boy nor man ever knew better the difference between a Cumberland cottage and a Venetian palace, or a Cumberland stream and the Rhône". Regrettably, neither diaries nor letters referring to his tours of the Lake District and Scotland 1837-38, have survived, but this important early contact on his part with British scenery has been ably reconstructed and illustrated for us by James S. Dearden in his *John Ruskin's tour to the Lake District in 1837*, Connoisseur, March 1968.＃ Also his sketch books of the period, and various other drawings, have survived (Ruskin Museum, CONISTON, Ruskin Galleries, Bembridge, Isle of Wight, and Brantwood), enabling us further to appreciate the significance of his tour in terms of his later artistic development; "this transitional period" he was to describe it in *Praeterita*, fifty years later.

Much as Ruskin was attracted to the Lake District, and often as he was to visit it throughout his rise to fame as art critic, and professor of fine art in the next three decades, it was not until 1871 that he finally decided to make his home there. The home which he chose was a damp, dilapidated cottage owned by William James Linton (q.v.), and this he progressively improved until it became a landmark on the shores of Coniston Water. Here he was to spend much of his remaining life, continuing his work in art criticism and teaching, showing his work at the Old Water Colour Society (he became an honorary member in 1873), and engaging in geological and other studies with his secretary, biographer and friend, William Gershom Collingwood (q.v.). He became increasingly eccentric in his appearance and behaviour as he aged, and eventually died at Brantwood insane.

Ruskin is well remembered in Cumbria and among the several monuments and establishments which commemorate his associations with the area are his memorial at Friar's Crag on Lake Windermere; the cross over his grave at St. Andrew's, CONISTON, designed by Collingwood and carved by H. T. Miles; his former home, Brantwood, and the Ruskin Museum at CONISTON, at both of which may be seen examples of his work, and personalia. The Abbot Hall Art Gallery, KENDAL, has a large collection of his work, and was responsible in 1969 for mounting a special exhibition to celebrate the 150th anniversary of his birth. His life and work are exhaustively detailed in several works by Collingwood, including *The Life and work of John Ruskin*, 1893 (republished in 1900 as *The Art Teaching of John Ruskin*, and *The Life of John Ruskin* – the latter portion of the original work much revised). Represented: British Museum; Tate Gallery; Victoria and Albert Museum; Fitzwilliam Museum, Cambridge; Abbot Hall A.G., Kendal; Ruskin Museum, Coniston, and various provincial art galleries.

ST. CLAIR, A. (fl. *c.*1850-1873)
Genre painter. This artist practised at CARLISLE about 1850, later living in London, where in 1873 he, or she, exhibited one work at the Suffolk Street Gallery. This work was entitled: *Setting Out*. Represented: Carlisle A.G.

*SALMON (SALOMON), Robert (1775- *c.*1844)
Marine painter in oil and watercolour. He was born at WHITEHAVEN, the son of silversmith Francis Salomon, and displayed an interest in painting and drawing from an early age. As a young man he is thought to have shared the same master (unknown) as John Clementson (q.v.), soon developing an outstanding skill as a marine painter. By 1800 he had moved to London, showing at the Royal Academy in 1802, one of his first dated pictures: *Whitehaven harbour, Cumberland,* entered as "R. Salomon, Painter". He was still using a London address when he exhibited two works at the British Institution in 1827, but it is believed that by this time, and having tired of the capital's dockland scene, he had moved to Liverpool. During his five years in Liverpool he painted about 100 pictures of Merseyside, but again finding the need for change, he moved to Greenock, in Scotland. Here he remained based from 1811 until 1822, making regular tours of the British coastline, and producing about 250 pictures of Clydeside alone.

In 1822 he returned to Liverpool, painting about 80 pictures in the following three years. Until 1828 he worked extensively throughout Britain, painting scenes at the Firth of Forth, Tyneside, Durham, the Channel Coast, and the South West of England Coast, but although his work sold well he decided to emigrate to America. On the eve of his departure for New York in June 1828, "Salomon" changed his name to "Salmon". His passage to New York took thirty-two days, and after remaining in the city until

Robert Salmon:
Man o' War at anchor in the
River Mersey, 1808.
Oil 23½×33½.
Richard Green Galleries.

early in the following year, he moved to Boston, where he became a scene painter before establishing a successful studio. Boston was then booming as a port, and in 1832 alone he made 650 dollars. In 1840 he was still actively painting at Boston, and enjoying a comfortable living, but his doctor advised him to stop painting small pictures because of his failing eyesight. Shortly after this he resolved to return to England.

Salmon's fourteen-year stay in America produced some of his finest work; the Old Boston State House has his *The Wharves of Boston*, and the Boston Museum of Fine Arts, his *Rocks at Nahant*, and there are many examples in North American public and private collections. The Americans recognise him as a major marine painter, and have inevitably shown this in the form of exhibitions and research material; an important exhibition of his paintings was held at the De Cordova Museum, Lincoln, Mass., in 1967, and a study of his work: *Robert Salmon, Painter of Ship & Shore*, by Professor John Wilmerding, was published by Boston Public Library in 1971. He returned to England about 1842, following which his movements remain a mystery, despite extensive research. Records indicate that he painted more than 1000 pictures, and that in addition to painting marine subjects, he produced a number of pure landscapes, and pictures of great fires. Several examples of his marine work were included in the "Marine Paintings & Models" exhibition at Whitehaven Public Library, in 1971, and a number have been reproduced in dictionaries of marine painters published in Britain in recent years. Represented: National Maritime Museum; Boston Museum of Fine Arts, U.S.A.; Carlisle A.G.; Glasgow A.G.; Walker A.G., Liverpool; Whitehaven Museum.

SANDERSON, Frank S. (fl. early 20th century)
This artist exhibited at Carlisle Art Gallery between 1929 and 1955, and at the Royal Scottish Academy in 1932,

while practising at CARLISLE. He later moved to KESWICK.

SAUL, George Hodgson (1838- after 1900)
Sculptor. He was born at CARLISLE, the son of a city solicitor, and studied in Italy before setting up a studio in Florence by 1871. While at Florence, he exhibited four works at the Royal Academy, and one work at the Grosvenor Gallery, between 1876 and 1887; he was also appointed professor of sculpture in Florence, in 1900. From 1897-1900 he was Vice President of the Cumberland & Westmorland Society of Arts and Crafts. The Walker Art Gallery, Liverpool, has his sculpture: *An Italian Girl*.

SCARROW, Thomas (b.1810)
Portrait painter in oil. Born at COCKERMOUTH, he became one of the six apprentices of Joseph Sutton (q.v.), before becoming a professional artist. By the age of twenty-one he was working in London, where in 1831 he showed his only work at the Royal Academy: *A Portrait*. It is not certain how long he remained in London, but he is known to have married at Annan, Dumfriesshire, in 1833, and to have repeated the ceremony at COCKERMOUTH in the same year. His movements after this date are unknown, and no examples of his work appear to have survived.

*SCHWITTERS, Kurt (1887-1948)
Abstract, portrait, landscape and still life artist in oil, and collage. One of the most outstanding figures in art this century, Kurt Schwitters was born in Hanover, and after studying at the Academy in Dresden, and at the Royal Gymnasium, decided to become a professional artist. He was much influenced by Kandinsky and the Dadaists in his early years, and about 1918 began to experiment with abstract pictures, using scraps of paper and other oddments. One of these scraps had the letters MERZ in red capitals torn from an advertisement of a Bank (*Commerz und Privatbank*), and from then on he termed

all similar compositions Merz. With the rise of the Nazi movement in Germany in the 1930's he found his beliefs in conflict with those of the regime, and after sacrificing all his posts and positions in Germany he fled to Norway. On the invasion of Norway he again found himself in peril, and escaped to England.

On his arrival in England he was interned on the Isle of Man, but after proving himself trustworthy he was freed, and allowed to travel to London. Here the blitz brought on an illness which required him to convalesce, and choosing the Lake District for this purpose, he settled at AMBLESIDE. His work to date had earned him little money, and during his stay in England he turned increasingly to figurative work, joining the Lake Artists' Society, and producing many fine portraits, landscapes, and still life paintings, which sold readily. These and the kindness of local people at AMBLESIDE enabled him to survive during the greater part of his stay, a generous grant from the Museum of Modern Art, New York, towards the cost of constructing a giant sculptural composition which he had christened his "Merzbau", later allowing him to live quite comfortably. This was, in fact, his third such construction; his first "Merzbau", at Hanover, was destroyed in 1943, and his second, at Lysaker, Norway, had to be abandoned because of the Nazi threat. Unfortunately this third construction, at ELTERWATER, near AMBLESIDE, was never completed, for Schwitters died in January, 1948, when he was still working on it. He was buried at AMBLESIDE, but his remains have since been returned to Germany at the wish of his son, and have been re-interred at Hanover.

In 1965 his "Merzbau" was presented to the Hatton Gallery, at King's College; now Newcastle University, its removal from its position in a small stone barn, transportation, and re-erection, posing great technical difficulties. Its caption card describes it as "... a powerful and moving statement, on an exceptional scale, by a major artist whose work derives from, and made an essential contribution to, some of the cardinal movements of 20th century art ...". Represented: Tate Gallery; Metropolitan Museum of Art, New York, U.S.A.; Schwitters Museum, Oslo; Abbot Hall A.G., Kendal; Hatton Gallery, Newcastle.

SCOTT, Benjamin (1823-1898)

Portrait and landscape painter in oil. He was a descendant of the well known Scott family of CALDBECK, from which sprang Hudson Scott (q.v.). He showed an interest in art from an early age, and was apprenticed to the drawing and engraving department of Messrs. Nathaniel Halliday & Co., of WIGTON, but lost his job when the company's works were destroyed by fire in 1847. He next became a commercial traveller for a drapery house, later taking a position in the drawing office of a Lancashire manufacturing company. Following this he became interested in photography, and started a business in CARLISLE in 1858, specialising in painted miniature photographs. From his studio in Cecil Street he moved to Devonshire Street, where he went into partnership with his eldest son, who was possibly John Blain Scott (q.v.). Most of his portraits and landscapes appear to have been painted in his spare time. His portrait of William Steel (1836-1904), son of one-time Mayor of CARLISLE, James Steel, was included in Carlisle Art Gallery's "Cumberland Artists 1700-1900" exhibition, in 1971, and his *Bowness Windmill*, was included in this gallery's "The Landscape of Cumbria" exhibition, in 1974. Represented: Carlisle A.G.

SCOTT, Hudson (1808-1891)

Amateur genre painter. He was born at CALDBECK, but moved to CARLISLE at an early age to serve an apprenticeship with his uncle, Benjamin Scott, who was a bookseller and printer in the city. During, and for a period after, his apprenticeship, he became interested in painting in his spare time, and showed one work at the Carlisle Academy in 1828. Later he worked in London as a printer, returning to CARLISLE about 1833 to take over the business of his uncle, and building it up into the giant

Kurt Schwitters:
Third Merzbau.
Stone, plaster, etc.
*Hatton Gallery, University
of Newcastle upon Tyne.*

John Scott:
Eagle carved in chestnut, on lectern of St. Mary's, Wreay.

printing firm of Hudson Scott & Sons, now the Metal Box Company. He died at CARLISLE.

*SCOTT, John (fl. 1842)

Wood carver. He was a cripple who lived at DALSTON, and was evidently gifted as a wood carver for he was engaged by Sarah Losh (q.v.) to carve various parts of the woodwork at St. Mary's, WREAY, the church which she erected in memory of her sister Katherine. His main contributions are said to have been (see *The King's England – Cumberland & Westmorland*, 1961, edited by Arthur Mee) the eagle carved in chestnut on the lectern,# and the pelican in chestnut on the reading desk. He charged five pounds each for these superb wood carvings, and eighteen pence for bringing them to the church in a farm cart. He may have been the uncle or grandfather of John Scott Junior (q.v.), the figure, genre and portrait painter.

SCOTT, John, Senior (1816- after 1880)

Wood carver, gilder, stained glass designer and decorative artist. He was born at CARLISLE, the son of John Scott (1780-1865), a "carver, gilder, and glass stainer", and joined his father's business as a partner some time before 1841. While working in the business he mainly designed stained glass windows for churches, but one of his last commissions was to paint the Decalogue on metal panels for All Saints' Church, COCKERMOUTH, in 1879. A comprehensive list of his works in stained glass, together with a general account of the history of the company for which he worked, prepared by M. I. M. MacDonald, M.A., was published in the Transactions of the Cumberland & Westmorland Antiquarian & Archaeological Society, Volume LXXII, 1972. He was the father of John Scott Junior (q.v.).

SCOTT, John, Junior, R.I., R.B.A. (1849-1919)

Figure, genre and portrait painter in watercolour. Scott was born at CARLISLE, the son of John Scott Senior (q.v.), wood carver, gilder and stained glass manufacturer, and after education in the city, decided on a career in art. He began by painting portraits and other works at CARLISLE, but later moved to London to study, first at Heatherlys, later at the Royal Academy Schools. By the age of twenty-three he had started exhibiting at the Royal Academy, showing his *Coming from Mass,* and from 1872 until 1908 he remained a regular exhibitor there, showing some twenty works. He also exhibited at the British Institution, the Suffolk Street Gallery, and the Royal Institute of Painters in Water Colours.

Scott spent most of his professional life in London. He was elected a member of the Royal Society of British Artists, in 1882, and a member of the Royal Institute of Painters in Water Colours, in 1885. He was a cousin of Sir James Linton, President of the latter, and the two artists worked together for many years. He was also friendly with many other leading artists of the day, including Yeend King, Edgar Bundy, Frederick Barnard, and Sir David Murray. He died in London, and is buried in St. Pancras Cemetery. He was possibly related, through his father, to John Scott (q.v.), the wood carver of DALSTON who was responsible for some of the woodcarvings at St. Mary's Church, WREAY. Represented: Carlisle A.G.

SCOTT, John Blain (fl. 1871)

He was described as an artist of Devonshire Street, CARLISLE, in the *Carlisle Patriot,* 16th June, 1871, when he married at North Shields, Northumberland, in that year. He was probably the eldest son of Benjamin Scott (q.v.). Nothing more is known of him.

SCOTT, Sydney (fl. 1880-1908)

Landscape painter. He practised at ULVERSTON between 1880 and 1896, and WINDERMERE between 1902 and 1908, and exhibited his work at the Royal Cambrian Academy, the Royal Hibernian Academy, the Glasgow Institute of Fine Arts, Manchester City Art Gallery, and Carlisle Art Gallery.

SCOTT, Thomas Taylor (d. 1930)

Architectural draughtsman. He was born in Cumberland, and was articled to an architect at CARLISLE before practising professionally in London. In 1882 he won the Royal Institute of British Architects' Silver Medal, and a prize, for measured drawings, his subject being St. David's Cathedral, Wales, and in the following year returned to CARLISLE to set up his own architect's practice. He was responsible for designing many buildings in the city between 1884 and 1904, several of which were illustrated in the professional press. His design for the stables at Carrs Biscuit Works, CARLISLE, appeared in *The Builder,* 1884, and other designs are in the Record Office, CARLISLE. He exhibited one work at the Royal Academy in 1904, this being his design for the interior of a house at LONGTOWN. He was buried in the family grave at IRTHINGTON.

SENHOUSE, George (c.1739- c.1794)

Portrait painter in oil. He was born at NETHERHALL, near MARYPORT, the son of Humphrey Senhouse II, the

76

landowner and gentleman who later was responsible for the founding of MARYPORT (formerly ELLENFOOT). Senhouse began to show an outstanding ability in drawing from an early age, and after a lengthy correspondence between his father and a friend in London, involving approaches to several leading artists of the day, he was placed as a pupil with Arthur Devis (for correspondence see *North Country Life in the Eighteenth Century*, Vol. II, E. Hughes, 1965, pp. 89-99). He joined Devis in May 1752, but in April 1753 he contracted smallpox, and though he made a complete recovery he did not resume tuition with Devis before he finally left London in 1755. Later in 1755 he became an ensign in the 20th Regiment Foot, commanded by Lieutenant Colonel James Woolfe. He subsequently disgraced himself, however, and had to be bought out of Canterbury Gaol by his father. A short time later he was sent to an Asylum near Preston, Lancashire, where he remained for the rest of his life. Two portraits of his are known, these being of Joseph and Catherine Dacre.

SEVERN, Joseph Arthur Palliser, R.I., R.O.I. (1842-1931)

Landscape and marine painter in oil and watercolour; illustrator. The younger son of Joseph Severn (1793-1879), the watercolour painter and engraver, he was born in Rome, and later studied there and in Paris, until 1868. He first began exhibiting his work by showing his *St. Paul's* at the Royal Academy in 1863, while living in London. In 1871 he married Joan Ruskin Agnew, niece of John Ruskin (q.v.), and as a result of this association, travelled with the latter to Italy in the following year, and thereafter spent much time with him at Brantwood, CONISTON. While living at Brantwood he was elected a member of the Royal Institute of Painters in Water Colours (1882), and a member of the Royal Institute of Oil Painters (1883), and resumed exhibiting at the Royal Academy, showing as one of his first two works in 1895, his *Sunset at Seascale, coast of Cumberland*. He remained a regular exhibitor at the major art institutions throughout the rest of his life, showing his work at the Royal Academy, the Royal Institute of Painters in Water Colours, the Fine Art Society, the Leicester Gallery, and other London and provincial galleries. He was a founder member of the Lake Artists' Society in 1904, and was subsequently elected to the first council and selection committee, with Arthur Tucker (q.v.). He spent much of his later life in London, dying there in 1931. His elder brother WALTER SEVERN (1830-1904), and sister, ANN MARY SEVERN (1832-1866), were also artists. Represented: British Museum.

*SHEFFIELD, George, Senior (1800-1852)

Portrait painter in oil. He was born at WIGTON, and became one of the six apprentices of Joseph Sutton (q.v.). On leaving Sutton he practised for a time at WHITEHAVEN as a painting and drawing master, later moving to London, where he entered the Royal Academy Schools. The *Carlisle Patriot*, 3rd July, 1824, reporting his move, said: "Mr Sheffield, the Cumberland artist, is now in London pursuing his studies in painting; and we dare predict that he will attain to considerable eminence in a few years...", but although befriended by Sir Thomas Lawrence at the Schools, and later working with him in London, Sheffield

George Sheffield, Senior: Portrait of Joshua Dixon, M.D., 1830. Lithograph $9\frac{1}{2} \times 8\frac{1}{2}$, by Samuel Crosthwaite (q.v.). *Whitehaven Museum.*

was not able to fulfil this prediction in the capital. He began showing his work at the Royal Academy in 1825, with his *Portrait of a Gentleman*, and continued to exhibit at the Academy, and at the Suffolk Street Gallery, until 1835, but two years before the latter date he decided that competition for portrait commissions was too fierce in London, and returned to WIGTON.

Because he had been a regular exhibitor at the Carlisle Academy, from just prior to his departure for London, (showing forty works between 1823 and 1833), and had also shown his work at the Whitehaven Exhibition of 1826, the Dumfries Exhibitions of 1828 and 1830, and the Newcastle Exhibition of 1830, Sheffield was soon able to establish himself as a portrait painter in Cumbria. He opened a studio in CARLISLE next to that of Samuel Bough (q.v.), and travelled from his home at WIGTON as commissions required. He painted many well known Cumbrian personalities in his career. In 1831 he painted a portrait of the Earl of Lonsdale, now in the County Law Courts, CARLISLE; West Cumberland Hospital, WHITEHAVEN, has his portraits of John Pennyfeather, and Dr. Dixon; a portrait of Paul Nelson (q.v.), with rolled plans and a compass in his hand, and that of John Wallas, "a sworn bailiff of Wigton", are in private collections. Many of his portraits were engraved, notably by Samuel Crosthwaite (q.v.).⁺

George Sheffield, Junior:
Taking on stores in
squally weather.
Sepia 12 × 19½.
Private collection.

Sheffield exhibited little in his later years, the only works which he showed publicly being the eight portraits which he sent to Carlisle Athenaeum in 1846. He died at WIGTON, and was buried at BRIDEKIRK. He was the uncle of George Sheffield Junior (q.v.). A number of portraits and letters by Sheffield have recently been discovered in the possession of his descendants, which promise to throw further light on the life and work of this distinguished Cumbrian portrait painter, and friend of the Carlyle and Nutter families. Represented: Carlisle A.G.

*SHEFFIELD, George, Junior (1839-1892)

Landscape and marine painter in oil and watercolour. The nephew of George Sheffield Senior (q.v.), he was born at WIGTON, but moved with his parents when young to Warrington, Lancashire, and later to Manchester. At Manchester he was apprenticed to a firm of calico makers, and took lessons at the Manchester School of Art. He could not settle in Manchester, however, and became a sailor, making voyages across the Atlantic and to Holland which were to give him a lifelong interest in marine painting. At the age of thirty-two he left the sea and settled at Bettws-y-Coed, from which he exhibited his work at the Manchester and Liverpool Institutions. In 1871 he was elected a member of the Manchester Institution, and by 1873 he had moved to Wilmslow, Cheshire, remaining there until his death. While living at Wilmslow, Sheffield exhibited at the Royal Academy, the Royal Society of British Artists, Manchester City Art Gallery, and the Walker Art Gallery, Liverpool; Ruskin is said to have expressed delight when some of his work was exhibited at Cambridge.

Although Sheffield painted fluently in oil and watercolour, some of his most admired work was executed in monochrome,# and featured a wide range of shipping and coastal scenes. Carlisle Art Gallery mounted a special exhibition of his work in 1933, and several examples were included in this gallery's "Cumberland Artists 1700-1900" exhibition, in 1971. Represented: British Museum; Tate Gallery; Birmingham A.G.; Carlisle A.G.; Manchester A.G.; Warrington A.G.

SHERIDAN, Harry (fl.1857)

Landscape painter. He exhibited one work at the Royal Academy in 1857, while living at WHITEHAVEN. His contribution was entitled: *The Fall of the Aar, at the Hander.*

SIBSON, Thomas (1817-1844)

Etcher; historical and subject painter in watercolour. He was born at CROSS CANONBY, near MARYPORT, the son of Francis Sibson, who had a teaching academy in the village. His first employment was in his uncle's counting house in Manchester, but by 1838 he had moved to London, where he shortly afterwards published a pair of etchings entitled: *The Anatomy of Happiness.* He remained in London until 1842, illustrating his own work: *Scenes from Life,* and a variety of works by others including those of Charles Dickens, and Sir Walter Scott. He also illustrated Samuel Carter Hall's *Book of Ballads.* While working in London he became a friend of the Pre-Raphaelite painter William Bell Scott, who may have been responsible for encouraging Sibson to place himself as a pupil under Kaulbach of Munich, in September 1842. He remained with Kaulbach for about two years before returning to London, later moving to Malta, where he died on the 28th November, 1844. An album of Sibson's sketches passed into the possession of Bell Scott after his death, and was presented to the British Museum in 1890. Represented: British Museum; Victoria and Albert Museum.

SIMPSON, Henry (died c.1929)

Painter of still life subjects. He was the brother of Joseph W. Simpson (q.v.), and was probably born at CARLISLE. He received some tuition from John James Hodgson (q.v.), and in Hodgson's opinion, was a better artist than his brother. Mrs. Simpson could not afford to support both of her sons as art students, however, so only Joseph was allowed to attend art school. Represented: Carlisle A.G.

SIMPSON, Henry Graham (fl.1882-1925)

Portrait and still life painter in oil and watercolour. He practised at Liverpool in 1882 and 1889, London in 1886 and 1892, and at PENRITH in 1891, and CARLISLE in 1908. During this period he showed his work at the Royal Academy, the Royal Institute of Painters in Water Colours, the Royal Scottish Society of Painters in Water Colours, and in the provinces.

*SIMPSON, Joseph W., C.B.E., R.I., R.B.A. (1879-1939)
Painter and etcher of portraits and landscapes; illustrator. One of Cumbria's most distinguished artists of the past century, Simpson was born at CARLISLE, and received his early training in art under Herbert Lees (q.v.), at Carlisle School of Art. For a short time after leaving the School he worked for Hudson Scott & Sons, now the Metal Box Company, but as a result of encouragement from John James Hodgson (q.v.), he left the company and became a student at Glasgow School of Art. On leaving Glasgow he lived for some years in Edinburgh, where he soon became a prominent figure among the city's young artists, and produced illustrations for books and lithographs.

Just after the turn of the century he moved to London, taking a studio next to that of his friend Frank Brangwyn, and quickly establishing a reputation for his black and white illustrations, and his gift for portraiture. Many of his portraits were in oil, or watercolour, but it was through his etchings that he first became well known – Bernard Shaw, for instance, claiming that Simpson's caricature of himself brought out his character better than others had delineated it. During the First World War he became an official war artist, and executed a considerable volume of work for the Russian and American Governments. He was awarded the C.B.E. for his work with the Flying Corps in France, and one of his war-time pictures: *The Bombed House*, was bought by Carlisle Art Gallery.

Although based in London, and for some time maintaining a studio at Kirkcudbright, in Scotland, Simpson retained close social and artistic links with his birthplace throughout his life. He remained friendly with all his early artist acquaintances, and painted portraits of many well known Cumbrian personalities, including Sir Frederick Chance, and Mr. F. P. Dixon. His work decorated the calendars of local printers Thurnam and Sons, for twenty-five years, and one of his most popular works was an etched portrait of John Peel which quickly became a collectors' item. He also exhibited widely throughout his life, showing his work at the Royal Scottish Academy, the Royal Scottish Society of Painters in Water Colours, the Glasgow Institute of Fine Arts, and at many London and provincial galleries. He was elected a member of both the Royal Institute of Painters in Water Colours, and the Royal Society of British Artists, and had several examples of his work purchased for national and other collections in his lifetime.

Simpson retained a lifelong interest in book illustrating, his works including: *A History of Fowling*,# 1897 – with John James Hodgson (q.v.); *Simpson – His Book*. 1903; *Lions*, 1908; *Literary Lions*, 1910; *Edinburgh*, 1911, and *War Poems from the Times*, 1915. He died in London on 30th January, 1939, and a major exhibition of his work was held later that year at Carlisle Art Gallery. His coloured lithograph of King Edward VII, a sketch for his portrait of Frank Brangwyn, and portraits of several of his artist friends at CARLISLE, were included in the "John James Hodgson" exhibition at Carlisle Art Gallery in 1970. He was the brother of Henry Simpson (q.v.). Represented:

British Museum; National Portrait Gallery of Scotland; Carlisle A.G.; Glasgow A.G., and various provincial and overseas art galleries.

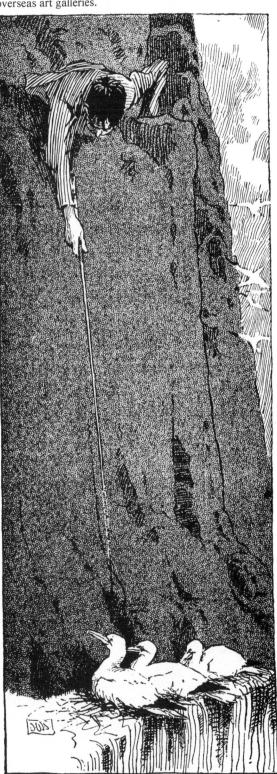

Joseph W. Simpson: Pelicans and Gannets.
Illustration from "A History of Fowling".

SLEE, Miss Mary (d.1943)

Miniature painter; art teacher. She was born at CARLISLE, the daughter of a painter and decorator, and after studying at the Royal College of Art, and at Heatherley's, she became an art teacher at Carlisle School of Art, and subsequently Carlisle Grammar School. She exhibited at the Royal Academy, the Royal Scottish Academy, the Royal Hibernian Academy, the Royal Miniature Society and various London and provincial galleries, and published three illustrated books on CARLISLE. Among her principal works in portraiture were H.R.H. Princess Mary, Viscount Selby, and Ellen Terry. She had a studio for many years at Lowther Street, CARLISLE. Represented: Carlisle A.G.

SLEVEN, J. (fl.1824)

Landscape painter. This artist showed one work at the Carlisle Academy in 1824, while living at MARYPORT.

SMIRKE, Robert, R.A., F.S.A. (1751-1845)

Historical and portrait painter in oil; illustrator. He was born at WIGTON, and after a brief apprenticeship with a local coach painter he travelled to CARLISLE to receive drawing lessons from Captain John Bernard Gilpin (q.v.). In 1766 his father took him to London, where he was again apprenticed to a coach painter, but his father soon realised that his son was determined to become an artist, and in 1772 placed him as a pupil in the Royal Academy Schools. He first began exhibiting his work by showing his *Juno's interview with the Furies*, at the Society of Artists, in 1775. In 1778 he was elected a member of the Free Society of Artists, and in the same year exhibited at the Society his *Portrait of a Gentleman*. Within a few years of leaving the Royal Academy Schools he had established a considerable reputation as an historical painter in London. In 1786 he began exhibiting for the first time at the Royal Academy, showing his *The Lady and Sabrina, from Milton's Comus*, and in the year he next exhibited at the Academy (1791), he was elected an associate. He was

elected a full member of the Royal Academy in 1793, and by 1804 his popularity had become such that he was elected "Keeper of the Royal Academy". Unfortunately, his appointment to the position was vetoed by George III, whose ill-feeling Smirke had provoked by expressing some "revolutionary opinions". He exhibited at the Royal Academy only once subsequently (1813), and although he continued to exhibit elsewhere (notably the Carlisle Academy, and the Suffolk Street Gallery, between 1827 and 1835), he increasingly turned to book illustration in his later life.

His numerous works are said to have been "well drawn, cleverly painted, and always pleasing", and he was not above offering his services freely on occasions. At one point in his career he offered to paint an altar-piece for St. Mary's Church, at WIGTON, at no cost to the parish, but when it was discovered that it would cost £30 to place in position, his offer was refused. Smirke was so angered by this insult that he vowed never to enter WIGTON again, and spent the remainder of his life in London. His first son, RICHARD SMIRKE (1778-1815), became a well known antiquarian draughtsman, and his second son, ROBERT SMIRKE Junior (1780-1867), became a famous architect, who not only was elected a member of the Royal Academy, but received a knighthood in 1831. His daughter, MARY SMIRKE (1779-1853), was also a talented artist, and occasional translator; her translation of *Don Quixote,* was published with illustrations by her father, in 1818.

*SMITH, John "Warwick", O.W.C.S. (1749-1831)

Landscape painter in watercolour. Smith was born at IRTHINGTON, where his father was gardener to the eldest sister of Captain John Bernard Gilpin (q.v.). The Captain took charge of his education, sending him to the grammar school at ST. BEES, and subsequently recommending him as a drawing master to a school near WHITEHAVEN. In the early 1770's he was apprenticed to the Captain's younger

John "Warwick" Smith:
St. Peter's from the
Villa Milleni, near Rome.
Watercolour $9\frac{5}{8} \times 13\frac{3}{4}$.
Tate Gallery.

80

son, Sawrey Gilpin (q.v.), in London, remaining with Gilpin until about 1775, when he came to the attention of Lord Warwick. Under the patronage of the latter he made extensive tours of Italy from 1776-1781, following which he returned to England, where he lived first at Warwick, later in London.

While living in London, Smith became a member of the Old Water Colour Society (1806), sending some 159 works to its exhibitions, and serving as secretary and treasurer before his resignation in 1823. Many of these works portrayed Italian views,# and although it is principally through these that he is best known, he produced many British views – sketching widely in Devonshire, Derbyshire and the Lake District, and visiting Wales every year from 1784 until 1788, and in many years subsequently, until 1806. Twenty of his *Views of the Lakes* were engraved by J. Merigot, and published between 1791 and 1795, by Richard Blamire. These enjoyed considerable popularity, and were re-published by Darling and Thompson in 1798; four of these views have recently been reproduced in *Early Prints of the Lake District*, by Kenneth Smith, Hendon Publishing, 1973 and 1976, and show the *Ferry on Windermere, Coniston Lake, Entrance to Borrowdale*, and *Wyburn Lake* (Thirlmere).

Smith is credited with being one of the first English watercolourists to break with the "tinted tradition of grey underpainting", favouring instead the use of blues and greens, though by no means a stranger to monochrome, pen and pencil. His Italian work caused him to become widely known as "Italian Smith". He was also, by virtue of the name of his birthplace, sometimes called "Irthington Smith". He died in London, and was buried under the vault of St. George's Chapel, Uxbridge Road. Represented: British Museum; Victoria and Albert Museum; Fitzwilliam Museum, Cambridge; Aberdeen A.G.; Carlisle A.G.; Exeter Museum; Grosvenor Museum, Chester; Laing A.G., Newcastle; Leicester A.G.; Manchester A.G.; and various provincial art galleries.

SMITH, J. (fl.1855-1858)

Landscape and architectural painter in watercolour. The *Carlisle Patriot*, 10th February, 1855, commenting on several of this artist's studies of landscapes and ruins in the neighbourhood of PENRITH, said: "Mr Smith far surpasses anything we have ever previously inspected", and the Post Office Directory of Cumberland & Westmorland for 1858 lists him as an artist of Arthur Street, PENRITH. He may have practised at SKINBURNESS, on the Solway, before moving to PENRITH, as an otherwise unidentified "Mr. Smith of Skinburness" is referred to in the *Carlisle Journal*, 18th November, 1853, as having produced: "... three beautiful watercolour sketches of Silloth Bay and lighthouse ... on view at the Journal office ... they display artistic powers of no common order".

SMITH, Thomas (fl.1726)

Sculptor. He practised at MARYPORT in the early 18th century, where one of his commissions in 1726 was to carve "... the Caesar's pillar in the fflower farding, the Sheild with the several marks of our ffamily ...", at Netherhall, the residence of Humphrey Senhouse I (grandfather of George Senhouse – see entry), near MARYPORT. Smith was assisted in his work by his son, also of MARYPORT.

Theodore Howard Somervell: Nanda Devi. Oil $32\frac{1}{4} \times 43\frac{1}{4}$. *Abbot Hall Art Gallery.*

*SOMERVELL, Dr. Theodore Howard (1890-1975)

Amateur landscape painter in oil and watercolour. Born at KENDAL, of a well known local family, Somervell was educated at Rugby, and later went on to Cambridge. During the First World War he went out to France as a surgeon, returning to KENDAL in 1917, from which, in this year, he showed at the New English Art Club, his: *W. Ypres, 1917*, and *Stone Quarry, Pas-de-Calais*. Following this, his interest in mountaineering led him to join one of the first post-war expeditions to Everest, and as a result of time spent in India between this, and a later expedition (on which, with Norton, in 1924, he set a new height record for the mountain), he decided to join the staff of the London Missionary Society's hospital at Neyyoor. He remained at the hospital for twenty years, returning to Britain in 1945, and lecturing widely on his experiences in India, on behalf of the Missionary Society. In the late 1940's he was asked by his close friend Pandit Nehru, to return to India to lecture on surgery at the medical college at Pellore. He accepted the invitation, subsequently leaving Pellore for Neyyoor, and remaining there until his retirement in 1957.

Somervell painted widely throughout India, Kashmir and Tibet, and was one of the first European artists of note to paint the Himalayas. He also painted a large number of Cumbrian landscapes on his visits to his birthplace, and during his retirement. Many of his works featured mountain scenery, and he was a regular exhibitor at the Alpine Club in London, as well as serving as President for several years. He died at AMBLESIDE. Represented: Abbot Hall A.G., Kendal.

SOMERVILLE, George Watson (1847-1905)

Landscape painter in oil; poet and printer. He was born at Edinburgh, and later settled in CARLISLE, where he worked for Hudson Scott & Sons, now the Metal Box Company, before setting up his own printing business. He was a keen painter of landscapes in his spare time, and showed five works at Carlisle Art Gallery in 1896.

STABLES, T. G. (fl. 1884-1886)

Landscape painter in watercolour. He exhibited one work at the Royal Academy, and several works at the Royal Institute of Painters in Water Colours, the Dudley Gallery, London, and the Walker Art Gallery, Liverpool,

Christopher Steele: Portrait of Mr. Bordley. Oil 30½×26½.
Private collection: photograph courtesy Abbot Hall Art Gallery, and The Iveagh Bequest.

while living at AMBLESIDE between 1884 and 1886. He may have been the father of THERESA J. STABLES, who was painting at AMBLESIDE in the same period, and showed two works at the Royal Academy in 1884.

*STEELE, Christopher "Count" (1733-1767).
Portrait painter in oil. The founder of the Kendal School of Portrait Painters, Steele was born at EGREMONT, and received his first tuition in art from a marine painter called Wright, of Liverpool. He then went to Paris to study under Charles André Vanloo (1705-1765), painter brother of the better known Jean Baptiste Vanloo (1684-1745), who visited London in 1737. In Paris, Steele came thoroughly under the influence of Parisian dress and manners, and is said to have taken lessons in deportment. As a result of this his appearance and flamboyant life style on his return to his native Cumberland quickly caused him to become dubbed by local people, the "Count".

On his return to England he first set up practice at York (c.1750), but he later moved to KENDAL, from where he toured widely throughout the Northern Counties painting portraits. While at KENDAL he established a studio in Redman's (or Redmayne's) Yard in the town, and there took as an apprentice on 20th March 1755, George Romney (q.v.). Shortly after this event he eloped to Gretna with a lady pupil, leaving Romney to placate the girl's parents, deal with his master's creditors, and finish off several portraits. Following their marriage the young couple decided to avoid immediate confrontation with the bride's parents, and settled at York. Romney joined them shortly afterwards, and resumed his apprenticeship with Steele. At York, Steele again started to paint portraits, one

of these being of Laurence Sterne (1713-1768), the first two volumes of whose "Tristram Shandy" were first published at York in 1759. Once more Steele got himself into financial difficulties, and he and his wife moved back to KENDAL in July 1757, leaving Romney behind to complete portraits and attend to other matters.

Romney followed Steele to KENDAL shortly afterwards, and after the two artists had quickly discovered that portrait commissions were scarce in the town, they moved to Lancaster. Work was even more scarce in Lancaster, and when Steele suggested that they should next move to Ireland, master and pupil parted company. Steele set off for Ireland in 1758, but stayed only a short time in Dublin before returning to England, where he stayed some time in Manchester and Liverpool before returning to EGREMONT. Towards the end of 1759 he moved to Middlewich in Cheshire, and in the April of the following year bought a small estate nearby. By December 1762, however, he had left Middlewich for Manchester and Liverpool, where, by all accounts he again got into financial difficulties, and was obliged to leave the country for the West Indies. Steele left his business and other affairs at Manchester and Liverpool to be settled by his friend Adam Walker, who, writing to Romney on 12th December, 1762, has left us with an amusing account of the artist's colourful life style, and idiosyncrasies:

"The Count now rides the vast Atlantic Ocean ... He sailed from Liverpool a few days ago for the West Indies, having left Manchester in too abrupt a way to make an end of his affairs. Accordingly he put me into commission to collect his scattered goods and Chattels; (an employ I could very well have dispensed with); and obliged his creditors, for the benefit of more things than their health, to take a ride out to Liverpool". Walker then went on to describe the seige of Steele's studio by a variety of creditors, and distressed women, ending by telling Romney: "With great difficulties I got all together (the few things belonging to Steele which had not been claimed by creditors), and a laced suit from the pawnbroker's; and sent all off, except a landscape after Poussin, two war pieces, a night piece, and a Dutch one; all of your performance, which I saved from the general wreck by giving him two guineas for them. My picture is in the same state in which you saw it. I do not think this thoughtless fellow has done a week's work in six months; sometimes a girl, and sometimes the prospect of matrimonial emolument, has kept him from all manner of business ...".

Steele returned to England from the West Indies but did not contact any of his old friends. He died at EGREMONT on 1st September, 1767, and was buried there. His work has been described as that of "an itinerant dauber", but Romney, who had little cause to like his former master, once admitted that Steele "drew correctly, was a neat painter", and that his work was "as good as Hudson's". Two of his few authenticated works were included in the "George Romney 1734-1802, Paintings and Drawings" exhibition, the Iveagh Bequest, Kenwood, in 1961, of which Professor Ellis Waterhouse remarks in *Painting in Britain 1530-1790*, pp. 306-7: "... the two portraits by him that I have seen are far from contemptible. They are neat and hard and crisply drawn, neither gauche nor provincial, and stylistically related to Highmore...". These two works were included in the Abbot Hall Art

Gallery's "Four Kendal Portrait Painters" exhibition, Summer, 1973, together with several attributed works (unfortunately, Steele seldom signed his pictures); among the latter was a portrait of T. Holmes, Mayor of KENDAL, 1756, from the Mayor's Parlour, Kendal Town Hall.

STEPHENSON, Joseph (1756-1792)

Landscape and portrait painter in oil. Stephenson was born at CARLISLE, and after some tuition in art from Captain John Bernard Gilpin (q.v.), he entered the Royal Academy Schools. Here he soon distinguished himself as an outstanding student, showing two works at the Royal Academy in 1785, before ill-health finally obliged him to return to CARLISLE. After leaving London he worked for some time at Beaufront, near Hexham, Northumberland, under the patronage of the Chief of Beaufront, and here produced one of his most impressive works; a view of scenery taken from an avenue in the grounds of the Chief's home, and measuring $7' \times 15'$. His health later deteriorated and he returned to CARLISLE, dying there in 1792. Stephenson copied the work of the Old Masters, and painted some portraits, but excelled mainly in landscape painting. Six of his copies were shown posthumously at the Carlisle Academy in 1823.

*STEWARDSON, Thomas (1781-1859)

Portrait, subject and genre painter in oil. Born at KENDAL, the son of a cobbler and clog maker, Stewardson was apprenticed briefly to John Fothergill (q.v.), and possibly made some contact with George Romney (q.v.),‡ before

Thomas Stewardson: Portrait of Mr. Jackson, c.1800. Oil on panel $13\frac{1}{2} \times 10\frac{3}{8}$. *Abbot Hall Art Gallery.*

setting off for London at the age of twenty. Here he quickly established himself as a portrait painter, exhibiting his first work at the Royal Academy by 1803, and the British Institution by 1807. During this early period in London he is also believed to have studied under John Opie (1761-1807); Opie painted his portrait c.1803, and it was later mezzotint engraved by W. W. Barney. His appointment as Court Painter to H.R.H. Princess of Wales, in 1810, soon brought him a distinguished clientele; in addition to painting portraits of George III and Queen Charlotte, he painted many members of the nobility, and a number of famous people. These included members of the family of the Duke of Marlborough, the Marquis of Winchester, Lord Skelmersdale, the Earl of Liverpool, the Rt. Hon. George Canning, Prime Minister, and George Grote, the historian. Several of these works were later engraved, adding yet further to his popularity and success.

He also found time to paint a variety of subject pictures, notable among which were his *The Indian Serpent Charmer,* shown at the Royal Academy in 1818, and *Aladdin,* shown in 1819. The latter was shown at the Academy in company with Wilkie's *Penny Wedding,* and Collins' *Fisherman on the Look Out,* and other crowd pulling works, but still managed to attract considerable attention. He last exhibited publicly at the British Institution in 1826, showing his *Boy running away with a puppy,* and *The Biter Bit,* following which he is said to have been prevented from painting any further pictures due to increasingly bad health. He died in London at his residence, and was buried at Kensal Green Cemetery. There is a memorial tablet to Stewardson and his mother in Holy Trinity Church, KENDAL, and a gravestone in memory of himself and his daughter (who predeceased him by eight years), at Kensal Green Cemetery. More than a dozen examples of Stewardson's work were included in the Abbot Hall Art Gallery's "Four Kendal Portrait Painters" exhibition, Summer, 1973, including this gallery's self portrait of Stewardson, and his portrait of his father. Represented: British Museum; National Portrait Gallery; Abbot Hall A.G., Kendal.

‡ *Romney returned to Kendal ill, in 1799, so it is unlikely that he could have given Stewardson much tuition, if any.*

STIRZAKER, Richard (1797-1833)

Landscape painter in oil and watercolour; architectural draughtsman and engraver. Born at Lancaster, Stirzaker moved at the age of twenty to KENDAL to take up a position in the firm of Francis Webster (q.v.), as a draughtsman. He remained with Webster only a short time, however, before opening his own drawing school, and working as a drawing master at the Friends' School. While working at KENDAL he painted Lake District views, and townscapes, showing five such works at the Carlisle Academy in 1823 and 1824, and attracting the comment in the local newspapers "... the artist is a young man rapidly advancing in his profession and is evidently destined for greater things than the pictures now exhibited". His work at KENDAL included his large watercolour: *General election, 3rd July, 1818,* and his oil: *King's Arms Hotel, 1823,* both of which, together with his tinted lithograph of Abbot Hall, KENDAL, were included in "The Artists' Kendal" exhibition, at the Abbot Hall Art

Gallery, KENDAL, Summer, 1975. The second of the two paintings was illustrated in the exhibition catalogue. He died at Manchester. Kendal Town Hall has several examples of his work.

STOKES, George Vernon, R.B.A. (1873-1954)

Animal and landscape painter in oil, watercolour and pastel; etcher. Born in London, Stokes was educated privately, and subsequently became a largely self-taught artist, working mainly in the South of England. He was working in London in 1895, and later lived at Emsworth, Hants., from which in 1907 he first began exhibiting at the Royal Academy. After the turn of the century he spent several years in Cumbria, living at CROSBY ON EDEN in 1911, and at IRTHINGTON in 1914. He produced a number of landscape and animal studies while living in Cumbria, and became so well known in the area that one of his best works: *Boredom*, was later purchased for Carlisle Art Gallery by W. Stead.

After leaving Cumbria he lived for many years at Great Mongeham, near Deal, Kent, from which he continued to exhibit at the Royal Academy, the Royal Society of British Artists, the Royal Miniature Society, and various other London and provincial institutions, from 1930 until his death. He was elected a member of the Royal Miniature Society in 1896, and a member of the Royal Society of British Artists, in 1930. From 1917 he was a member of the Lake Artists' Society. Stokes' work was reproduced in a number of sporting and other publications, including the *Graphic, Sphere,* and *Sketch,* and in a number of books, among them *How to Draw & Paint Dogs*. Three of his drawings of dogs were reproduced in "Qualities of the modern Bird-dog", by Geoffrey Armitage. *Country Life*, 18th September, 1969. Represented: Carlisle A.G.

STOURTON, The Hon. Mrs. (Howard, Miss) (fl.1825-1829)

Amateur landscape painter. She was the daughter of Henry Howard, of Corby Castle, near WETHERAL, and exhibited one work at the Carlisle Academy in 1825, as "Miss Howard". One of her sketches of Corby Castle, executed after her marriage to The Honourable Philip Stourton, eldest son of Lord Stourton, in 1829, was lithographed by Matthew Ellis Nutter (q.v.) later in the year, and published as No. 1 in a series of *Gentlemen's Seats* in Cumberland, by Charles Thurnam, the CARLISLE printer. Her Carlisle Academy exhibit is in the collection of Corby Castle.

STUBBS, James (fl.1822-1832)

Portrait and landscape painter. He was the son of Ralph Stubbs (1734-1822), Keeper of the Circulating Library in KESWICK, and practised as a painter in the town in the early 19th century. He exhibited four landscapes at the Carlisle Academy between 1823 and 1827, and a number of his works were engraved in 1832.

*SUNDERLAND, Thomas (1744-1823)

Amateur painter of landscapes in watercolour. He was born at Whittington Hall, near Carnforth, Lancashire, and subsequently became a keen amateur painter of Lake District and other views in pale grey and blue washes. On his father's death he sold the family home and built Littlecroft, ULVERSTON, in 1782, using this as a base from which to tour Scotland, Wales and other parts of Britain on sketching trips. Possibly during this period he was for some time a pupil of John Robert Cozens, and may also have studied under Joseph Farington; certainly he was at least acquainted with these two artists, and, indeed, many of their contemporaries in art. He was Deputy Lieutenant of Lancashire, and in 1803, formed the Ulverston Volunteer Corps. He may have been the "T. Sunderland" who engraved several of the North East of England coastal views of Thomas Miles Richardson (1784-1848). Sunderland is popularly thought to have toured widely abroad, but there is no direct evidence that he ever left Britain, and almost all of his continental views can be shown to have been copied from the work of other artists. He died at Littlecroft, and was buried at ULVERSTON. Represented: British Museum; Victoria and Albert Museum; Abbot Hall A.G., Kendal; Carlisle Library;

Thomas Sunderland:
Beetham Mill.
Watercolour $9\frac{1}{2} \times 14\frac{7}{8}$.
Tyne & Wear County Museums, Laing Art Gallery.

Coventry A.G.; Laing A.G., Newcastle; Leeds City A.G.; Leicester A.G.; Newport A.G.; Ulster Museum, Belfast; William A.G., Birkenhead.

SUTTON, Joseph (1762-1843)
Portrait, genre and historical painter in oil; copyist. He was born at COCKERMOUTH in the same house as Joseph Faulder (q.v.), and later became one of Faulder's most outstanding pupils. Little is known of his life and work before he began exhibiting at the Royal Academy in 1798, showing his *Portrait of an Artist,* though there is some suspicion that he spent part of this time in London, and may have studied there. He was living at COCKERMOUTH when he began exhibiting at the Academy, and such was his success from this point forward, that he never left his native Cumbria. His first patron of note was Lord Mulcaster, who provided him with a studio at Mulcaster Hall, and here Sutton painted what is considered to be one of his finest copies: *Charles I, in three attitudes*, after Van Dyck.

Following his marriage, Sutton went to live on his own estate at ROGERSCALE, near LORTON, and built a "painting house" on the banks of the River Cocker. Here he enjoyed such a demand for his paintings among the local gentry that he was able to article six apprentices: George Sheffield Senior (q.v.), Robert Taylor (q.v.), Robert Hird (q.v.), Thomas Scarrow (q.v.), John Lewthwaite (q.v.), and a "Mr Askew". Sutton did not exhibit at the Royal Academy after 1801, but showed a number of works at the Carlisle Academy in 1823, 1824, 1825, 1826 and 1830, and at the Whitehaven Exhibition of 1826. Most of these later works were portraits, and included a self portrait, and portraits of "Mr Sheffield when a pupil of Mr Sutton" (George Sheffield Senior), and Joseph Faulder (q.v.). One of his most popular works was his *The Blind Beggar of Bethnal Green, and his daughter.* Represented: Carlisle Library.

TAIRE, *of Kendal* (fl.1817)
Sculptor. Taire signs a large tablet to Margaret Chippindale, 1817, at Skipton, Yorkshire.

*TALBOT, George Quartus Pine (1853-1888)
Landscape and figure painter in oil and watercolour. He was born at Bridgwater, in Somerset, and subsequently lived in Venice and Paris while practising as an artist. He exhibited at the Royal Academy from 1881, and also showed his work at the Royal Hibernian Academy, the Royal Institute of Painters in Water Colours, the Fine Art Society, the Grosvenor Gallery, London, and in the provinces. He lived for a time at GRASMERE, dying there in 1888. Represented: Carlisle A.G.; Walker A.G., Liverpool.

TAYLOR, Robert (*c.*1811- *c.*1870)
Portrait painter in oil. Taylor was possibly born at COCKERMOUTH, where he became one of the six apprentices of Joseph Sutton (q.v.). His only known works are his portrait of Mary Henderson, painted in 1836, and a copy of a portrait of Lord Byron, for Cockermouth

George Quartus Pine Talbot: In a Moorish Graveyard. Watercolour 9×12. *Carlisle Museum & Art Gallery.*

Castle in 1838. He was admitted to the Garlands Asylum near CARLISLE in his later life, and was there in 1866. Represented: Carlisle A.G.

TEASDALE, John, Senior (fl.1777-1809)
Sculptor. He was born at GREYSTOKE, near PENRITH and, in 1780 came to the notice of the Duke of Norfolk, owner of Greystoke Castle, who placed him under the tuition of a London sculptor. About 1790 he began work as a "sculptor of ornaments in marble" at Arundel Castle, which was then being rebuilt, and undertook much of the ornamental work. (Dallaway's *Western Sussex*, Vol. II, Part One, p. 162). He was the father of John Teasdale Junior (q.v.), with whom he undertook restoration work at Westminster Abbey.

TEASDALE, John, Junior (1777- after 1809)
Sculptor. The son of John Teasdale Senior (q.v.), he was born at GREYSTOKE, near PENRITH, and in 1801 attended the Royal Academy Schools. In 1809 Teasdale and his father were employed as chief stone carvers in the restoration of King Henry VII's Chapel in Westminster Abbey. (Brayley's *Westminster Abbey,* Vol. I, Part II; p. 26).

TEBAY, Robert (fl.1757)
Animal painter in oil. This artist practised as a painter of horses in 1757. His *The Bell Mare,* painted in a very primitive style, is in the collection of Kendal Museum, and portrays a pack-man and his pack-horse. The work is signed and dated 1757, and was in the collection of his descendants until 1952.

THOMPSON, Alex (fl.1829)
Sculptor. He practised as a sculptor of ornamental stones, tombstones, and monuments at CARLISLE in 1829, following service with W. Gate.

*THOMPSON, Jacob (1806-1879)
Genre, landscape, portrait and religious painter in oil and watercolour; wood engraver; copyist. Thompson was born at PENRITH, the son of a Quaker factory owner, and later attended the Queen Elizabeth Grammar School in the town. On leaving school he was intended to join printer

Charles Thurnam, at CARLISLE, but was instead placed with a local grocer. He disliked his employment with the grocer and left to become an apprentice to a "coach, house, sign and ornamental painter and gilder" in PENRITH. After two years with the latter he abandoned his apprenticeship and started out in business on his own account, painting signboards and furniture. He visited CARLISLE in 1824 to see the Carlisle Academy exhibition of that year, and was so impressed by what he saw there that he himself began to exhibit at the Academy in the following year. He soon came to the notice of the Earl of Lonsdale, who invited him to copy some paintings in Lowther Castle. One of these copies was sent to Sir Thomas Lawrence in London, who advised Thompson to move to the capital to further his career.

In 1829 he was placed under Henry Sass, and attended classes at the British Museum, later becoming a student at the Royal Academy Schools, where he was encouraged by William Hilton, R.A. When Lawrence died, and Robert Smirke (q.v.) became head of the Schools, Smirke advised him to leave its classes before his originality was destroyed. He first began exhibiting by showing his *View in Cumberland* at the Suffolk Street Gallery in 1824. By 1831 he was exhibiting at the Royal Academy, and in 1832 he had shown his first work at the British Institution. Most of these early works were landscapes or portraits, but by the 1840's and having now moved to The Hermitage at HACKTHORPE, near PENRITH (a cottage presented to him in 1844 by Lord Lonsdale), he had started to paint the type of works by which he is best remembered. These included *The Highland Ferry,* shown at Westminster Hall, 1847; *The Highland Bride's*

Departure, shown at the Royal Academy in 1851, and *The Course of true Love never did run smooth,* shown at the Academy in 1854. These and many other of his exhibited works were reproduced as engravings and enjoyed substantial sales, but Thompson was not tempted to leave his native Cumbria again, except occasionally to handle commissions.

In his later years he produced several memorable works associated with the area of his birth, including his *Drawing the Net at Hawes Water* (1867), *The Rush Bearers* (1872),# and views of Wordsworth's home at Rydal Mount, and grave at GRASMERE. Also while living at The Hermitage, he replaced the murals originally painted by Matthias Read (q.v.) for St. Andrew's Church, PENRITH, with two paintings: *The Annunciation of the Shepherds,* and the *Agony in the Garden.* He died at The Hermitage, and is buried in St. Michael's Churchyard, LOWTHER. His wife ANN PARKER THOMPSON has been described as a "clever painter in watercolours"; his son Jacob was the author of *Eldmuir,* illustrated with engravings after Thompson Senior's Scottish work. His life is well documented in Llewellyn Jewitt's *Life and Works of Jacob Thompson,* 1882. Examples of his work were included in Carlisle Art Gallery's "Cumberland Artists 1700-1900" exhibition, in 1971. Represented: Carlisle A.G.; Penrith Public Library.

THOMPSON, John Christmas (1824-1906)
Portrait and landscape painter in oil. Thompson was born at CARLISLE, and after education at the Grammar School there, trained at the Royal Institution, Edinburgh, under Sir William Allen and Professor D. O. Hill. He was awarded the Art Master Certificate of the New School of

Jacob Thompson: The Rush Bearers, 1872. Oil 34½×55½. *B. Cohen & Sons.*

Practical Art, and after practising as an artist in CARLISLE for some time he took up an appointment as Headmaster of the Warrington School of Art, remaining there from 1855 until his retirement twenty-nine years later. Before leaving CARLISLE he exhibited at the 1846 and 1850 exhibitions of Carlisle Athenaeum, showing portraits, and joined the city's Albert Club with William Jordan Fairlie (q.v.). Under his headmastership the Warrington School had five National Medals awarded to its pupils. Among those who received their early training there were Sir Luke Fildes, R.A., and Henry Woods, R.A. He lived at Warrington following his retirement, dying there in 1906. Two examples of his work in landscape were shown at Warrington Art Gallery in 1951, in connection with the Festival of Britain, together with a portrait of the artist by W. Herbert Johnson. Represented: Warrington A.G.

THOMPSON, Miles (fl.1800-1872)
Sculptor and architect. He joined George Webster (q.v.), in the Webster family business at KENDAL in the 1820's, and became a partner in the firm in 1845. He apparently undertook a number of sculptural commissions of the firm apart from his architectural design work, and signs tablets at St. Anthony's Church, Cartmel Fell, near CARTMEL: John Gibson, 1834; and at St. John's, GRAYRIGG, near KENDAL: Henry Shepherd, 1850, and Geo. Wilson, 1860. He continued the work of the Webster & Thompson practice after the death of George Webster in 1864, but closed the sculptural department in 1872.

THOMPSON, Ruth (1806-1827)
Miniature and flower painter. She was the granddaughter of Thomas Carlyle (q.v.), the sculptor and wood carver, and the niece of Robert Carlyle Senior (q.v.), and was probably born at CARLISLE. Her uncle Robert taught her drawing but she appears to have learnt miniature painting from her cousins Thomas Carlyle Junior (q.v.), Robert Carlyle Junior (q.v.), and George Carlyle (q.v.). She taught at a school in CARLISLE, and in 1825 was giving lessons at her uncle's drawing school in the city. When her uncle died in the latter year she took over his classes. She exhibited at the Carlisle Academy from 1823 until 1825, showing landscapes and flower studies. Her obituary notice in the *Carlisle Journal* two years after the latter date stated: "Her productions in flower-painting have frequently been exhibited at the annual exhibitions of this place and have been favourably noticed in this paper". She died at CARLISLE.

TODD, T. (fl.1874)
Fruit painter. This artist showed one work at the Suffolk Street Gallery in 1874, while living at ULVERSTON. The work was entitled: *Grapes and apples*.

TOPPING, James (b.1879- after 1945)
Landscape painter in oil. He was born at CLEATOR MOOR, and is said to have received some tuition in art from Richard Herd (q.v.), before moving to America. He exhibited in America for some years, where he was a member of the Chicago Society of Artists, and received a number of prizes for his work. He was recorded as living at Chicago in a dictionary of American artists published in 1945.

*TUCKER (MAILE), Alfred Robert, Bishop of Uganda (1849-1914)
Genre and landscape painter in watercolour; illustrator. The second eldest son of Edward Tucker Senior (q.v.), Alfred Robert was possibly born at Woolwich, and moved with his family to Clapham (1850), Bristol (c.1857), Brighton (1866), Derby (1867), then to Langdale, near AMBLESIDE, in 1868. Like his brothers – Edward, Hubert, Frederick and Arthur – he was tutored in art by his parents, but unlike them he decided on a career in the Church, attending Christchurch, Oxford, until his early twenties, and obtaining his M.A. During or shortly after Oxford, he began exhibiting his work using the pseudonym "Alfred Maile" ("Maile" being his mother's maiden name), sending a work entitled: *Silver How, Grasmere, from Loughrigg*, to the Suffolk Street Gallery in 1871/2. Whether he used this pseudonym to avoid confusion with other members of his family, who also showed at the same exhibition, is not known. Whatever its original purpose, he used it again in sending other works to the Suffolk Street Gallery in 1874, and for all five of his contributions to the Royal Academy from that date, until 1889. Only after a long and successful ecclesiastical career (see below) did he revert to his baptismal name, contributing his *Victoria Nyanza* to the Royal Academy exhibition of 1894.

Maile's work was probably the most individual of any produced by the Tucker family. Apart from the fact that his sojourn in Africa as 3rd Bishop of East Equatorial Africa, or Mombasa (1890-1899), and subsequently Bishop of Uganda (1899-1911), presented him with many unusual subjects for his brush and pencil – leading him to illustrate his autobiographical work *Eighteen Years in Uganda*, 1908 – with several examples of his skill, his lifelong concern for the welfare of other human beings gave him a special interest in drawing and painting them, while the rest of the family remained preoccupied with pure landscape. Also he had a marked predilection for drawing and painting romantic views of old cathedrals, churches# and other buildings, spending several periods abroad for this purpose. Following his period in Africa, Tucker was appointed Canon of Durham, dying on his way to a meeting at Westminster Abbey some three years later. He was buried outside the main entrance to Durham Cathedral, where a tall stone cross marks his grave. An excellent account of his life as both artist and clergyman is contained in *Tucker of Uganda – Artist and Apostle*, by Arthur P. Shepherd, 1929, while other details of his life may be found in the autobiographical work mentioned earlier, and his other published writings. The Church Missionary Society, London, is said to have a fine collection of his work.

*TUCKER, Arthur, R.B.A. (1864-1929)
Landscape painter in watercolour; etcher. Born at Bristol, the youngest son of Edward Tucker Senior (q.v.), Arthur moved with his family to Brighton (1866), Derby (1867), then to Langdale, near AMBLESIDE, in 1868. Like his brothers – Edward, Alfred Robert, Hubert and Frederick – he was tutored in art by his parents, and from 1883 showed his work at the Royal Academy, the Suffolk Street Gallery, the New Water Colour Society, and Carlisle Art Gallery. In 1895 he was elected a member of the Royal Society of British Artists, and in 1904 he became a

founder member of the Lake Artists' Society, subsequently becoming Vice-President. His work was almost exclusively in watercolour, and is characterised by its superb directness, clarity of colouring, and self assurance. Much of it was executed on a small scale, and featured landscapes, river scenes, seascapes and old buildings# throughout the British Isles. Most of these smaller works he signed "A. Tucker", reserving the signature "Arthur Tucker" for his larger works. Nearly fifty of his drawings were used to illustrate *Wordsworthshire*, 1911, by the Rev. Eric Robertson, a former Vicar of WINDERMERE. He lived all his professional life at WINDERMERE. Represented: Abbot Hall A.G., Kendal; Laing A.G., Newcastle, and various provincial art galleries.

*TUCKER, Edward, Senior (*c.*1825-*c.*1909)

Painter of landscapes and seascapes in watercolour. The father of one of Cumbria's most talented families of artists (see also the Gilpins, Carlyles, Nutters, and Collingwoods), Edward Tucker did not settle in the area until about 1868, and after many years of work in other parts of Britain as a professional artist. He was born at or near Bristol, but is first recorded living at Woolwich, from which in 1849 he began exhibiting at the Royal Academy, and the Suffolk Street Gallery, showing English and continental seascapes and landscapes. By 1850 he had moved to Clapham, and commenced exhibiting at the British Institution. Then he moved to Bristol (*c.*1857), Brighton (1866), Derby (1867), then to Langdale, near

88

Edward Tucker, Senior:
Barnard Castle,
Co. Durham.
Watercolour 10½×18.
Dean Gallery.

AMBLESIDE in 1868. He was by now the father of five sons – Edward Junior, Alfred Robert, Hubert, Frederick and Arthur – all of whom were taught to draw and paint in his Langdale studio. He continued to show his work at the Suffolk Street Gallery following the family's move to Langdale, but did not show again at the Royal Academy or the British Institution.

Most of Tucker's work consisted of seascapes, continental coastal, lake and river scenes, and North Country landscapes, all of them executed very much in the style of fellow Bristolian James Baker Pyne (1800-1870), whose views of the Lake District published in *The English Lake District*, 1853, and *Lake District Scenery*, 1859, may have been responsible for attracting him to settle in the area. According to the biographer of his son Alfred Robert Tucker (q.v.), both Edward Tucker Senior and his wife were "landscape painters". It is believed that they both died at AMBLESIDE. Represented: Victoria and Albert Museum, and various provincial and overseas art galleries.

*TUCKER (ARDEN), Edward, Junior (*c.*1847-1910)

Landscape painter in watercolour. The eldest son of Edward Tucker Senior (q.v.), the birthplace of Edward Junior is unknown. He is believed to have been born before his father's move to Woolwich, however, and to have accompanied the growing family in its various moves to Clapham (1850), Bristol (*c.*1857), Brighton (1866), and Derby (1867), before arriving at Langdale, near AMBLE-SIDE, in 1868. Like his brothers – Alfred Robert, Hubert, Frederick and Arthur – he was tutored in art by his parents, first exhibiting his work at the Suffolk Street Gallery in 1871/2, showing his *Elterwater*. This work was submitted as that of "E. Tucker Jun.", and he evidently continued to sign his work in this way for several years, until its increasing confusion with that of his father prompted him to change his professional name to that of EDWARD ARDEN. His first recorded use of the latter name dates from 1881, when he began exhibiting at the New Water Colour Society, the Grosvenor Gallery, and the Royal Hibernian Academy, but it is by no means

certain that he did not occasionally revert to his real name in later years.

Certainly he is known to have exhibited under the name ARDEN for the remainder of his professional life, showing his work widely throughout the North of Britain, including Carlisle Art Gallery, the exhibitions of the Lake Artists' Society (of which he was a founder member), and Paisley Art Institute; at the last named, his exhibits in 1893, along with those of his brother Hubert, attracted the comment that his work showed "all the finish and attention to detail characteristic of the school of water-colourists to which he belongs...", clearly indicating that his pseudonym was successful in masking his relationship to Hubert, and other members of the Tucker family. Unfortunately, his work varied widely in quality. At its best it compares extremely well with that of his father; at its worst it descends to the very mediocre. He is believed to have died at the family home at AMBLESIDE, and to have been buried in that town. Represented: Carlisle A.G.

*TUCKER, Frederick (*c.*1860-*c.*1935)

Landscape painter in watercolour. The fourth eldest son of Edward Tucker Senior (q.v.), the whereabouts of his birthplace is unknown, but is thought to have been Bristol. From Bristol he moved with his family to Brighton (1866), Derby (1867), then to Langdale, near AMBLESIDE, in 1868. Like his brothers – Edward, Alfred Robert, Hubert and Arthur – he was tutored in art by his parents, but unlike most of his brothers there is little evidence that he subsequently became a full-time professional artist. He exhibited eleven works at the Royal Academy, showing his first work: *Upon the Lonely Hills of Cumberland*, in 1881. He also showed his work at the Royal Scottish Academy, the Royal Institute of Painters in Water Colours, the New Gallery, and a number of other London and provincial galleries. Many of these works featured Cumbrian subjects* but an equal number were of Scottish and West of England scenery. He frequently lived away from the family home at AMBLESIDE during his early life, and it is believed that a few years after becoming a founder member of the Lake Artists' Society in 1904, he moved

permanently to Gloucestershire. Little is known of him after his move except that he painted well into the 1930's. His place of death is at present unknown.

*TUCKER (COUTTS), Hubert, R.I. (1851-1921)

Landscape painter in watercolour. Born at Clapham, the third eldest son of Edward Tucker Senior (q.v.), Hubert moved with his family to Bristol (c.1857), Brighton (1866), Derby (1867), then to Langdale, near AMBLESIDE, in 1868. Like his brothers – Edward, Alfred Robert, Frederick and Arthur – he was tutored in art by his parents, his first exhibited work being his *Kirkstall Abbey,* shown at the Suffolk Street Gallery in 1871/2. This work was submitted as that of "Hubert Tucker", but by 1874, and again exhibiting at Suffolk Street, he had started to sign his work HUBERT COUTTS, presumably to avoid confusion with that of his father and brothers, who also were professional artists.

In 1892 he married a wealthy spinster, Mary Anne Grundy Wrigley, at WINDERMERE, and shortly after changed his name by deed-poll to COUTTS. He is not known to have reverted to that of Tucker throughout the rest of his long and successful career as an artist, during which he was elected a member of the Royal Institute of Painters in Water Colours (1912), and was an exhibitor at the Royal Academy for forty years from 1876, showing some seventy-four works. He also showed his work at the Royal Institute of Painters in Water Colours, the Royal Scottish Academy, and various London and provincial galleries. He was a founder member and President of the Lake Artists' Society, and regularly showed work at its exhibitions from its inception in 1904. In addition to his busy artistic life he also served as a magistrate and local councillor. Although many of his watercolours are of Cumbrian subjects,# some of his most highly praised work was executed in Scotland, in particular on the Island of Iona, which he visited for forty years in succession to paint. He died at WINDERMERE, and was buried in St. Mary's churchyard.

TUER, Joseph (fl.1842-1855)

Historical portrait painter in oil; copyist. Tuer practised at

KENDAL in the middle years of the 19th century. Kendal Town Hall has several examples of his work, including his *Charles II and Royal Party going Hawking,* dated 1855.

TURNER, William Lakin (1867-1936)

Landscape painter in oil. He was born at Barrow-on-Trent in Derbyshire, and first studied art under his father, George Turner. He subsequently attended the West of London Art School, later practising as a professional artist at Barrow-on-Trent, London, HAWKSHEAD, LEVENS, KESWICK, Madeley, Salop, and Leamington, Warwickshire, specialising in woodland and mountain scenes. He exhibited at the Royal Academy from 1886, and also showed work at the Royal Society of British Artists, the Royal Hibernian Academy, and in the provinces. One of his Royal Academy exhibits was his *Mid mountain solitudes; near Coniston,* shown in 1899, while he was living at HAWKSHEAD. While living in the Lake District he served as Treasurer of the Lake Artists' Society. He died at Sherborne in Dorset.

TYLER, Will, (William E.) (c.1870-c.1930)

Landscape and portrait painter in oil; decorative designer. Born at Bridgnorth, Shropshire, Tyler became a designer for a carpet manufacturer, working at Bridgnorth and London for H. & M. Southwell. While working with the company he wove the first piece of Axminster in the country. At the turn of the century Southwell's discontinued the manufacture of handmade carpets and sold the equipment to a company at CARLISLE. Tyler moved with the equipment and became chief designer of the company. Throughout his career as a carpet designer he had taken a keen interest in landscape and portrait painting, exhibiting his work at the Royal Society of British Artists, the Royal Institute of Oil Painters, and in the provinces. This interest led him shortly after arriving in CARLISLE to form friendships with John James Hodgson (q.v.), and Paul Greville Hudson (q.v.), all three sharing an exhibition at Scott & Son's Gallery in the city in 1904. In addition to being a spare-time painter Tyler also took an active interest in the cultural life of CARLISLE, becoming a member of the Hellenic Society, and giving lectures on art at Carlisle Art Gallery. His oil painting *Candle Light,* from a private collection, was shown at the "John James Hodgson" exhibition at Carlisle Art Gallery in 1970. This gallery has the Paul Greville Hudson (q.v.) portrait of Tyler, illustrated page 44. Represented: Carlisle A.G.

Thomas Wade: An Old Mill. Watercolour 21×21¾.
Tate Gallery.

*WADDINGTON, Frank (c.1897-1952)

Architectural draughtsman. He was born at Blackburn, Lancashire, and later qualified as an architect. He exhibited at the Royal Scottish Academy, and the Walker Art Gallery, Liverpool, between 1927 and 1932, later settling near ST. BEES, where he produced a number of drawings of local architectural subjects. He died at Maidstone, Kent, after taking ill on a holiday in Belgium.

WADDINGTON, William Hartley (1883-1961)

Landscape and portrait painter in oil and water-colour. Waddington was born at Bradford, and later studied at the Slade, where he received the School's portrait prize. He practised as an artist in Yorkshire before making his home in Cumbria following his marriage in 1914, living first at HAWKSHEAD, later at NEAR SAWREY, near WINDERMERE, where his neighbour and landlord was Beatrix Potter (q.v.). He next moved to WINDERMERE, where he remained for the rest of his life. He first began exhibiting his work while living in Bradford in 1907, and exhibited at the Royal Academy, the Royal Scottish Academy, and the New English Art Club, until 1938. He was a member of the Lake Artists' Society, and President from 1949 until his death. He died at WINDERMERE. His eldest son, ROY WADDINGTON (b.1917), has also practised as a professional artist. Represented: Abbot Hall Art Gallery, Kendal.

*WADE, Thomas (1828-1891)

Landscape and rustic genre painter in oil and watercolour. Wade was born at Wharton, in Cheshire, and became a self-taught artist practising first at Preston, Lancashire, and after 1879 at WINDERMERE. He is said to have been influenced by the Pre-Raphaelites, and exhibited many rustic genre works indicating this influence at the Royal

Academy, the British Institution, and elsewhere before moving from Preston to WINDERMERE. From 1879, however, all his exhibits at the Royal Academy were Cumbrian, Scottish and Welsh landscapes; the first of these exhibits, *An old Mill,*# was purchased for the Tate Gallery by the Chantrey Bequest, in the year in which it was shown. Wade lived at WINDERMERE almost continuously until his death in 1891. His *Carting Turf from the Moss* (Preston A.G.), has been described by Christopher Wood, in *Victorian Panorama* (p. 118, with illustration) as: "an outstanding example of his work . . . a landscape of ravishing Pre-Raphaelite detail . . .". His wife was also a talented artist, and showed two works at Manchester Art Gallery in 1884. Represented: Tate Gallery; Manchester City A.G.; Preston A.G.

WALDECK, T. (fl.1817-1825)

Painter of portrait miniatures and landscapes. This artist came to CARLISLE from Paris in 1817, describing himself as an *Academician,* and inserting an advertisement in the

Frank Waddington:
Beacon Mills, Whitehaven.
Pen and ink 12¼×25½.
Whitehaven Museum.

Carlisle Patriot, 29th November, of that year, stating that he would "receive Orders for Painting Miniatures on the most moderate terms". He took lodgings in the city, near the Court Houses, at which visitors might examine "some excellent drawings and paintings, among which a miniature likeness of Bonaparte", and in the following year advertised that he was prepared to offer drawing and painting lessons. Also in 1818 he painted a "fine oil painting of 'A View of Carlisle', four feet nine inches by three feet six inches", which he exhibited at the Bush Inn during the city Assizes, with the intention of attracting orders for a large engraving of his work. In 1823 he exhibited his "From Ossian" at the Carlisle Academy, attracting much favourable comment in the local press, and in 1825 he showed one other work at the Academy. He may have been the "Waldeck" identified in other dictionaries as JEAN FREDERICK WALDECK (1766-1875), or COUNT FREDERICK DE WALDECK, exhibitor of portraits at the Royal Academy in 1853.

WALKER, *of Kendal* (fl.1825-1841)
Sculptor. Tablets bearing the signature "Walker of Kendal", are to be found in several parts of Northern England, including a relief of *Hope,* to Thomas Parkin, 1825, at Ecclesfield, Yorkshire, and another, with a relief of mourning soldiers to Captain Considine, 1841, in Chester Cathedral.

WALKER, Bernard Eyre – see EYRE-WALKER, Bernard.

WALLACE, Robin, Hon. R.B.A. (1897-1952)
Landscape and still life painter in oil and watercolour; etcher. He was born at KENDAL, and after first working for a local horticulturist, and serving in the First World War, studied art at the Byam Shaw and Vicat Cole School of Art. Here he made such good progress that his scholarship was renewed annually until 1926. During his period as a student he paid regular visits to KENDAL, and produced several landscapes featuring Cumbrian subjects which he showed at the Royal Academy from 1922, and included in his first one-man show at the Rembrandt Gallery, Liverpool, in 1926. A second one-man show followed in 1931, and until 1940 he was a regular exhibitor at the Royal Academy, the Royal Institute of Painters in Water Colours, the Royal Institute of Oil Painters, the New English Art Club, and in the provinces.

At the outbreak of the Second World War he decided to leave London, and moved to a cottage at Kern Bridge, Ross on Wye. Here he initially worked the land surrounding the cottage, painting in his spare time. In the middle of the War, however, he taught art at Langford Grove Girls School in Gloucestershire, eventually moving back to London to become a part time teacher at the Channing School. He resumed exhibiting at the Royal Academy from 1946, and had a one-man show at Colnaghi's on March 12th, 1952, but the mental and physical strain of preparing for the latter is believed to have seriously undermined his health, and he died in London a few months later. He was an honorary member of the Royal Society of British Artists from 1948, and for many years a member of the Lake Artists' Society. Represented: British Museum; Abbot Hall A.G., Kendal; Carlisle A.G.

WALTON, George (1855-1891)
Portrait painter in oil. Born at Blenkinsop, near Haltwhistle, Northumberland, Walton studied at the Newcastle School of Art, the Royal Academy Schools, and in Paris, before becoming a distinguished painter of portraits. He practised in Australia, London and Newcastle, exhibiting at the Royal Academy, the Royal Scottish Academy, and the Suffok Street Gallery, before settling at APPLEBY, after 1888, where he is presumed to have continued painting until his death.

WARD, James, *of Kendal* (1784-1850)
Portrait, genre and landscape painter in oil. Born at ODDENDALE, near CROSBY RAVENSWORTH, Ward showed a love for drawing and painting from his childhood, and possibly received some tuition from portrait painters practising at KENDAL before becoming a professional artist. When he was twenty-five he decided to move to London, attending the Royal Academy Schools, and quickly abandoning his early love of landscape painting in favour of portraiture. Within a short period he had successfully established himself as a portrait painter and began to receive commissions from various parts of the country. He also formed several friendships with brother artists, among these John Jackson, R.A., and James Northcote, R.A. Ward's friendship with the latter, started in 1810, was to last throughout Northcote's life, their discussions together about artistic matters encouraging Ward to keep copious notes which later found their way into print as his little known *Conversations of James Northcote, R.A.* (see below).

By 1817 Ward was exhibiting at the Royal Academy, and ten years later, at the Suffolk Street Gallery, showing portraits and genre works, notable among which was his *Portrait of the late Mary Noble, of Penrith, Cumberland, in her 107th year,* shown at the former in 1823, and the latter in 1828. He last exhibited at both the Royal Academy, and Suffolk Street, in 1831, in this year leaving London following the death of Northcote. Also while working in London he exhibited at the Carlisle Academy, showing nine works between 1824, and 1826. Ward was evidently no stranger to his native county during his sojourn in London, for in 1819 he was at NATLAND, near KENDAL, where he married Ann Berry, and Kendal Town Hall has three portraits dated 1823 and 1830. On finally returning to Cumbria, Ward settled at KENDAL, and was living at the town's Highgate just prior to his death on 19th December, 1850. Several of his later works were landscapes. Two of these works: *View in Crosby Ravensworth, Westmorland; and Crosby Ravensworth, Westmorland, from Hopper Hill,* dated 1843 and 1845, were sold at Christie's on the 22nd November, 1974. He was buried at the churchyard of St. Lawrence, CROSBY RAVENSWORTH.

Conversations of James Northcote, R.A. with James Ward on Art and Artists, edited and arranged from the manuscripts and note books of James Ward, by Edward Fletcher, was published by Methuen in 1901. The book contains much interesting information about Ward, and includes among its illustrations a self portrait, and a portrait of Northcote by his hand. John Ruskin (q.v.), originally offered to handle the editing of Ward's notes for publication in 1883, but was unable to proceed with the work due to ill-health.

WATSON, John Dawson, R.W.S., R.B.A. (1832-1892)

Figure and genre painter in oil and watercolour; illustrator. He was born at SEDBERGH, and showed a talent for drawing and painting from an early age. In 1847 he left home to study at Manchester School of Art, moving on to the Royal Academy Schools four years later. By 1851 he was exhibiting at the Manchester Royal Institution, showing *The Wounded Cavalier* – a work which attracted the attention of publisher George Routledge. Routledge commissioned him to produce illustrations for an edition of *The Pilgrim's Progress*, following which Watson decided to settle permanently in the London area. Here he pursued a highly successful career, becoming elected a member of the Royal Society of Painters in Water Colours in 1870, and a member of the Royal Society of British Artists in 1882, and exhibiting his work at the Royal Academy, the British Institution, the Suffolk Street Gallery, the Old Water Colour Society (later the Royal Institute of Painters in Water Colours), the Grosvenor Gallery, and various other London galleries. He was also a prolific illustrator of furniture and stage costumes. Some of his furniture designs were for the home of his brother-in-law, Myles Birket Foster, and in 1872, he designed the costumes for Charles Calvert's *Henry V* at the Prince's Theatre, Manchester. Among his best known works in oil were: *The Parting, The Old Clock,* and *Women's Work*. Several of his oil paintings and watercolours were engraved. He was the brother of Thomas J. Watson (q.v.). He died at Conway, North Wales. Represented: Victoria and Albert Museum; Manchester City A.G.; Walker A.G., Liverpool; Worcester City A.G.

*WATSON, Musgrave Lewthwaite (1804-1847)

Sculptor; genre painter in oil and watercolour. He was born at Hawksdale Hall, near DALSTON, the son of a yeoman, and received his education at the village school. He showed a talent for carving in wood, drawing and engraving from an early age, but his father decided that he should practise law, rather than art, and he was articled to a solicitor in CARLISLE. Here he remained for two years, receiving considerable encouragement from his employer to pursue his studies in art, and for some time attending the modelling classes of David Dunbar Senior (q.v.) at the Carlisle Academy. When his father died in 1823 he left CARLISLE for London, where John Flaxman, the sculptor, advised him to enter the Royal Academy Schools. He stayed at the Schools for only a short while, however, leaving London for Italy, and remaining there for three years.

In 1828 he returned to London, and shortly afterwards exhibited at the Carlisle Academy some of the work he had done in Rome, and a bust of J. Heysham the naturalist, carved on a short visit to the city before the exhibition. After leaving CARLISLE on this visit he took a studio near the British Museum in London, where he produced various poetical works, including compositions from Homer, Chaucer and Spencer, and began to exhibit at the Royal Academy. In 1833 he entered the studio of Sir Francis Chantrey as a modeller. Chantrey entrusted him with some important commissions but was not prepared to meet Watson's request for better wages. He left Chantrey shortly after being refused his request, and

next worked for W. Behnes and E. H. Bailey, also finding time to work at W. Croggan's terra-cotta works at Lambeth. His work for Croggan included the designing and modelling of friezes for the Wyndham family, statues *Aesculapius* and *Hygeia* for a hall in Liverpool, and a group for Dublin.

In 1842 he received his first independent commission. This was to carve the frieze on the façade of Moxhay's Hall of Commerce in Threadneedle Street. The commission was to mark the turning point in his career, statues of Lord Eldon and Lord Stowell following shortly afterwards, and his *Death and Sleep bearing off the body of Sarpedon*✝ receiving the praise of all the critics of the time when it was shown at the Royal Academy in 1844. (His group portrait of the Lords Eldon and Stowell was not completed in his lifetime, the remaining work being carried out by George Nelson (q.v.), and Charles Summers, but many regard it as his finest work). Among his other important works before he died, only three years after achieving this success, were his statues of the Earl of Lonsdale (1845),✝ and Major Aglionby (1845), both for CARLISLE, and his *Hebe* and *Iris* for the gates at Bowood,

Musgrave Lewthwaite Watson:
Statue of Earl of Lonsdale outside Assize Courts, Carlisle.
Photograph courtesy Carlisle Museum & Art Gallery.

93

Calne, Wiltshire, seat of the Marquess of Lansdowne (1847). His health in these final years was evidently poor and while working on the Lonsdale statue he wrote: "The labour I go through is beyond all that I would wish any friend to suffer. I do suffer and deeply, too. It is impossible for me to say what I feel, fourteen hours a day are not enough ... The letters, the work, the conversation, the anxiety, the excitement, the debility, the broken spirit, my own sorrows, will, I am sure, cut me down". He died of heart disease at his home in London and was buried in Highgate cemetery. His memorial tablet in Carlisle Cathedral by George Nelson bears the inscription "... The elegance, simplicity and purity of his works are sufficient to impose all that by his death, art has lost one of her most gifted exponents".

Watson's monument to his father at St. Mary's Church, SEBERGHAM, has been described by Pevsner in *Cumberland & Westmorland*, as "one of the most effective monuments of the 1820's in all England, even if all but copied from Fuseli" (Pevsner also illustrates the work at plate 57), and the monument to his schoolmaster, at RAUGHTON HEAD, "Equally fine". He was also an able painter and draughtsman "as competent with pencil, watercolour and oils as he was with the chisel". Three of his oil paintings were included among the twenty-four works which he exhibited at the Carlisle Academy between 1824 and 1833, and he exhibited sketches at the Suffolk Street Gallery in 1829 and 1830. Examples of his work in sculpture and lithographs illustrating his work have been included in several recent exhibitions at Carlisle Art Gallery, notably the "Cumberland Artists 1700-1900" exhibition, in 1971. His biography by Henry Lonsdale: *The Life and Works of Musgrave Lewthwaite Watson*, 1866, contains much additional information about this, Cumbria's most outstanding sculptor of the 19th century. Represented: Carlisle A.G.

WATSON, Thomas J., R.B.A., A.R.W.S. (1847-1912)
Landscape, genre and marine painter in oil and watercolour. The younger brother of John Dawson Watson (q.v.), he was born at SEDBERGH, and after studying under a private tutor in London for a short time, entered the Royal Academy Schools. He later lived and painted with his elder brother before moving to the North East of England, where for several years he painted local coastal and fishing scenes, exhibiting the first of these at the Royal Academy in 1870 while living at Cullercoats. About 1877 he moved once more to the South of England, living first at Godalming, Surrey, with his brother, later at nearby Witley, where he came considerably under the influence of his brother-in-law, Myles Birket Foster, who was living there. While living at Witley he became an associate of the Royal Water Colour Society (1880), and a member of the Royal Society of British Artists (1882). He later lived at various places in the South East of England, and from which he continued to show his work at the Royal Academy, the Suffolk Street Gallery, and the Old Water Colour Society (later the Royal Institute of Painters in Water Colours), the Dudley Gallery, and elsewhere. He died at Ombersley, Worcester. Represented: Williamson A.G., Birkenhead; Melbourne A.G., Australia.

WEBSTER, Francis (1767-1827)
Sculptor and architect. He was born at Quarry Flatt on the edge of Morecambe Bay. He moved to KENDAL as a young man to work for William Holme, a mason and building contractor, later becoming Holme's architectural partner. His earliest identifiable work is the obelisk of 1788 on Castle How in KENDAL, and dedicated to liberty. By this year, however, he had already been developing the marble working activities of the firm to a remarkable degree, and had been the first to polish Kendal Fell limestone as marble to be made into chimney-pieces. Under his direction the marble works became extremely successful, surviving until 1872, and at various times maintaining showrooms throughout the North of England, as well as for some time employing as its principal sculptor Thomas Duckett (q.v.).

Musgrave Lewthwaite Watson: Sarpedon. Plaster $15 \times 19\frac{1}{2}$ (oval). *Carlisle Museum & Art Gallery.*

Webster was responsible for many monuments throughout Cumbria before becoming increasingly involved in architectural design in his later life, many of these being signed "Webster, Kendal" and dating from 1781-c.1825. (From 1817 many of the firm's monuments were signed "Websters, Kendal", making some attributions to his hand doubtful). In 1818, Webster's son, George Webster (q.v.), joined the family business, and Webster Senior bought a small house at LINDALE, midway between KENDAL and ULVERSTON. The firm shortly afterwards became known as "Francis Webster & Sons". Webster was Mayor of KENDAL 1823-1824, and a short time later retired from the family business. He died at LINDALE. His drawing of Lowther Castle, c.1800 – a building for which he apparently prepared a number of drawings while employed as architect and surveyor at Lowther in the 1790's and early 1800's – was included in "The Websters of Kendal" exhibition, held at the Abbot Hall Art Gallery, KENDAL, Autumn, 1973. This work was reproduced in the exhibition catalogue, together with a comprehensive list of the works in sculpture and architecture for which he was responsible.

WEBSTER, George (1797-1864)

Architectural draughtsman; architect. The son of Francis Webster (q.v.), he possibly trained as an architect with Thomas Harrison of Chester before joining his father's business in 1818. By then he was a proficient draughtsman, and is said to have possessed "a sensitive grasp of the latest taste in Grecian architecture . . .". One of his earliest works of note after joining the family business, was his design for Underley Hall, KIRKBY LONSDALE, his drawing for which was exhibited at the Royal Academy in 1826. He was also responsible for designing many other buildings in the North of England, several of his drawings for these displaying a high degree of drawing and colouring ability. Webster lived for much of his life at LINDALE, his father's former home, but he also had from 1840 an occasional residence at GRANGE-OVER-SANDS, two miles away. After 1846 his poor health led him to leave much of the architectural work of the family business to others. He died at LINDALE, and is buried in the family vault in the churchyard of St. Paul's Church, at LINDALE. Several of his drawings of buildings, and many photographs of his work, were included in "The Websters of Kendal" exhibition, held at the Abbot Hall Art Gallery, KENDAL, Autumn, 1973. Some of these drawings and photographs were reproduced in the exhibition catalogue, together with a comprehensive list of the works for which he was responsible.

WEBSTER, Robert (1794- c.1810)

Landscape draughtsman. A member of the well known Webster family of KENDAL (see Francis Webster and George Webster), he studied at Kirkby Lonsdale Grammar School, and received some tuition from William Green (q.v.), at AMBLESIDE. His sketch book of drawings c.1807-9, was included in "The Websters of Kendal" exhibition, at the Abbot Hall Art Gallery, KENDAL, Autumn, 1973.

WESTON, Rev. George Frederick (1819-1887)

Amateur landscape and architectural painter in watercolour. Educated at Christ's College, Cambridge, Weston graduated in 1844, and two years later became Curate at Holy Trinity Church, KENDAL. In 1848 he was appointed Vicar of St. Lawrence, CROSBY RAVENSWORTH, later becoming Rural Dean of LOWTHER, and an Honorary Canon of CARLISLE (1879). Throughout his life as a clergyman he took a keen interest painting in watercolour, producing many views of Cumbria, and several views taken on visits to Greece, Egypt, Gilbraltar and Spain.

He exhibited on only one occasion, showing his *A sketch of a Village,* at the Suffolk Street Gallery in 1840, but it has been said of him that "few painters have equalled him in the delicacy of his touch and the exactness of his representation . . .". He also lithographed his work, two of his subjects being views of Holy Trinity Church, KENDAL, before its restoration in 1851. These two works in lithography, and his *Nether Bridge,* 1852, from a private collection were included in "The Artists' Kendal" exhibition, at the Abbot Hall Art Gallery, KENDAL, Summer, 1975.

WILKINSON, Rev. Joseph (1764-1831)

Amateur landscape painter in watercolour. Born at CARLISLE, Wilkinson was educated at Corpus Christi College, Cambridge, graduating in 1794. He became a Fellow of the College, and after serving as a minor Canon at CARLISLE, and living for some time at ORMATHWAITE, near KESWICK, he was appointed Rector of Wrethams, Norfolk, in 1803. He was also Perpetual Curate of Beccles, and domestic Chaplain to the Marquess of Huntley. Wilkinson evidently painted and drew considerably in his spare time, many of his works appearing in Ackermann's *Select Views of Cumberland, Westmorland and Lancashire,* 1810, with descriptive letterpress by William Wordsworth (1770-1850). His drawings were etched by W. F. Wells, and hand coloured by Ackermann's young artists. (The latter circumstance may account for Wordsworth's unjustified remark after their publication: "They will please many who in all the arts are taken with what is most worthless"). The only subsequent publication of note which used his drawings was *The Architectural Remains of the Ancient Town and Borough of Thetford, etc.,* published by subscription in 1822 while he was still Rector of the Wrethams. He died at Thetford.

Wilkinson is not known to have exhibited his work, though there is a possibility that he was the "Wilkinson – Junr. . . . An Honorary Exhibitor", who showed a landscape drawing at the Royal Academy in 1783. His *Cockermouth Castle* (private collection), and *Rydal Water* (Carlisle Library), were included in Carlisle Art Gallery's "The Landscape of Cumbria" exhibition, in 1974. Represented: Victoria and Albert Museum; Abbot Hall A.G., Kendal; Carlisle A.G.; Carlisle Library.

WILKINSON, Matthew (1773-1807)

Painter of portrait miniatures. He was born at WHITEHAVEN, the son of Isaac Wilkinson, clerk of St. Nicholas Church in the town. According to his obituary notice in the *Cumberland Pacquet,* 15th September 1807, he was a "drawing and writing master", and apparently succeeded to his father's position at St. Nicholas on the latter's death in 1795. In *A Picture of Carlisle,* by Henderson, 1810, it is stated that Wilkinson moved to CARLISLE, in 1798, "and practised as a portrait painter in miniature with great success . . . he had a singular facility in drawing a likeness and his manner was forcible and expressive". Wilkinson died at CARLISLE at the age of thirty-four. Examples of his work were exhibited posthumously at the Carlisle Academy in 1823, and 1824, as a mark of respect to this evidently talented artist.

WILLIAMSON, Daniel Alexander (1823-1903)

Landscape painter in oil and watercolour. He was born at Liverpool, the son of Daniel Williamson (1783-1843), a landscape painter, and first worked as a designer for a firm of cabinet-makers. He then started painting portraits, showing several examples of his work at the Walker Art Gallery, Liverpool, between 1848 and 1851, before turning to landscape painting. In 1852 he moved to London, where he came under the influence of the Pre-Raphaelites before developing a more personal style of painting. He exhibited at various London galleries between 1849 and 1871, later settling at BROUGHTON-IN-FURNESS, where from 1880 he showed his work at the Royal Scottish Society of Painters in Water Colours, the Royal Institute of Painters in Water Colours, the Glasgow Institute of Fine Arts, and the Suffolk Street Gallery. He was the uncle of Oliver Hall (q.v.), and had considerable influence on his nephew's early style. He died at BROUGHTON-IN-FURNESS. Represented: Walker A.G., Liverpool; Williamson A.G., Birkenhead.

WILSON, John (fl.1790)

Landscape painter in oil. He was a self-taught artist of MARYPORT, commonly called "Painter Wilson". His only known work is his *St. Mary's Chapel, Maryport, as it was originally built, painted from nature by John Wilson.*

WILSON, Captain R. (d.1838)

Amateur landscape painter in watercolour. He painted landscapes in the Lake District in the early 19th century. Twenty of his paintings were disposed of by lottery in CARLISLE on his death, the *Carlisle Journal,* 10th November, 1838, commenting: "As an amateur artist Mr Wilson has few equals". He exhibited two landscapes at the Whitehaven Exhibition in 1826.

WILSON, William (1815-1849)

Landscape painter. All that is known of this artist is contained in his obituary notice in the *Carlisle Journal,* 7th September, 1849: "In Virginia, U. States, on the 12th July of Cholera. Deceased was formerly a cotton spinner, but for some time past followed with considerable success the profession of a landscape painter. He was also known among the naturalists of this district as an indefatigable entomologist".

WINDER, William Smallwood, R.B.A. (fl.1896-1910)

Landscape painter. Winder practised as an artist in Cumbria at the turn of the century, following tuition at Carlisle School of Art, and lived at CARLISLE in 1900, and KENDAL in 1904. He exhibited his work at the Royal Academy, the Royal Scottish Academy, the Royal Society of British Artists, the Royal Institute of Oil Painters, the Dudley Gallery, and Carlisle Art Gallery, between 1896 and 1910. He became a member of the Royal Society of British Artists in 1903.

WISE, John (fl.1824-1830)

Genre and landscape painter in oil. Wise contributed three works to the exhibitions of the Carlisle Academy between 1824 and 1830, while living at ABBEYTOWN.

*WOOD, A. J. Carter (d.1915)

Landscape painter in oil and watercolour. Wood worked in the Penzance area of Cornwall before moving to

A. J. Carter Wood:
Solway Shore, Winter.
Oil 18×24.
Norham House Gallery.

Cumbria, living first at ULVERSTON (1910), and later at SKINBURNESS, on the Solway. He exhibited at the Royal Academy, and the Walker Art Gallery, Liverpool, while living in Cornwall and Cumbria. He enlisted in the army at the outbreak of the First World War, and was killed in action in 1915. His *Hoop Maker*, 1910, was included in Carlisle Art Gallery's "The Landscape of Cumbria" exhibition, in 1974, courtesy of Norham House Gallery, COCKERMOUTH.

*WOOD, Francis Derwent, R.A. (1871-1926)

Sculptor; painter and engraver; art professor. Wood was born at KESWICK, and after education in Switzerland and Germany, decided on a career in art. He studied first at Karlsruhe, Germany, later returning to England, where in 1889, he enrolled as a student at the Royal College of Art under Lanteri. From 1890 until 1892 he assisted Legros at the Slade, subsequently entering the Royal Academy Schools, where he won a gold medal and a travelling scholarship in 1895. He was assistant to Sir Thomas Brock, R.A., from 1894 until 1895, in the latter year working for some time in Paris, and showing his first work at the Royal Academy: *Circe; relief. By baleful wine the swinelike horde, etc.* In 1897 he was chosen as Modelling Master at Glasgow School of Art, remaining there until 1901, when he returned to London.

He was elected an associate of the Royal Academy in 1910, and a member in 1920. He served in the Royal Army Medical Corps from 1915, receiving his commission in the following year, and working on the remodelling of faces of wounded soldiers. On his release from the army in 1918 he was appointed Professor of Sculpture at the Royal College of Art, remaining in this position until 1923. He spent the remaining years of his life mainly in London, dying there in 1926. In addition to exhibiting his work in sculpture at the Royal Academy, the Royal Scottish Academy, the Royal Hibernian Academy, and elsewhere, Wood also exhibited several of his works in oil, watercolour and engraving at the Royal Institute of Painters in Water Colours, the Royal Institute of Oil Painters, and in the provinces. Several of his sculptures were purchased for public collections in his lifetime, including his *Henry James, Psyche, Bess Norriss,* and *Colonel T. E. Lawrence (Lawrence of Arabia),*# for the Tate Gallery, some by the Chantrey Bequest. Represented: British Museum; Tate Gallery; Victoria and Albert Museum; Aberdeen A.G.; Glasgow A.G.; Paisley A.G.; Walker Art Gallery, Liverpool, and various provincial and overseas art galleries.

WOOD, John Barlow (1862-1949)

Landscape and portrait painter in watercolour. He was a painter of ceramics for Mintons before becoming a professional landscape and portrait painter, and lived at Oxford (1894), Woodbridge, Suffolk (1897), and Ipswich, Suffolk (1905), before moving to KENDAL after his marriage in 1911. Prior to moving to KENDAL he exhibited at the Royal Academy, the Royal Society of British Artists, and in the provinces. Kendal Museum has his *Yard 59, Stramongate,* and *Yard 6, Stricklandgate,* both of which works were included in "The Artists' Kendal" exhibition, the Abbot Hall Art Gallery, KENDAL, Summer, 1975; his *A Kendal Yard, Highgate* (private collection), was illustrated in the exhibition catalogue.

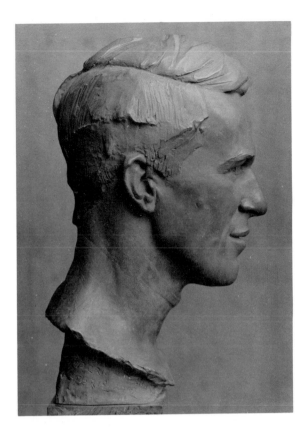

Francis Derwent Wood: Colonel T. E. Lawrence, 1919. Plaster $14\frac{1}{4} \times 7 \times 9$. *Tate Gallery.*

WOOD, William (1774-1857)

Illustrator, zoologist and doctor. He was born at KENDAL and later became a zoologist and doctor. He illustrated a number of zoological books, and is known to have drawn some views of Calcutta. He died at Ruislip, Middlesex.

WOODALL, Christopher (1795-1859)

Sculptor. He was probably born at DENT, and practised at CARLISLE following some twenty years in the employment of Nixson & Denton. He set up as a sculptor and stone mason on his own account in 1838. One of his earliest commissions after this date was a monument to Dr. Blamire at RAUGHTON HEAD, in 1839. In the same year he sculptured a monument to William Campbell, a "Barrack Master", which was sent to the Isle of St. Vincent in the West Indies. Later works were his monument to William Hildebrand for Carlisle Cathedral in 1842, and his bust of C. Wannop in 1843. He subsequently became Master of St. Mary's Workhouse, CARLISLE, in which capacity he was employed until his death.

WORDSWORTH (Quillinan), Dora (1804-1847)

The first daughter of William Wordsworth (1770-1850), she was a talented amateur artist much given to sketching in spare moments. One of her sketch books was included in the "Wordsworth Bicentenary Exhibition" organised by the Arts Council in 1970, and shown at the Abbot Hall Art Gallery, KENDAL, and various other galleries in Britain, and an example of her work may be seen at Rydal

Mount, AMBLESIDE.‡ Dora married Edward Quillinan, poet and translator, in 1841. She died six years later.

‡ *A sketch book which she used in Portugal, with a note by her mother referring to her death, was included in the Abbot Hall Gallery's "Cumbrian Characters" exhibition, 1968.*

*YATES, Frederic (1854-1919)

Painter of portraits and landscapes in oil, watercolour and pastel; etcher. Yates was born at Southampton, and subsequently lived for a time at Liverpool. About 1881 he went to America with his parents, where at the age of twenty-eight he became a professional artist. Two periods of study followed in Paris, where he exhibited at the Salon, and paid a visit to Italy. Returning to the U.S.A. he painted portraits and landscapes and taught art in San Francisco. From 1890 he made his home in England, though portrait commissions took him back to America several times. He also worked in Japan and several other places in the Far East. In 1892 he began exhibiting at the Royal Academy, eventually showing twenty works, and became a regular exhibitor at the Pastel Society, the New English Art Club, the New Gallery, and Walker's Gallery. Following a commission to paint the portrait of Miss Charlotte Mason (founder member of the P.N.E.U.), at AMBLESIDE, he fell in love with the area and settled with his wife and daughter there in 1902. Much of his portrait work was still done in his London studio, for the convenience of sitters, but he also produced a considerable number of landscapes in Cumbria, and became a founder member of the Lake Artists' Society in 1904. His output in portraiture was prodigious, and featured many well known personalities of the day. A large exhibition of his work was held at the Abbot Hall Art Gallery, KENDAL, in 1975, along with that of his daughter, Mary Yates (q.v.), who was also a talented artist. Represented: National Portrait Gallery; Abbot Hall A.G., Kendal.

YATES, Mary (1891-1974)

Landscape painter in pastel; sculptor. Born at Chiselhurst, the only daughter of Frederic Yates (q.v.), Mary travelled as a child with her parents to America, and the Far East, before returning to England. In 1892 she settled with her family, first at AMBLESIDE, later at RYDAL, which remained her home for the rest of her life. She showed a talent for drawing, painting and sculpture from her childhood, and received tuition from her father, who refused to have her originality spoilt by an art school. She later exhibited at the Royal Academy, and the Royal

Frederic Yates: Girl with a pigeon (Mary Yates q.v.). Oil 12½ × 10. *Abbot Hall Art Gallery.*

Scottish Academy between 1918 and 1924, and was a regular exhibitor at the Pastel Society, and the Lake Artists' Society, until her death. A large exhibition of her work was held at the Abbot Hall Art Gallery, KENDAL, in 1975, along with that of her father. Represented: Abbot Hall A.G., Kendal.

YEADON, Richard (1896-1937)

Landscape painter in oil, watercolour and pastel. He was born at Brierfield, Lancashire, and later studied art at the Allen Technical School, KENDAL. On completing his studies he made his home at KENDAL, painting many local subjects, and exhibiting his work at the Royal Academy, and in the provinces, from 1926. The Abbot Hall Art Gallery, KENDAL, has several examples of his work, including his *Sparrowmire Farm, Kendal,* dated 1930, in pastel and watercolour. His watercolour: *Kings Arms Yard* (private collection), was included in "The Artists' Kendal" exhibition, at the Abbot Hall Art Gallery, KENDAL, Summer, 1975.

Bibliography

Please see individual artists' entries for the titles of books, articles, newspaper comments, etc., of particular interest in connection with their lives and work, and which may not be listed below.

GENERAL WORKS (selected):

BOASE, T. S. R. *English Art 1800-1870*. London, 1959.
BROOK-HART, DENYS. *British 19th Century Marine Painting*. Woodbridge, Suffolk, 1974.
BURKE, JOSEPH. *English Art 1714-1800*. London, 1976.
FOSKETT, DAPHNE. *British Portrait Miniatures*. London, 1963. Reprinted 1968.
GAUNT, WILLIAM. *A Concise History of English Painting*. London, 1964. Reprinted 1976.
HARDIE, MARTIN. *Water Colour Painting in Britain*. 3 vols. London, 1966. Reprinted 1969 and 1975.
HUGHES, EDWARD. *North Country Life in the Eighteenth Century, vol. II: Cumberland & Westmorland 1700-1830*. London, 1965.
LONG, BASIL S. *British Miniaturists*. London, 1929.
MEE, ARTHUR (Editor). *The King's England: Lake Counties*. London, 1937. Seventh impression: 1961; *The King's England: Lancashire*. London, 1936. New revised edition: 1973.
PEVSNER, NIKOLAUS. *Buildings of England: Cumberland & Westmorland*. Harmondsworth, Middlesex, 1967. Reprinted 1973 and 1977; *Buildings of England: North Lancashire*, 1969.
REYNOLDS, GRAHAM. *A Concise History of Watercolours*. London, 1971. Reprinted 1978.
RICE, H. A. L. *Where rise the mountains – a Cumbrian miscellany*. Newcastle upon Tyne, 1969.
SMITH, KENNETH. *Early Prints of the Lake District*. Nelson, Lancashire, 1973. Reprinted 1976.
WATERHOUSE, PROFESSOR ELLIS. *Painting in Britain 1530 to 1790*. Harmondsworth, Middlesex, 1953. Second edition: 1962; third edition: 1969; fourth (integrated) edition: 1978.
WOOD, CHRISTOPHER. *Victorian Panorama: Paintings of Victorian Life*. London, 1976.

DICTIONARIES:

BENEZIT, E. *Dictionnaire des Peintres, Sculpteurs, Dessinateurs et Graveurs*. 8 vols. Paris, 1976.
BRYAN, M. *Dictionary of Painters and Engravers*. First edition: 2 vols. London, 1816. Revised edition in 5 vols. London, 1903-4.
COLVIN, HOWARD. *A Biographical Dictionary of British Architects 1600-1840*. London, 1954. Reprinted 1978.
DICTIONARY OF NATIONAL BIOGRAPHY. London, 1885-1937.
E. P. PUBLISHING. *Royal Academy Exhibitors 1905-1970*. 3 vols. A-HAR; London, 1973-78.
FIELDING, MANTLE. *A Dictionary of American Painters, Sculptors and Engravers*. New York, 1945.
FOSKETT, DAPHNE. *A Dictionary of British Miniature Painters*. 2 vols. London, 1972.
FOSTER, J. J. *A Dictionary of Painters of Miniatures 1525-1850*. London, 1926.
GRANT, COLONEL MAURICE HAROLD. *A Dictionary of British Sculptors from 13th-20th Century*. London, 1953.
GRAVES, ALGERNON. *The British Institution 1806-1867*. London, 1875. Facsimile edition, Bath, 1969. *A Dictionary of Artists 1760-1893*. London, 1884. Enlarged 1901.

Facsimile edition, Bath 1969; *The Royal Academy of Arts 1769-1904*. 8 vols. London, 1905. Facsimile edition in 4 vols. Bath, 1970; *The Society of Artists of Gt. Britain 1760-1791; The Free Society of Artists 1761-1783*. London, 1907. Facsimile edition, Bath, 1969.
GROCE, GEORGE C. and WALLACE, DAVID H. *The New York Historical Society's Dictionary of Artists in America, 1564-1860*. New Haven, and London, 1957.
GUNNIS, RUPERT. *Dictionary of British Sculptors 1660-1851*. London, 1951. New revised edition 1964.
HALL, MARSHALL. *The Artists of Northumbria*. Newcastle upon Tyne, 1973.
JOHNSON, JANE. *Works exhibited at the Royal Society of British Artists 1824-1893*. Woodbridge, Suffolk, 1975.
JOHNSON, J. and GREUTZNER, A. *The Dictionary of British Artists 1880-1940*. Woodbridge, Suffolk, 1976.
MALLALIEU, HUON L. *The Dictionary of British Watercolour Artists up to 1920*. Woodbridge, Suffolk, 1976.
MALLETT, DANIEL TROWBRIDGE. *Mallett's Index of Artists*. New York, 1935. Facsimile edition, Bath, 1976.
PAVIERE, SYDNEY H. *A Dictionary of British Sporting Painters*. Leigh on Sea, 1965; *A Dictionary of Victorian Landscape Painters*. Leigh on Sea, 1968.
REDGRAVE, SAMUEL. *A Dictionary of Artists of the English School*. London, 1878. Facsimile edition, Bath, 1970.
RINDER, FRANK. *The Royal Scottish Academy 1826-1916*. London, 1917. Facsimile edition, Bath, 1975.
SPARROW, W. SHAW. *British Sporting Artists*. London, 1922. Reprinted 1965.
STRICKLAND, WALTER G. *A Dictionary of Irish Artists*. 2 vols. Dublin, 1913.
TURNBULL, HARRY. *Yorkshire Artists: A short dictionary*. Snape Bedale, Yorks, 1976.
WATERS, GRANT. *A Dictionary of British Artists Working 1900-1950*. Vol. 1. Eastbourne, 1975. Vol. 2 (with illustrations) 1977.
WILSON, ARNOLD. *A Dictionary of British Marine Painters*. Leigh on Sea, 1967; *A Dictionary of British Military Painters*. Leigh on Sea, 1972.
WHO'S WHO IN ART. First published 1927. 18th edition. Havant, Herts, 1977.
WOOD, CHRISTOPHER. *The Dictionary of Victorian Artists*. Woodbridge, Suffolk, 1971. Revised and enlarged edition 1978.
WOOD, LIEUTENANT J. C. *A Dictionary of British Animal Painters*. Leigh on Sea, 1973.

CATALOGUES AND OTHER PUBLICATIONS:

ABBOT HALL ART GALLERY, KENDAL.
Eminent Amateurs (John Harden, William James Blacklock, Christopher Machell and Henry Melville Gaskell), 1965.
Beatrix Potter 1866-1943. Centenary Exhibition, 1966.
Cumbrian Characters. An exhibition of famous people of the Lake District, 1968.
John Ruskin 1819-1900. An exhibition to celebrate the 150th anniversary of his birth, 1969.
Wordsworth. A bicentenary exhibition organised by the Arts Council (also Southampton), 1970.
Works by W. G. Collingwood and Mrs. E. M. D. Collingwood, 1971.
Hilde Goldschmidt. Paintings, Pastels and Monotypes, 1935-1971 (also Lancaster, Blackburn and Preston), 1973.

Bernard Eyre-Walker Retrospective Exhibition, 1973.
Four Kendal Portrait Painters (Christopher Steele, George Romney, Daniel Gardner and Thomas Stewardson), 1973.
The Websters of Kendal, 1973.
Oil Paintings and Pastels by Fred Yates and Mary Yates, 1975.
The Artists' Kendal, 1975.
Paintings, Watercolours, Drawings, Sculpture (catalogue of gallery collection), 1978.
Quarto: the Quarterly Bulletin of the Abbot Hall Art Gallery:
   Volume IX, No. 2, July 1971: Editorial re: Arthur Ransome, by M. E. Burkett (Director); "The Collingwoods at Coniston", by Janet B. Gnosspelius.
   Volume XI, No. 3, October 1973: " 'Count' Steele", by Vicky Slowe.
   Volume XIII, No. 1, April 1975: "Whitehaven Artists" (part one), by Daniel Hay; "Howard Somervell", by R. A. Somervell.
   Volume XIII, No. 2, July 1975: "Whitehaven Artists" (continued), by Daniel Hay.

CARLISLE MUSEUM & ART GALLERY, CARLISLE:

Frederick George Meekley Memorial Exhibition, 1952.
George Howard, Ninth Earl of Carlisle (also at Leighton House, London), 1954.
Paul Greville Hudson 1876-1960. A Retrospective Exhibition, 1961.
Robert Rule. Retrospective Exhibition, 1962.
George Howard and his circle, 1843-1911. 1968.
John James Hodgson of Carlisle, 1871-1905. 1970.
Cumberland Artists 1700-1900 Exhibition, 1971.*
The Nutter Family and their friends, 1971-2.
The Carlisle Exhibitions – 1823-1850. 1973.
Eighteenth Century Carlisle, 1973.
The Landscape of Cumbria, 1974.
The Etruscan School 1870-1900. English Artists in Rome, 1978.

DE CORDOVA MUSEUM, U.S.A.
Robert Salmon Exhibition, 1967.

FITZWILLIAM MUSEUM, CAMBRIDGE.
Drawings by George Romney, 1977 (shown at Newcastle upon Tyne, etc.).

LAING ART GALLERY, NEWCASTLE UPON TYNE.
Catalogue of the permanent collection of watercolour drawings, 1939.

NATIONAL PORTRAIT GALLERY, LONDON.
Concise catalogue 1856-1969; Concise catalogue 1970-76.

NATIONAL GALLERY, IRELAND, DUBLIN.
Irish Portraits 1660-1860, 1969 (also at National Gallery, London, and Ulster Museum, Belfast, 1970).

PUBLIC LIBRARY AND MUSEUM, WHITEHAVEN.
Exhibition of Marine Paintings & Models, 1971.

TATE GALLERY, LONDON.
British Painting; Modern Painting & Sculpture, 1975.

TOWN HALL, KENDAL.
James Bateman, 1893-1959, 1960.

* This important catalogue lists in its bibliography several catalogues of earlier gallery exhibitions, including: Frederick Clive Newcome, 1894; Thomas Bushby, 1895; Samuel Bough, 1896, and George Sheffield, Junior, 1933.

*Key to Map**

Abbeytown	6D	Irthington	4H
Ainstable	6H		
Ambleside	12F	Kendal	13H
Appleby	9J	Keswick	9E
Armathwaite	6H	Kirkbride	5D
Asby	10J	Kirkby Lonsdale	14I
Aspatria	7C	Kirkby Stephen	11K
Bassenthwaite	9D		
Bowness-on		Levens	14H
Windermere	12G	Longtown	4F
Brampton	4H	Lorton	9C
Bridekirk	8C	Lowther	9H
Broughton-in-			
Furness	14D		
		Maryport	8B
Caldbeck	7E	Melmerby	7I
Carlisle	5F	Millom	15D
Cartmel	14F		
Cleator Moor	10B	Penrith	8H
Cockermouth	8C		
Coniston	12E		
Crosby on Eden	5G	Raughton Head	6F
Crosby		Renwick	7I
Ravensworth	10I	Rusland	13F
Cumwhitton	6H	Rydal	11F
Dalston	6F	Sebergham	7F
Dalton-in-Furness	15D	Sedbergh	13I
Dean	9B	Shap	10H
Dent	13J	Sizergh	13H
		Skinburness	5C
Egremont	11B	Staveley	12G
		St. Bees	11A
Frizington	10B		
Furness	E14 etc.	Thursby	6E
Grange-over-Sands	15G		
Grasmere	11F	Ulverston	15E
		Urswick	15E
Hallthwaites	14D		
Harrington	9A	Wetheral	5G
Hawkshead	12F	Whitehaven	10A
Hensingham	10A	Wigton	6E
Hesket-Newmarket	7F	Windermere	12G
Houghton	5G	Workington	9A
Hutton-in-the-Forest	8G	Wreay	6G

Note: Only place names set thus in artists' entries: AMBLESIDE, are given map location points above. Where it has not been possible to accommodate a place name on the map, the nearest large town or village has been named in the entry, and can be located by reference to the key.

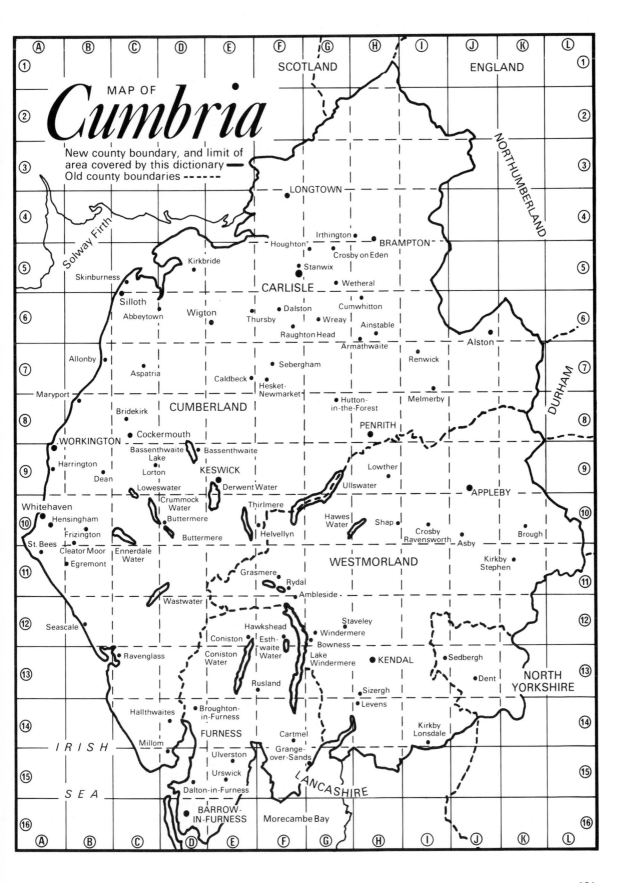

MAP OF
Cumbria

New county boundary, and limit of
area covered by this dictionary —
Old county boundaries - - - -

SCOTLAND

ENGLAND

NORTHUMBERLAND

LONGTOWN

Houghton   Irthington   BRAMPTON
Crosby on Eden
Kirkbride   Stanwix
Skinburness   Wetheral
CARLISLE
Silloth   Dalston   Cumwhitton
Abbeytown   Wigton   Thursby   Wreay   Ainstable
Raughton Head   Armathwaite
Allonby   Sebergham   Renwick
Aspatria   Caldbeck   Hutton-   Melmerby   Alston
Maryport   Hesket-   in-the-Forest
Newmarket
Bridekirk   CUMBERLAND
PENRITH
Cockermouth
WORKINGTON   Bassenthwaite   Bassenthwaite
Lake
Harrington   Lorton   Lowther
Dean   KESWICK   APPLEBY
Loweswater   Derwent Water   Ullswater
Whitehaven   Crummock   Thirlmere
Water   Hawes   Shap   Crosby   Brough
Hensingham   Buttermere   Water   Ravensworth
Frizington   Buttermere   Helvellyn   Asby   Kirkby
St. Bees   Stephen
Cleator Moor   Ennerdale   WESTMORLAND
Egremont   Water
Grasmere
Rydal
Wastwater   Ambleside
Seascale   Staveley
Hawkshead   Windermere
Coniston   Esth-   Bowness   Sedbergh
Ravenglass   Coniston   waite   Lake   KENDAL   NORTH
Water   Water   Windermere   Dent   YORKSHIRE
Rusland   Sizergh
Hallthwaites   Levens
Broughton-   Kirkby
in-Furness   Lonsdale
Millom   FURNESS   Cartmel
IRISH   Ulverston   Grange-
over-Sands
Urswick
SEA   Dalton-in-Furness   LANCASHIRE
BARROW-
IN-FURNESS   Morecambe Bay

Solway Firth

Exhibiting organisations

The following are some brief notes on the principal exhibiting organisations referred to in this dictionary:

British Institution. The Institution was established in London in 1806 as a rival to the *Royal Academy.* It survived until 1867.

Carlisle Academy. Built in 1823, and considerably enlarged in 1824, the Academy staged exhibitions until 1833, and assumed a dominant role in showing and encouraging the work of Cumbria's artists, as well as attracting exhibits from many nationally famous artists.

Carlisle Athenaeum. Built in 1841, its first exhibition of paintings was held in 1843. Two exhibitions were held subsequently, in 1846 and 1850.

Dudley Gallery. Established in London in 1865, it first specialised in watercolours; in 1867 it extended its exhibiting scope to include works in oil, and in 1872, works in black and white.

Free Society of Artists. Although it will be remarked later that the Society of Artists staged the first large scale exhibition of artists' work in Britain, it was in reality the Free Society which should be entitled to this claim, as the future members of the latter society seceded from the first, leaving the main body exhibiting at the same place as before. As, however, the 1760 catalogue has always been considered to belong to the *Society of Artists,* the Free Society's exhibiting life is usually stated as having started in 1761. Like the *Society of Artists* it attracted many of the nation's leading artists both before, and after, the establishment of the *Royal Academy.* It held exhibitions almost uninterruptedly until 1783. Members styled: F.S.A.

Glasgow Institute of Fine Arts. Founded in 1862, its annual exhibitions attracted artists from all over Britain. It was created Royal in 1896.

Grosvenor Gallery. Although this London gallery, founded in 1877, survived for only 13 years, it became a focal point for the Aesthetic Movement of the 1880's, and a favourite of Pre-Raphaelite followers.

Lake Artists' Society. Founded at AMBLESIDE in 1904, this society continues to attract the membership of some of Cumbria's finest artists.

Liverpool Academy of Fine Arts. Founded 1810.

Manchester Academy of Fine Arts. Founded 1859.

New English Art Club. Founded in 1885 by a body of predominantly young artists, who selected works for exhibition themselves, rather than by committee, this became one of the most important art clubs in Britain, with many outstanding artists among its members. Its first exhibition was staged at the Grosvenor Gallery in 1886. Members styled: N.E.A.C.

New Gallery. Founded in London in 1888 as a splinter of the Grosvenor Gallery, this gallery attracted many of the latter's members when the Grosvenor closed in 1890.

New Water Colour Society. This society,was founded in 1832, in competition with the *Old Water Colour Society.* In 1863 it changed its name to "Institute of Painters in Water Colours", and in 1883 it was authorised to use the title: Royal. Members styled R.I.

Northern Academy of Arts (Newcastle upon Tyne). Founded 1828 (originally *Northumberland Institution*).

Old Water Colour Society. Founded in London in 1804 by a group of artists who had become dissatisfied with the *Royal Academy,* it became Royal in 1881. Members styled: R.W.S.

Pastel Society. Founded 1898.

Royal Academy of Arts. Founded in 1768, this institution has played an important part in the development of British Art for more than two centuries. Its most influential period was during the Victorian era, when its exhibitions were among the most widely discussed topics of the day. As a teaching institution, the Academy has been responsible for the early training of some of the country's best known painters, sculptors, draughtsmen and engravers. Members styled: R.A.

Royal Birmingham Society of Artists. Founded 1812.

Royal Cambrian Academy. This academy was founded in 1881, and was granted a Royal Charter in 1882. Members styled: R.Cam.A.

*Royal Hibernian Academy.*This academy was founded in 1822, and has included some of Ireland's finest artists among its members. Members styled: R.H.A.

Royal Institute of Painters in Oils. Founded in 1883, this institute was shortly afterwards awarded a Royal Charter. Members styled R.O.I.

Royal Institute of Painters in Water Colours: see *New Water Colour Society.*

Royal Scottish Academy. Founded in Edinburgh in 1826, it received its Royal Charter in 1839. Closely modelled on the *Royal Academy,* it was not, however, until the 1850's that it established anything like the position of its English counterpart. Members styled: R.S.A.

Royal Scottish Society of Painters in Water Colours. Founded in Glasgow in 1878, it was granted permission to term itself Royal, ten years later. Members styled: R.S.W.

Royal Society of Painter-Etchers and Engravers. Founded in 1880. Members styled: R.E.

Royal Society of Painters in Water Colours: see *Old Water Colour Society.*

Royal Ulster Academy. Founded 1879.

Royal West of England Academy. Founded 1845.

Society of Artists. One of the first societies in Britain to stage regular exhibitions of artists' work, this society was founded in 1760, and survived for 31 years. Its first exhibition in the premises of the Society for the Encouragement of Arts, Manufactures and Commerce, in London, has been described as the earliest large scale exhibition of artists' work in Britain. It subsequently established its own premises, and in the eight years before the establishment of the Royal Academy showed the work of the nation's leading artists; some continued to exhibit with the Society for the rest of its life. Fellows styled: F.S.A. (before 1791).

Suffolk Street Gallery. The exhibition venue and headquarters of the *Society of British Artists,* this London Gallery held its first exhibition in 1824, and quickly became a popular alternative to the Royal Academy for artists seeking exhibiting facilities. Its governing Society became Royal in 1887, whereafter its members were styled: R.B.A. (note that the description "Suffolk Street Gallery" is used throughout this dictionary in referring to works sent to the Society's exhibitions before 1887, and "Royal Society of British Artists", in subsequent years.

GEORGE HOWARD
9th Earl of Carlisle

PAUL GREVILLE HUDSON

JULIUS CAESAR IBBETSO

MATTHEW ELLIS NUTTER

BEATRIX POTTER

ARTHUR RANSOME

GEORGE SHEFFIELD JUNIOR

ROBERT SMIRKE R.A.

THOMAS STEWARDSON